STUDY GUIDE

Marc Healy

Elgin Community College

THE CULTURAL LANDSCAPE

An Introduction to
HUMAN GEOGRAPHY
TENTH EDITION

James M. Rubenstein

Prentice Hall

Boston   Columbus   Indianapolis   New York   San Francisco   Upper Saddle River
Amsterdam   Cape Town   Dubai   London   Madrid   Milan   Munich   Paris   Montréal   Toronto
Delhi   Mexico City   São Paulo   Sydney   Hong Kong   Seoul   Singapore   Taipei   Tokyo

Geography Editor: Christian Botting
Editorial Director: Frank Ruggirello
Marketing Manager: Maureen McLaughlin
Project Editor: Crissy Dudonis
Assistant Editor: Kristen Sanchez
Managing Editor, Geosciences and Chemistry: Gina M. Cheselka
Project Manager, Science: Maureen Pancza
Operations Specialist: Maura Zaldivar
Supplement Cover Designer: Paul Gourhan
Cover Image: epa/Corbis

Printed in the United States of America

10 9 8 7 6 5 4 3

ISBN-13:   978-0-321-68173-7
ISBN-10:   0-321-68173-8

Prentice Hall
is an imprint of

www.pearsonhighered.com

CONTENTS

PREFACE

It is suggested that this study guide be used as a framework to outline the chapters for a full grasp of concepts and as a means to integrate the material with course notes. The terms at the end of the chapters will be helpful for review.

The basic design goal of the present study guide is to provide a uniformly distilled version of the text. The goal is to facilitate recall for anyone who previously read the entire text. It is not assumed that beginning students will find the study guide useful without referring to the main text.

Comments, inquiries, and suggestions from students and professors about any aspect of the study guide are most welcome. E-mail: Mhealy@elgin.edu

(June, 2010)

Chapter 1
Thinking Geographically

Key Issues
1. How do geographers describe where things are?
2. Why is each point on Earth unique?
3. Why are different places similar?

(4)

The ancient Greek scholar Eratosthenes coined the word geography from two Greek words, *geo* meaning *earth* and *graphy* meaning *to write.* Geography asks two simple questions: *where* and *why*.

Geography is divided broadly into two categories — *human* geography and *physical* geography. Human geography studies where and why human activities are located as they are. Physical geography studies where and why natural forces occur as they do. This book focuses on human geography, but it never forgets Earth's atmosphere, land, water, vegetation, and other living creatures. To introduce human geography, we concentrate on two main features of human behavior — culture and economy.

(5)

Distinctive geographic approaches concentrate on five aspects in thinking about the world: **place**, **regions**, **scale**, **space**, and **connections**. These five distinctive ways that geographers think about the world are discussed in detail in this chapter.

Key Issue 1. How Do Geographers Address *Where* Things Are?
*   **Maps**
*   **Contemporary tools**

Geographers think about the arrangements of people and activities found in space and try to understand why those people and activities are distributed across space as they are. Geographers use maps as a method of depicting the distribution of features and as a tool for explaining observed patterns.

(6)
Maps
Geography's most important tool for thinking spatially about the distribution of features across Earth is a map. A **map** is a two-dimensional or flat-scale model of Earth's surface, or a portion of it. For centuries geographers have worked to perfect the science of mapmaking, called **cartography**. A map serves two purposes: a tool for storing reference material and a tool for communicating geographic information. A map is often the best means for depicting the distribution of human activities or physical features, as well as for thinking about reasons underlying a distribution.

Early Mapmaking
The earliest surviving maps were drawn in the Middle East in the seventh or sixth century B.C.

Mediterranean sailors and traders made maps of rock formation, islands, and ocean currents as early as 800 B.C.

Aristotle (384–322 B.C.) was the first to demonstrate the earth was spherical. He observed the curved shadow of the earth on the moon during an eclipse and the fact that the visible groups of stars change as one travels north or south.

Eratosthenes (276?–194? B.C.), the first person on record to use the word geography, calculated the circumference of the earth and made one of the earliest maps of the known world, correctly dividing Earth into five climatic regions.

Ptolemy (A.D. 100?–170?) wrote an eight-volume *Guide to Geography*, taking advantage of information collected by merchants and soldiers who traveled throughout the Roman Empire.

Non-European After Ptolemy little progress in mapmaking or geographic thought was made in Europe for several hundred years, although geographic inquiry continued outside of Europe.

Phei Hsiu (Fei Xiu), the "father of Chinese cartography," produced an elaborate map of China in A.D. 267.

al-Idrisi, the Muslim geographer, (1100–1165?) prepared a world map and geography text in 1154, building on Ptolemy's long-neglected work.

Ibn-Battutah (1305–1368?) wrote *Rihlah* (Travels) based on three decades of journeys.

Age of Exploration and Discovery Geography and mapmaking enjoyed a revival during the Age of Exploration and Discovery. By the seventeenth century, maps accurately displayed the outline of most continents and the position of oceans.

Map Scale
Map scale is represented in three ways: a fraction (1/24,000) or ratio (1:24,000) shows the numerical ratio between distances on the map and the Earth's surface; a written statement ("1 inch equals 1 mile") describes this relationship between map and Earth distances in words; or a graphic bar scale, which usually consists of a bar line marked to show distance on Earth's surface.

(8)
Projection
To communicate geographic concepts effectively through maps, cartographers must design them properly and assure that users know how to read them. Earth's spherical shape poses a challenge for cartographers because drawing Earth on a flat piece of paper unavoidably produces some distortion. The scientific method of transferring location on Earth's surface to a flat map is called **projection**.

Four types of distortion can result: *shape* can be distorted, *distance* may be increased or decreased, *relative size* may be altered, and *direction* between points can be distorted.

Most of the world maps in this book are *equal area projections*.

(9)
Other commonly used projections are the Robinson and Mercator. Each has advantages and disadvantages. The Appendix explains decisions made when developing a map.

U.S. Land Ordinance of 1785
In addition to the global system of latitude and longitude, other mathematical indicators of locations are used in different parts of the world. In the United States, the Land Ordinance of 1785

divided much of the country into a system of townships and ranges to facilitate the sale of land to settlers in the West.

In this system, a township is a square 6 miles on each side. Some of the north-south lines separating townships are called principal meridians and some east-west lines are designated base lines. Each township has a number corresponding to its distance north or south of a particular base line. Each township has a second number, known as the range, corresponding to its location east or west of a principal meridian. A township is divided into 36 sections, each of which is 1 mile by 1 mile. Each section is divided into four quarter-sections. A quarter-section, which is 0.5 mile by 0.5 mile, or 160 acres, was the amount of land many western pioneers bought as a homestead.

Contemporary Tools
Two important technologies that developed during the past quarter century are remote sensing from satellites (to collect data) and geographic information systems (computer programs for manipulating geographic data).

(12)
GIS
A **geographic information system (GIS)** is a high-performance computer system that processes geographic data. Each type of information (topography, political boundaries, population density, manufacturing, soil type, earthquake faults, and so on) is stored as an information layer. GIS is most powerful when it is used to combine several layers, to show relations. The term "mash-up" refers to the practice of overlaying data from one source on top of one of the mapping services.

GPS
The **Global Positioning System (GPS)** is an example of applying new technology to an old human habit: consulting a map to get to a desired destination. The GPS can pinpoint a location using signals from a group of satellites.

Remote Sensing
The acquisition of data about Earth's surface from a satellite orbiting Earth or from other long-distance methods is known as **remote sensing**. The smallest feature on Earth's surface that can be detected by a sensor is the resolution of the scanner. Some can show an object 1 meter across. Weather satellites take a broader view, looking at several kilometers at a time.

Key Issue 2. Why Is Each Point on Earth Unique?
- **Place: Unique location of a feature**
- **Regions: Areas of unique characteristics**
- **Spatial association**

The interplay between the uniqueness of each place and the similarities among places lies at the heart of geographic inquiry into why things are found where they are. Two basic concepts help geographers to explain why every point on Earth is in some ways unique: place and region. The difference between the two concepts is partly a matter of scale: a place is a point, whereas a region is an area.

Humans possess a strong sense of place — that is, a feeling for the features that contribute to the distinctiveness of a particular place, perhaps a hometown or vacation spot.

Place: Unique Location of a Feature
Geographers identify the location of something in four ways: by place-name, site, situation, and mathematical location.

Place Names
Geographers call the name given to a portion of Earth's surface its **toponym** (literally, place-name). The name of a place may give us a clue about its founders, physical setting, social customs, or political changes. Some place-names derive from features of the physical environment. Places can change names. The Board of Geographical Names, operated by the U.S. Geological Survey, was established in the late nineteenth century to be the final arbiter of names on U.S. maps. Names can also change as a result of political upheavals.

Site
The second way that geographers describe the location of a place is by **site**, which is the physical character of a place. Important site characteristics include climate, water sources, topography, soil, vegetation, latitude, and elevation. Humans have the ability to modify the characteristics of a site. The central areas of Boston and Tokyo have been expanded through centuries of landfilling in nearby bays.

Situation
Situation is the location of a place relative to other places. Situation is a good way to indicate location for two reasons — finding an unfamiliar place and understanding its importance. Many locations are important because they are accessible to other places.

(15)
Mathematical Location
The location of any place on Earth's surface can be described precisely by meridians and parallels, two sets of imaginary arcs drawn in a grid pattern on Earth's surface. A **meridian** is an arc drawn between the North and South poles. A **parallel** is a circle drawn around the globe parallel to the equator. The location of each meridian is identified on Earth's surface according to a numbering system known as **longitude**. The **prime meridian**, 0° longitude, passes through the Royal Observatory at Greenwich, England. All other meridians have numbers between 0° and 180° east or west of Greenwich.

The numbering system to indicate the location of a parallel is called **latitude**. The equator is 0° latitude, the North Pole is 9° north latitude, and the South Pole is 90° south latitude. The mathematical location of a place can be designated more precisely by dividing each degree into 60 minutes and each minute into 60 seconds.

(15-16)
Measuring latitude and longitude is a good example of how geography is partly a natural science and partly a study of human behavior. Latitudes are scientifically derived by Earth's shape and its rotation around the Sun. On the other hand, 0° longitude is a human creation. The 0° longitude runs through Greenwich because England was the world's most powerful country when longitude was first accurately measured and the international agreement was made.

(16-17)
Longitude plays an important role in calculating time. Traveling 15° east is the equivalent of traveling one hour forward on the clock, and 15° west is one hour backward.

(18)
Earth is divided into 24 standard time zones, one for each hour of the day, so each time zone represents 15° of longitude. Before standard time zones were created, each locality set its own time. The international agreement (in 1884) designated the time at the prime meridian as **Greenwich Mean Time (GMT)** or **Universal Time (UT)**. The eastern United States, which is near 75° west longitude, is five hours earlier than Greenwich Mean Time.

When you cross the **International Date Line**, which for the most part follows 180° longitude, you move the clock back 24 hours, or one entire day, if you are heading eastward toward America. You turn the clock ahead 24 hours if you are heading westward toward Asia.

Regions: Areas of Unique Characteristics

The "sense of place" that humans posses may apply to a larger area of Earth than to a specific point. An area of Earth defined by one or more distinctive characteristics is a **region**.

A region derives its unified character through the **cultural landscape,** a combination of cultural features such as language and religion, economic features such as agriculture and industry, and physical features such as climate and vegetation.

Cultural Landscape

The contemporary **cultural landscape** approach in geography — sometimes called the **regional studies** approach — was initiated in France. It was later adopted by several American geographers, who argued that each region has its own distinct landscape that results from a unique combination of social relationships and physical processes.

Types of Regions

Geographers most often apply the concept region at one of two scales: either several neighboring countries that share important features, such as those in Latin America, or many localities within a country, such as those in southern California. A particular place can be included in more than one region depending on how the region is defined. Geographers identify three types of regions: formal, functional, and vernacular.

Formal Region. A formal region, also called a uniform region or a homogeneous region, is an area within which everyone shares in common one or more distinctive characteristics.

(19)
Some formal regions are easy to identify, such as countries or local government units. In other kinds of formal regions a characteristic may be predominant rather than universal. For example, the wheat belt of North America also grows other crops. A cautionary step in identifying formal regions is the need to recognize the diversity of cultural, economic, and environmental factors, even while making a generalization.

Functional Region. A functional region, also called a nodal region, is an area organized around a node or focal point. The region is tied to the central point by transportation or communications systems or by economic or functional associations. An example of a functional region is the circulation area of a newspaper. New technology is breaking down traditional functional regions. Newspapers such as *USA Today* and the *New York Times* are transmitted by satellite to printing machines in various places.

(20)
Vernacular Region. A **vernacular region**, or perceptual region, is a place that people believe exists as part of their cultural identity. Such vernacular regions emerge from people's informal perceptions of place, rather than from scientific models. A **mental map** depicts what a person knows about a place. As an example of a vernacular region, Americans frequently refer to the South as a place with environmental, cultural, and economic features perceived to be quite distinct from the rest of the United States.

Spatial Association

Different conclusions may be reached concerning a regions characteristics depending on scale. For example, death rates vary widely among scales within the United States.

At the national scale, the eastern regions of the United States have higher levels of cancer than the western ones. At the scale of the state of Maryland, the city of Baltimore and counties in the east have higher levels of cancer than the western and suburban counties. At the scale of the city of Baltimore, lower levels of cancer are found in the zip codes on the north side. To explain why regions possess distinctive features, such as a high cancer rate, geographers try to identify cultural, economic, and environmental factors that display similar spatial distributions. Geographers conclude that factors with similar distributions have spatial association.

(21)
Regional Integration of Culture
In thinking about *why* each region on Earth is distinctive, geographers refer to **culture**, which is the body of customary beliefs, material traits, and social forms that together constitute the distinct tradition of a group of people.

Intellectually challenging culture is often distinguished from *popular culture*, such as television programs. *Culture* also refers to small living organisms, such as those found under a microscope or in yogurt. *Agriculture* is a term for growing things on a much larger scale. The origin of the word *culture* is the Latin *cultus*, which means "to care for," which has two very different meanings.

Culture. Some geographers study what people care about (their ideas, beliefs, values, and customs), whereas other geographers emphasize what people take care of (their ways of earning a living and obtaining food, clothing and shelter).

What People Care About. Especially important cultural values derive from a group's language, religion, and ethnicity. Language is a system of signs, sounds, gestures, and marks that have meanings understood within a cultural group. Religion is an important cultural value because it is the principle system of attitudes, beliefs, and practices through which people worship in a formal, organized way. Ethnicity encompasses a group's language, religion, and other cultural values, as well as its physical traits, products of common traditions, and heredity.

(22)
What People Take Care Of.
The second cultural element of interest to geographers is production of material wealth — the food, clothing, and shelter that humans need to survive and thrive. Different cultural groups obtain their wealth in different ways. Geographers divide the world into regions with countries that are more (or relatively) developed economically (abbreviated MDCs), and regions with less developed (or developing) countries (abbreviated LDCs). Agriculture predominates in LDCs, while manufacturing and performing services for wages predominates in MDCs. Some manufacturing is leaving MDCs and relocating in LDCs. Geographers are also interested in the political institutions that protect material artifacts, as well as cultural values. As discussed in Chapter 8, cultural groups in the modern world are increasingly asserting their rights to organize their own affairs at the local scale rather than submit to the control of other cultural groups.

(24)
Cultural Ecology: Integrating Culture and Environment
In constructing regions, geographers consider environmental factors as well as cultural. **Cultural ecology** is the geographic study of human–environment relations. Some nineteenth century geographers argued that human actions were *scientifically caused* by environmental conditions, an approach called **environmental determinism**. Modern geographers reject environmental determinism in favor of **possibilism**, arguing that the physical environment may limit some human actions but people can adjust to their environment. People choose a course of action among alternatives in the environment and endow the physical environment with cultural values by

treating it as substances for use, a collection of **resources**. For example, the climate of any location influences human activities, especially food production.

Human and Physical Factors. Human geographers use this cultural ecology, or humanenvironment, approach to explain many global issues. People can adjust to the capacity of the physical environment by controlling their population growth, adopting new technology, consuming different foods, migrating to new locations, and other actions.

A people's level of wealth can also influence its attitudes toward modifying the environment. A rocky hillside is an obstacle to a farmer with a tractor, but an opportunity to a farmer with a hoe. Modern technology has altered the historic relationship between people and the environment.

Physical Processes: Climate. Human geographers need some familiarity with global environmental processes to understand the distribution of human activities.

Climate is the long-term average weather condition at a particular location. Geographers frequently classify climates according to a system developed by German climatologist Vladimir Köppen. The modified Köppen system divides the five main climate regions into several subtypes.

The climate of a particular location influences human activities, especially production of the food needed to survive.

(25)
Physical Processes: Vegetation. Plant life covers nearly the entire land surface of Earth. Earth's land vegetation includes four major forms of plant communities, called biomes: forest, savanna, grassland, and desert. Their location and extent are influenced by both climate and human activities. Vegetation and soil, in turn, influence the types of agriculture that people practice in a particular region.

(26)
Physical Processes: Soil. Soil, the material that forms on Earth's surface, is the thin interface between the air and the rocks. Not merely dirt, soil contains the nutrients necessary for successful growth of plants, including those useful to humans.

The U.S. Comprehensive Soil Classification System divides global soil types into ten orders. The orders are subdivided into suborders, great groups, subgroups, families, and series. More than 12,000 soil types have been identified in the United States alone. Two basic problems contribute to the destruction of soil: erosion and depletion of nutrients.

Physical Processes: Landforms. Geographers find that the study of Earth's landforms — a science known as geomorphology — helps to explain the distribution of people and the choice of economic activities at different locations.

Geographers use topographic maps to study the relief and slope of localities. Relief is the difference in elevation between any two points, and it measures the extent to which an area is flat or hilly.

Modifying the Environment. Modern technology has altered the historic relationship between people and the environment. Humans can now modify the environment to a greater extent than in the past. Geographers are concerned that people sometimes use modern technology to modify the environment insensitively.

(27)

The Netherlands: Sensitive Environmental Modification. The Dutch have modified their environment with two distinctive types of construction projects: polders and dikes. A **polder** is a piece of land that is created by draining water from an area. The building of dikes and polders began in the thirteenth century as private enterprise and has been continued by the government during the last 200 years. In the north, a dike built in 1932 has turned the Zuider Zee from a saltwater sea to a freshwater lake. An ambitious 30-year project in the southwest, begun after a devastating flood in 1953, built dams to close off most of the water ways in the huge Delta formed by the Rhine, the Maas, and the Scheldt rivers. With these two massive projects finished, attitudes toward modifying the environment have changed in the Netherlands. The Dutch are deliberately breaking some dikes to flood fields. But modifying the environment will still be essential to the survival of the Dutch.

(28)

South Florida: Not-So-Sensitive Environmental Modification. Sensitive environmental areas in South Florida include barrier islands, the Everglades wetlands, and the Kissimmee River.

The barrier islands are essentially large sandbars that shield the mainland from flooding and storm damage. Despite their fragile condition, the barrier islands are attractive locations for constructing homes and recreational facilities.

People build seawalls and jetties to fight erosion, but these projects result in more damage than protection. A seawall causes erosion on the down-current side of the island, by trapping sand along the up-current side.

A 2000 plan called for restoring the historic flow of water through South Florida while improving flood control and water quality. A 2008 plan called for the state to acquire hundreds of thousands of acres of land from sugarcane growers. But to date, few elements of the plan have been implemented.

Key Issue 3. Why Are Different Places Similar?
- **Scale: From local to global**
- **Space: Distribution of features**
- **Connections between places**

Although accepting that each place or region on Earth is unique, geographers recognize that human activities are rarely confined to one location. This section discusses three basic concepts — scale, space, and connections — that help geographers understand why two places or regions can display similar features.

Scale: From Local to Global
All scales from local to global are important in geography — the appropriate scale depends on the specific subject. At a local scale, such as a neighborhood within a city, geographers tend to see unique features. At the global scale, encompassing the entire world, geographers tend to see broad patterns. Geography matters in the contemporary world because it can explain human actions at all scales, from local to global.

(29)

Globalization of Economy
Scale is an increasingly important concept in geography because of **globalization**, which is a force or process that involves the entire world and results in making something worldwide in scope.

Globalization means that the scale of the world is shrinking — not literally in size, of course, but in the ability of a person, object, or idea to interact with a person, object, or idea in another place.

A few people living in very remote regions of the world may be able to provide all of their daily necessities. But most economic activities undertaken in one region are influenced by interaction with decision makers located elsewhere. Globalization of the economy has been led primarily by **transnational corporations**, sometimes called multinational corporations.

Modern technology provides the means to easily move money — as well as materials, products, technology, and other economic assets — around the world. Every place in the world is part of the global economy, but globalization has led to more specialization at the local level.

A locality may be especially suitable for a transnational corporation to conduct research, to develop new engineering systems, to extract raw material, to produce parts, to store finished products, to sell them, or to manage operations. Globalization of the economy has heightened economic differences among places. The deep recession that began in 2008 has been called the first global recession. Past recessions were typically confined to one country or region.

(31)
Globalization of Culture
Geographers observe that increasingly uniform cultural preferences produce uniform "global" landscapes of material artifacts and of cultural values. The survival of a local culture's distinctive beliefs, forms, and traits is threatened by interaction with such social customs as wearing jeans and Nike shoes, consuming Coca-Cola and McDonald's hamburgers, and other preferences in food, clothing, shelter, and leisure activities.

Yet despite globalization, cultural differences among places not only persist but actually flourish in many places. The communications revolution that promotes globalization of culture also permits preservation of cultural diversity.

With the globalization of communications, people in two distant places can watch the same television program. At the same time, with the fragmentation of the broadcasting market, two people in the same house can watch different programs. Culturally, people residing in different places are displaying fewer differences and more similarities in their cultural preferences. But the desire of some people to retain their traditional cultural elements has led to political conflict and market fragmentation in some regions.

Strong determination on the part of a group to retain its local cultural traditions in the face of globalization of culture can lead to intolerance of people who display other beliefs, social forms, and material traits. A much more extreme opposition to globalization led to the attack by al-Qaeda terrorists against the United States on September 11, 2001, with support from the Taliban, then in control of Afghanistan. Human geographers understand that many contemporary social problems result from a tension between forces promoting global culture and economy on the one hand and, on the other, preservation of local economic autonomy and cultural traditions.

(32)
Space: Distribution Features
Geographers think about the arrangements of people and activities found in space and try to understand why those people and activities are distributed across space as they are.

Distribution
The arrangement of a feature in space is known as **distribution**. Geographers identify three main properties of distribution across Earth: density, concentration, and pattern.

Density. The frequency with which something occurs in space is its density. **Arithmetic density**, which is the total number of objects in an area, is commonly used to compare the distribution of population in different countries. Arithmetic density involves two measures: the number of people and the land area. A large *population* does not necessarily lead to a high *density*. **Physiological density** is the number of persons per unit of area suitable for agriculture. The number of farmers per unit of area is called **agricultural density**.

(33)
Concentration. The extent of a feature's spread over space is the **concentration**. *Clustered* objects in an area are close together; *dispersed* are far apart. Geographers use concentration to describe changes in distribution.

Pattern. Some features are organized in a geometric pattern, while others are distributed irregularly.

(34)
Gender and Ethnic Diversity in Space
Spatial interaction may be limited even among people in close proximity to one another. Consider first the daily movement of an "all-American" family.

Dad drives to work, spends the day and drives home. The mother's local-scale travel patterns are likely to be far more complex than the father's, as she transports children and organizes family life. Most American women are now employed at work outside the home, adding a substantial complication to an already complex pattern of moving across urban space.

If the hypothetical family consists of persons of color, its connections with space would change. In most U.S. neighborhoods the residents are virtually all whites or virtually all persons of color. Segregation persists partly based on cultural preference, partly based on fears.

Cultural identity is a source of pride to people at the local scale and an inspiration for personal values. Even more than self-identification, personal traits matter to other people. For geographers, concern for cultural diversity is not merely a politically correct expediency; it lies at the heart of geography's spatial tradition.

(35)
Connections Between Places
Geographers apply the term **space–time compression** to describe the reduction in the time it takes for something to reach another place. Geographers explain the process, called diffusion, by which connections are made between regions, as well as the mechanism by which connections are maintained through networks.

Spatial Interaction
In the past, most forms of interaction among cultural groups required the physical movement of settlers, explorers, and plunderers from one location to another. Today travel by motor vehicle or airplane is much quicker and we can communicate instantly with people in distant places. When places are connected to each other through a network, geographers say there is spatial interaction between them.

Networks are chains of communication that connect places. A well-known example is the television network. Transportation systems also form networks that connect places to each other. Typically, the farther away one group is from another, the less likely the two groups are to interact. This trailing-off phenomenon is called **distance decay**.

Diffusion
Diffusion is the process by which a characteristic spreads across space from one place to another over time. The place from which an innovation originates is called a **hearth**. The dominant cultural, political, and economic features of contemporary United States and Canada can be traced primarily to hearths in Europe and the Middle East. Other regions of the world also contain important hearths. An idea, such as agriculture, may originate independently in more than one hearth. Geographers observe two basic types of diffusion: relocation and expansion.

(37)
Relocation Diffusion. The spread of an idea through physical movement of people is termed relocation diffusion. Relocation diffusion can explain the rapid rise in the number of AIDS cases in the United States during the 1980s and early 1990s but not the rapid decline beginning in the mid-1990s. The decline resulted from the rapid diffusion of preventive methods and medicines. The rapid spread of these innovations is an example of expansion diffusion rather than relocation diffusion.

(38)
Expansion Diffusion. The spread of a feature from one place to another in a snowballing process is **expansion diffusion**. This expansion may result from one of three processes: hierarchical diffusion, contagious diffusion, and stimulus diffusion.

Hierarchical diffusion is the spread of an idea from persons or nodes of authority or power to other persons or places. **Contagious diffusion** is the rapid, widespread diffusion of a characteristic throughout the population.

Stimulus diffusion is the spread of an underlying principle, even though a characteristic itself apparently fails to diffuse.

Modern methods of communications encourage hierarchical diffusion; the Internet has encouraged contagious diffusion, and all the new technologies support stimulus diffusion.

Diffusion of Culture and Economy. In a global culture and economy, transportation and communications systems have been organized to rapidly diffuse raw materials, goods, services, and capital from nodes of origin to other regions. The global culture and economy is increasingly centered on three core or hearth regions of North America, Western Europe, and Japan. The global economy has produced greater disparities than in the past between the levels of wealth and well-being enjoyed by people in the core and in the periphery. The increasing gap in economic conditions is known as **uneven development**.

Key Terms

Agricultural density (p.33)
Arithmetic density (p.32)
Base line (p.9)
Cartography (p.5)
Concentration (p.33)
Connections (p.5)
Contagious diffusion (p.39)
Cultural ecology (p.24)
Cultural landscape (p.17)
Culture (p.21)
Density (p.32)
Diffusion (p.36)

Distance decay (p.36)
Distribution (p.32)
Environmental determinism (p.24)
Expansion diffusion (p.38)
Formal region (p.17)
Functional region (p.19)
Geographic Information System (GIS) (p.12)
Global Positioning System (GPS) (p.9)
Globalization (p.29)
Greenwich Mean Time (p.18)
Hearth (p.36)
Hierarchical diffusion (p.39)

International Date Line (p.18)
Land Ordinance of 1785 (p.9)
Latitude (p.15)
Location (p.13)
Longitude (p.15)
Map (p.4)
Mental map (p.20)
Meridian (p.15)
Parallel (p.15)
Pattern (p.33)
Physiological density (p.33)
Place (p.5)
Polder (p.27)
Possibilism (p.24)
Prime meridian (p.15)
Principal meridian (p.9)
Projection (p.8)

Region (p.5)
Regional studies (p.17)
Relocation diffusion (p.37)
Remote sensing (p.9)
Resource (p.24)
Scale (p.5)
Section (p.9)
Site (p.14)
Situation (p.14)
Space (p.5)
Space-time compression (p.35)
Stimulus diffusion (p.39)
Toponym (p.13)
Township (p.9)
Transnational corporation (p.30)
Uneven development (p.39)
Vernacular region (p.19)

Test Prep Questions

1) Map projections can cause these kinds of distortion EXCEPT:
A) relative size
B) color
C) distance
D) shape

2) Contemporary mapping tools are based upon all of the following technologies EXCEPT:
A) polders
B) GPS
C) remote sensing
D) GIS

3) Geographers describe the location of a place by:
A) mathematical location, toponyms, and site
B) situation, site, and toponyms
C) mathematical location, site, and situation
D) all of the above

4) Which of the following is NOT an example of a formal region?
A) the state of New Mexico
B) Dade County, Florida
C) "The South"
D) a school district

5) Which of the following is an example of a functional, or nodal, region?
A) a television market
B) a time zone
C) a geographic region
D) a postal zip code

6) Which of the following is true about vernacular regions?
A) They have distinct central points.
B) Their boundaries are always discrete.
C) Their boundaries are not always agreed upon.
D) They embody the geographical concept of "distance decay."

7) Which of the following statements about possibilism is true?
A) It was founded by the German geographers von Humbolt and Ritter.
B) Modern geographers reject it in favor of environmental determinism.
C) It posits that the environment causes social development.
D) It rejects the idea that humans can alter their physical environment.

8) What is true about globalization?
A) It has largely affected the economy at the global scale and culture at the local scale.
B) It has made different places more similar.
C) It has reduced the instances of terrorism in the world today.
D) It has insulated local economies from economic downturns in other regions.

9) Distribution is a geographic concept that has what three main properties?
A) arithmetic, physiological and agricultural
B) density, dispersion, and regularity
C) clusters, dispersions, and geometric pattern
D) density, concentration, and pattern

10) Which type of diffusion is not a type of expansion diffusion?
A) relocation
B) hierarchical
C) stimulus
D) contagious

Short Essay

1) Explain the concepts of scale, projection, and distortion as they pertain to cartography.

The earth is not flat, its round. When the world is projected on a flat surface like a map, shape and relative size will be changed. When there is scaling finer detailes may be gained or tosed lost.

2) Explain how geographers describe the mathematical location of a place, and give a specific example of how they would use the concepts of site and situation in relation to a particular place, such as "Manhattan."

Mathematical location is described by longitude, latitude, minutes & seconds, N/S or E/w. Situation is a place in relation to another place. Site is physical character of a place. Ie Manhattan is a hevily populated island That was man made and is located east of New Jersy

_____
_____
_____
_____
_____
_____
_____
_____

3) Describe the concept of globalization and explain its impact on culture and the economy.

Due to advances in technology, comunication over vast distance became possible along ~~travel~~ with travel. I leads to combining of combining culture both good and bad values, also ~~cause~~ has trading with other countries, leads to a countric's economy depending on another country.

_____
_____
_____
_____
_____
_____
_____

Chapter 2
Population

(44)
Key Issues
1. Where is the world's population distributed?
2. Where has the world's population increased?
3. Why is population increasing at different rates in different countries?
4. Why might the world face an overpopulation problem?

(46)
The study of population is critically important for three reasons:
- More people are alive at this time — over 6 3/4 billion — than at any time in human history;
- The world's population increased at a faster rate during the second half of the twentieth century than ever before in history;
- Virtually all global population growth is concentrated in less developed countries.

At a global *scale*, the world's so-called **overpopulation** problem is not simply a matter of the total number of people but the relationship between number of people and available resources. At a local scale, geographers find that overpopulation is a threat in some regions of the world but not in others. Regions with the most people are not necessarily the same as the regions with an unfavorable balance between population and resources.

Key Issue 1. Where Is the World's Population Distributed?
- **Population concentrations**
- **Sparsely populated regions**
- **Population density**

We can understand how population is distributed by examining two basic properties: concentration and density.

(47)
Population Concentrations
Approximately two-thirds of the world's population is clustered in four regions: East Asia, South Asia, Southeast Asia, and Western Europe. The four regions display some similarities. Most of their people live near an ocean or near a river with easy access to an ocean. The four population clusters occupy generally low-lying areas, with fertile soil and temperate climate. Despite these similarities, we can see significant differences in the pattern of occupancy of the land.

East Asia
One-fifth of the world's people live in East Asia, the largest cluster of inhabitants. Five-sixths of the people in this concentration live in the People's Republic of China, the world's most populous country. The Chinese population is clustered near the Pacific Coast and in several fertile river valleys. Three fourths of the people live in rural areas where they work as farmers.

In Japan and South Korea, population is not distributed uniformly either. More than three-fourths of the Japanese and Koreans live in urban areas.

South Asia
Nearly one-fourth of the world's people also live in South Asia, which includes India, Pakistan, Bangladesh, and the Island of Sri Lanka. India, the world's second most populous country, contains more than three-fourths of the South Asia population concentration. Much of this area's

15

population is concentrated along the plains of the Indus and Ganges rivers. Population is also concentrated near India's two long coastlines. Like the Chinese, most people in South Asia are farmers.

(48)
Southeast Asia

A third important Asian population cluster, and the world's fourth-largest population cluster, after Europe, is in Southeast Asia, mostly on a series of islands that lie between the Indian and Pacific Oceans. The largest concentration is on the island of Java, inhabited by more than 100 million people. Indonesia, which consists of 13,677 islands, is the world's fourth most populous country. Several Philippine islands contain high population concentrations. The Indochina population is clustered along several river valleys and deltas at the southeastern tip of the Asian mainland. A high percentage of people in Southeast Asia work as farmers.

The three Asian population concentrations together comprise over half of the world's total population, but together they live on less than 10 percent of Earth's land area. The same held true 2,000 years ago.

(49)
Europe

Europe, including the European portion of Russia, forms the world's third-largest population cluster, one-ninth of the world's people. Three-fourths of Europe's inhabitants live in cities. Europeans import food and other resources. The search for additional resources was a major incentive for Europeans to colonize other parts of the world during the previous six centuries.

Other Population Clusters

The largest population concentration in the Western Hemisphere is in the northeastern United States and southeastern Canada. About 2 percent of the world's people live in the area. Less than 2 percent are farmers.

Another 2 percent of the world's population is clustered in West Africa, especially along the south-facing Atlantic coast. Approximately half is in Nigeria, and the other half is divided among several small countries west of Nigeria. Most people work in agriculture.

Sparsely Populated Regions

Relatively few people live in regions that are too dry, too wet, too cold, or too mountainous for agriculture. Approximately three-fourths of the world's population lives on only 5 percent of Earth's surface. The portion of the Earth's surface occupied by permanent human settlement is called the **ecumene**.

(50)
Dry Lands

Areas too dry for farming cover approximately 20 percent of Earth's land surface. Deserts generally lack sufficient water to grow crops although some people survive there by raising animals, such as camels, that are adapted to the climate. Dry lands may contain natural resources notably, much of the world's oil reserves.

Wet Lands

Lands that receive very high levels of precipitation may also be inhospitable for human occupation. These lands are located primarily near the equator. The combination of rain and heat rapidly depletes nutrients from the soil, thus hindering agriculture. In seasonally wet lands, such as those in Southeast Asia, enough food can be grown to support a large population.

Cold Lands
Much of the land near the North and South poles is perpetually covered with ice or the ground is permanently frozen (permafrost). Few animals can survive the extreme cold, and few humans live there.

High Lands
Relatively few people live at high elevations. We can find some significant exceptions, especially in Latin America and Africa.

Population Density
Density, the number of people occupying an area of land, can be computed in several ways, including arithmetic density, physiological density, and agricultural density.

Arithmetic Density. Geographers most frequently use **arithmetic density**, which is the total number of people divided by total land area. Arithmetic density enables geographers to make approximate comparisons of the number of people trying to live on a given piece of land in different regions of the world.

(51)
Physiological Density. A more meaningful population measure is afforded by looking at the number of people per area of a certain type of land in a region. Land suited for agriculture is called *arable land*. The number of people supported by a unit area of arable land is called the physiological density.

Comparing physiological and arithmetic densities helps geographers to understand the capacity of the land to yield enough food for the needs of people.

(52)
Agricultural Density. Two countries can have similar physiological densities, but they may produce significantly different amounts of food because of different economic conditions. **Agricultural density** is the ratio of the number of farmers to the amount of arable land. To understand the relationship between population and resources in a country, geographers examine its physiological and agricultural densities together.

(53)
The Netherlands has a much higher physiological density than does India but a much lower agricultural density.

Key Issue 2. Where Has the World's Population Increased?
- **Natural increase**
- **Fertility**
- **Mortality**

Population increases rapidly in places where many more people are born than die, increases slowly in places where the number of births exceeds the number of deaths by only a small margin, and declines in places where deaths outnumber births.

The population of a place also increases when people move in and decreases when people move out.

Natural Increase

Geographers most frequently measure population change in a country or the world as a whole through three measures: **Crude birth rate (CBR)** is the total number of live births in a year for every 1,000 people; **Crude death rate (CDR)** is the total number of deaths in a year for every 1,000 people; and **Natural increase rate (NIR)** is the percentage by which a population grows in a year. The term *natural* means that a country's growth rate excludes migration. The world NIR during the twenty-first century was 1.2 percent. The world NIR is lower today than at its all-time peak of 2.2 percent in 1963. However, the NIR during the second half of the twentieth century was high by historical standards. The number of people added each year has dropped much more slowly than the NIR, because the population base is much higher now than in the past. The rate of natural increase affects the **doubling time**, which is the number of years needed to double a population. When the NIR was 2.2 percent back in 1963, doubling time was 35 years.

(54)

More than 95 percent of the natural increase is clustered in LDCs. To explain these differences in growth rates, geographers point to the regional differences in fertility and mortality rates.

Fertility

The highest crude birth rates are in sub-Saharan Africa, and the lowest are in Europe. The word *crude* in *crude birth rate* and *crude death rate* means that we are concerned with society as a whole rather than a refined look at particular individuals or groups. Geographers also use the **total fertility rate (TFR)** to measure the number of births in a society. The TFR is the average number of children a woman will have throughout her childbearing years. The total fertility rate for the world as a whole is approximately three. The TFR exceeds six in many countries of sub-Saharan Africa, compared to less than two in nearly every European country.

Mortality

Two useful measures of mortality in addition to the crude death rate are the infant mortality rate and life expectancy. The **infant mortality rate (IMR)** is the annual number of deaths of infants under one year of age, compared with total live births, usually expressed as the number of deaths per 1,000 births rather than as a percentage. Infant mortality rates exceed 100 in some LDCs.

In general, the IMR reflects a country's healthcare system. Minorities in the United States have infant mortality rates that are twice as high as the national average, comparable to levels in Latin America and Asia.

(55)

Life expectancy at birth measures the average number of years a newborn infant can expect to live at current mortality levels. Babies born today can expect to live to around 80 in Western Europe but only to around 50 in sub-Saharan Africa.

Higher natural increase, crude birth, total fertility rates, IMRs, and lower average life expectancy are found in LDCs. The final world map of demographic variables—crude death rate—does not follow the familiar pattern. The combined crude death rate for all less developed countries is actually lower than the combined rate for MDCs. Furthermore, the variation between the world's highest and lowest CDRs is much less extreme than the variation in CBRs. The populations of different countries are at various stages in an important process known as the demographic transition.

(56)

Key Issue 3. Why Is Population Increasing at Different Rates in Different Countries?
- **The demographic transition**
- **Population pyramids**

- **Countries in different stages of demographic transition**
- **Demographic transition and world population growth**

Although rates vary among countries, a similar process of change in a society's population, known as the **demographic transition,** is operating.

The Demographic Transition

The demographic transition has a beginning, middle, and end. Historically, once a country has moved from one stage to the next, it has not reverted to an earlier stage. However, a reversal may be occurring in some African countries because of the AIDS epidemic.

Stage 1: Low Growth

Most of humanity's several-hundred-thousand-year occupancy of Earth was characterized by stage 1 of the demographic transition. Crude birth and death rates varied considerably from one year to the next and from one region to another, but over the long term they were roughly comparable, at very high levels.

Between 8000 B.C. and A.D. 1750, Earth's human population increased from approximately 5 million to 800 million. The burst of population growth around 8000 B.C. was caused by the **agricultural revolution**. Despite the agricultural revolution, the human population remained in stage 1 of the demographic transition because food supplies were still unpredictable.

(57)

Stage 2: High Growth

For nearly 10,000 years after the agricultural revolution, world population grew at a modest pace. After around A.D. 1750 the world's population suddenly began to grow ten times faster than in the past. In stage 2, the crude death rate suddenly plummets, while the crude birth rate remains roughly the same as in stage 1.

Some demographers divide stage 2 into two parts. During the second part, the growth rate begins to slow, although the gap between births and deaths remains high. Countries entered stage 2 of the demographic transition after 1750 as a result of the **Industrial Revolution**. The result of this transformation was an unprecedented level of wealth, some of which was used to make communities healthier places to live.

Countries in Europe and North America entered stage 2 of the demographic transition around 1800, but stage 2 did not diffuse to most countries in Africa, Asia, and Latin America until around 1950. The late twentieth-century push of countries into stage 2 was caused by the **medical revolution**. Improved medical practices suddenly eliminated many of the traditional causes of death in LDCs and enabled more people to experience longer and healthier lives.

Stage 3: Moderate Growth

A country moves from stage 2 into stage 3 of the demographic transition when the crude birth rate begins to drop sharply. European and North American countries moved from stage 2 to stage 3 during the first half of the twentieth century. Most countries in Asia and Latin America have moved to stage 3 in recent years, while most African countries remain in stage 2. A society enters stage 3 when people choose to have fewer children. Medical practices introduced in stage 2 societies greatly improved the probability of infant survival, but many years elapsed before families reacted by conceiving fewer babies. Economic changes in stage 3 societies also induce people to have fewer offspring. Farmers often consider a large family to be an asset. In contrast, children living in cities are generally not economic assets.

Stage 4: Low Growth

A country reaches stage 4 when the crude birth rate declines to the point where it equals the crude death rate. The condition is called **zero population growth (ZPG)**. Demographers more precisely define zero population growth as the total fertility rate (TFR) that results in a lack of change in the total population over a long term. A TFR of approximately 2.1 produces ZPG, although a country that receives many immigrants may need a lower total fertility rate to achieve ZPG.

Most European countries have reached stage 4 of the demographic transition. The United States has moved slightly below ZPG since 2000. Several Eastern European countries, most notably Russia, have negative natural increase rates, a legacy of a half-century of Communist rule.

As memories of the Communist era fade, Russians and other Eastern Europeans may display birth and death rates more comparable to those in Western Europe. Alternatively, demographers in the future may identify a fifth stage, characterized by higher death rates than birth rates and an irreversible population decline.

(59)
Population Pyramids

Population in a country is influenced by the demographic transition in two principal ways: the percentage of the population in each age group, and the distribution of males and females. A country's population can be displayed by age and gender groups on a bar graph called a **population pyramid**. The shape of the pyramid is determined primarily by the CBR.

Age Distribution

The age structure of a population is extremely important in understanding similarities and differences among countries. The most important factor is the **dependency ratio**, which is the number of people who are too young or too old to work, compared to the number of people in their productive years.

(60)

Young dependents outnumber elderly ones by 10:1 in stage 2 countries, but the numbers of young and elderly dependents are roughly equal in stage 4 countries. The large percentage of children in sub-Saharan Africa and other stage 2 countries strains the ability of poorer countries to provide needed services. As countries pass through the stages of the demographic transition, the percentage of elderly people increases. More than one-fourth of all government expenditures in the United States, Canada, Japan, and many European countries go to Social Security, health care, and other programs for the older population.

Sex Ratio

The number of males per hundred females in the population is the sex ratio. The ratio of men to women is about 93:100 in Europe and 97:100 in North America. In LDCs the ratio is 103:100.

In stage 2 countries, the high mortality rate during childbirth partly explains the lower percentage of women. The difference also relates to the age structure. The shape of a community's population pyramid tells a lot about its distinctive character.

(61)
Countries in Different Stages of Demographic Transition

No country today remains in stage 1 of the demographic transition, but it is instructive to compare countries in each of the other three stages.

Cape Verde: Stage 2 (High Growth). Cape Verde, a collection of 12 small islands in the Atlantic Ocean off the coast of West Africa, moved from stage 1 to stage 2 about 1950. During the first half of the twentieth century Cape Verde's population declined.

The large gap between births and deaths most years produced a high natural increase rate typical of stage 2, yet Cape Verde remained in stage 1 because famines dramatically disrupted the typical patterns of birth, death, and natural increase.

(62)

Cape Verde moved on to stage 2 when an antimalarial campaign was launched.

Cape Verde's crude birth rate has remained relatively high and still fluctuates wildly.

(63)

The wild fluctuations in Cape Verde's crude birth rate are a legacy of the severe famine during the 1940s. The population pyramid shows that Cape Verde has a large number of females age 5-14 who will soon start moving into their prime childbearing years. For Cape Verde to enter stage 3 these females must bear considerably fewer children than did their mothers.

Chile: Stage 3 (Moderate Growth). Like most countries outside Europe and North America, Chile entered the twentieth century still in stage 1. Much of Chile's population growth resulted from European immigration. Chile's crude death rate declined sharply in the 1930s, moving the country into stage 2. Chile's crude death rate was lowered by the infusion of medical technology from MDCs. Chile has been in stage 3 since about 1960 primarily because of a vigorous government family planning policy.

Reduced income and high unemployment also induced couples to delay childbearing. The country is unlikely to move into stage 4 in the near future. Chile's government reversed its policy and renounced support for family planning during the 1970s. The government policy was that population growth could help promote national security and economic development. Also most Chileans belong to the Roman Catholic Church, which opposes the use of what it calls artificial birth-control techniques.

(64)
Denmark: Stage 4 (Low Growth). Denmark entered stage 2 in the nineteenth century, when the CDR began its permanent decline. The CBR then dropped in the late nineteenth century, and the country moved on to stage 3.

Since the 1970s the country has reached ZPG, and the population is increasing almost entirely because of immigration. Instead of a classic pyramid shape, Denmark has a column, demonstrating that the percentages of young and elderly people are nearly the same.

Demographic Transition and World Population Growth
Worldwide population increased rapidly during the second half of the twentieth century. The demographic transition is characterized by two big breaks with the past. The first break—the sudden drop in the death rate — has been accomplished everywhere. The second break —t he sudden drop in the birth rate — has yet to be achieved in many countries.

(66)
Medical technology was injected from Europe and North America into Africa, Asia, and Latin America instead of arising within those regions as part of an economic revolution. In the past, stage 2 lasted for approximately 100 years in Europe and North America, but today's stage 2

countries are being asked to move through to stage 3 in much less time to curtail population growth.

Key Issue 4. Why Might the World Face an Overpopulation Problem?
- **Malthus on overpopulation**
- **Declining birth rates**
- **World health threats**

Why does global population growth matter? Geographers observe that diverse local culture and environmental conditions may produce different answers in different places.

Malthus on Overpopulation
English economist Thomas Malthus (1766–1834) was one of the first to argue that the world's rate of population increase was far outrunning the development of food supplies. In *An Essay on the Principle of Population*, published in 1798, Malthus claimed that population increased geometrically, while food supply increased arithmetically. He concluded that population growth would press against available resources in every country, unless "moral restraint" produced lower crude birth rates or unless disease, famine, war, or other disasters produced higher crude death rates.

(67)
Contemporary Neo-Malthusians. Malthus's views remain influential today because of the unprecedented rate of natural increase in LDCs. Neo-Malthusians argue that two characteristics of recent population growth make Malthus' thesis more frightening than when it was first written. First, Malthus failed to anticipate that poor countries would have the most rapid population growth. The gap between population and resources is wider in some countries than even Malthus anticipated. The second argument made by neo-Malthusians is that population growth is outstripping such resources as clean air, suitable farmland, and fuel as well as food.

Malthus's Critics. Criticism has been leveled at both the population growth and resource depletion sides of Malthus's equation. Contemporary analysts such as Esther Boserup and Julian Simon argue that a larger population could stimulate economic growth and therefore the production of more food. The Marxist theorist Friedrich Engels argued that the world possessed sufficient resources to eliminate global hunger and poverty, if only these resources were shared equally. Malthus' critics argue that a large population of consumers can generate a greater demand for goods, which results in more jobs. Some political leaders, especially in Africa, argue that more people will result in greater power.

Malthus Theory and Reality
Vaclav Smil has shown that Malthus was fairly close to the mark on food production but much too pessimistic on population growth. Many people in the world cannot afford to buy food or do not have access to sources of food, but these are problems of distribution of wealth rather than insufficient global production of food, as Malthus theorized. Population has been increasing at a much slower rate during the past two decades than it was during the previous half-century. However, neo-Malthusians point out that despite the lower NIR during the 1990s, the world added approximately the same number of people as during the 1980s.

Declining Birth Rates
Although the world as a whole may not be in danger of "running out" of food, some regions with rapid population growth do face shortages of food. Two strategies have been successful in reducing birth rates. One alternative emphasizes reliance on economic development, the other on

distribution of contraceptives. Because of varied economic and cultural conditions, the most effective method varies among countries.

Reasons for Declining Birth Rates
One approach to lowering birth rates emphasizes the importance of improving local economic conditions. With improved healthcare programs, IMRs would decline and with the survival of more infants ensured, women would be more likely to limit the number of children.

(69)
Reducing Births Through Contraception
In LDCs, demand for contraceptive devices is greater than the available supply.

(70)
About one-fourth of African women employ contraceptives, compared to about two-thirds in other less developed countries. Very high birth rates in Africa and southwestern Asia also reflect the relatively low status of women.

Many oppose birth control programs for religious and political reasons. Analysts agree that the most effective means of reducing births would employ both alternatives.

But LDC governments and international family planning organizations have limited funds so they must set priorities.

(71)
World Health Threats
Lower CBRs have been responsible for declining NIRs in most countries. However, in some countries of sub-Saharan Africa lower natural increase rates have also resulted from higher crude death rates, especially through the diffusion of AIDS. Medical researchers have identified an **epidemiologic transition** that focuses on distinctive causes of death in each stage of the demographic transition.

Epidemiologic Transition Stages 1 and 2
Stage 1 of the epidemiologic transition has been called the stage of pestilence and famine. Infectious and parasitic diseases were principal causes of human deaths.

Black Plague. The Black Plague, or bubonic plague, originated in present-day Kyrgyzstan and was brought from there by a Tatar army when it attacked an Italian trading post on the Black Sea. About 25 million Europeans died between 1347 and 1350, at least one-half of the continent's population. Five other epidemics in the late fourteenth century added to the toll in Europe. In China, 13 million died from the plague in 1380.

Stage 2 of the epidemiologic transition has been called the stage of receding pandemics. A **pandemic** is disease that occurs over a wide geographic area and affects a very high proportion of the population. Cholera became an especially virulent epidemic in urban areas during the Industrial Revolution.

Construction of water and sewer systems eradicated cholera by the late nineteenth century. However, cholera reappeared a century later in rapidly growing cities of less developed countries as they moved into stage 2 of the demographic transition.

(72)
Epidemiologic Transition Stages 3 and 4
Stage 3 of the epidemiologic transition, the stage of degenerative and human-created diseases, is characterized by a decrease in deaths from infectious diseases and an increase in chronic disorders

associated with aging. The two especially important chronic disorders in stage 3 are cardiovascular diseases, such as heart attacks, and various forms of cancer.

The decline in infectious diseases has been sharp in stage 3 countries. Effective vaccines were responsible for these declines. As less developed countries have moved recently from stage 2 to stage 3, infectious diseases have also declined.

The epidemiologic transition was extended to stage 4, the stage of delayed degenerative diseases. The major degenerative causes of death — cardiovascular diseases and cancers — linger, but the life expectancy of older people is extended through medical advances.

Epidemiologic Transition Possible Stage 5
Some medical analysts argue that the world is moving into stage 5 of the epidemiologic transition, the stage of reemergence of infectious and parasitic diseases. Infectious diseases thought to have been eradicated or controlled have returned, and new ones have emerged. Three reasons help to explain the possible emergence of a stage 5 of the epidemiologic transition

1. Evolution. Infectious disease microbes have continuously evolved and changed in response to environmental pressures by developing resistance to drugs and insecticides.

2. Poverty. Tuberculosis (TB) is an example of an infectious disease that has been largely controlled in relatively developed countries like the United States but remains a major cause of death in less developed countries.

3. Improved travel. As they travel, people carry diseases with them and are exposed to the diseases of others. Several dozen "new" infectious diseases have emerged over the past three decades and have spread through travel. Most prominent currently is H1N1, commonly known as swine flu, which was first identified in Mexico in early 2009 and spread around the world rapidly.

(73)
AIDS. The most lethal epidemic in recent years has been AIDS (acquired immunodeficiency syndrome), caused by the human immunodeficiency virus (HIV). The impact of AIDS has been felt most strongly in sub-Saharan Africa. With one-tenth of the world's population, sub-Saharan Africa has two-thirds of the world's HIV-positive population and nine-tenths of the world's infected children. CDRs in many sub-Saharan Africa countries rose sharply during the 1990s as a result of AIDS, from the mid-teens to the low twenties.

Key Terms

Agricultural density (p.52)	Industrial Revolution (p.57)
Agricultural revolution (p.57)	Infant mortality rate (IMR) (p.55)
Arithmetic density (p.50)	Life expectancy (p.55)
Census (p.62)	Medical Revolution (p.58)
Crude birth rate (CBR) (p.53)	Natural increase rate (NIR) (p.53)
Crude death rate (CDR) (p.53)	Overpopulation (p.46)
Demographic transition (p.56)	Pandemic (p.71)
Demography (p.45)	Physiological density (p.51)
Dependency ratio (p.59)	Population pyramid (p.59)
Doubling time (p.53)	Sex ratio (p.60)
Ecumene (p.49)	Total fertility rate (TFR) (p.54)
Epidemiologic transition (p.71)	Zero population growth (ZPG) (p.58)
Epidemiology (p.71)	

Test Prep Questions

1) The world's fourth largest population cluster is located in:
A) Southeast Asia
B) Europe
C) South Asia
D) East Asia

2) The number of people supported by a unit of land suitable for agriculture is called:
A) agricultural density
B) physiological density
C) population density
D) arithmetic density

3) The Natural Increase Rate of the world during the early 21st century has been:
A) 4 percent
B) 2.2 percent
C) .5 percent
D) 1.2 percent

4) The Industrial revolution caused countries to move into what stage of the demographic transition?
A) stage 1
B) stage 2
C) stage 3
D) stage 4

5) Stage four of the demographic transition is characterized by what?
A) high TFR
B) high IMR
C) ZPG
D) CDR that are much lower than CBR

6) What type of country is likely to have a population pyramid that resembles a true pyramid?
A) a stage 4 country
B) a stage 1 country
C) a stage 3 country
D) a stage 2 country

7) How have Africa, Asia and Latin America moved into stage two of the demographic transition?
A) through the Industrial Revolution
B) through the medical revolution
C) through economic development
D) through the agricultural revolution

8) What was Thomas Malthus's idea regarding population?
A) That population growth was necessary to stimulate the economy.
B) That population was falling due to lack of food.
C) That population and food supply needed to be maintained at equal levels.
D) That population grew geometrically while food supply grew arithmetically.

9) Which of the following conditions does NOT contribute to reducing birth rates?
A) improved healthcare programs
B) economic development
C) empowerment of men
D) distribution of contraceptives

10) Which of the following is NOT a reason for the possible addition of a stage five to the epidemiological transition?
A) poverty
B) decreased nutrition
C) evolution
D) improved travel

Short Essay

1) Explain the three types of population density geographers use, noting why each is useful.

Arithmetic: # of people ÷ area, Helps try to compare people occupying land in different places.

Physiological: # of people per type of land. Good for comparing lands & arability.

Agricultural: Ratio # of farmers to amount of arable land. Helps determine economic conditions by comparing amounts of food.

2) Describe the geographic distribution of population across the Earth, noting the major population clusters.

The population is mostly located in costal areas with arid climates.

Most major clusters are, Western Europe, East, South & Southeast Asia

3) Discuss Thomas Malthus' contribution to population studies, as well as the major criticisms of his work.

Showed that the population grows faster than food production. Teaches us to be careful on how we populate and try to moderate our CBU.

Criticisms: Boserup & Simon argue that this population explosion may stimulate economic growth for food production.

Me: More growth = more urbanization. Infrastructure seals over arable land rendering it useless for food production.

Chapter 3
Migration

Key Issues
1. Why do people migrate?
2. Where are migrants distributed?
3. Why do migrants face obstacles?
4. Why do people migrate within a country?

(80)

The subject of this chapter is a specific type of relocation diffusion called **migration**, which is a permanent move to a new location. **Emigration** is migration *from* a location; **immigration** is migration *to* a location. The difference between the number of immigrants and the number of emigrants is the **net migration**. Migration is a form of **mobility**, which is a more general term covering all types of movements. Short-term, repetitive, or cyclical movements that recur on a regular basis, such as daily, monthly, or annually, are called **circulation**.

The changing *scale* generated by modern transportation systems, especially motor vehicles and airplanes, makes relocation diffusion more feasible than in the past. Within a global culture, people migrate to escape from domination by other cultural groups or to be reunited with others of similar culture.

Key Issue 1. Why Do People Migrate?
- **Reasons for migrating**
- **Distance of migration**
- **Characteristics of migrants**

Geography has no comprehensive theory of migration, although a nineteenth-century outline of 11 migration "laws" written by E. G. Ravenstein is the basis for contemporary migration studies. Ravenstein's "laws" can be organized into three groups: reasons, distance, and migrant characteristics.

Reasons for Migrating
People decide to migrate because of push factors and pull factors. A **push factor** induces people to move out of their present location, whereas a **pull factor** induces people to move into a new location. Both push and pull factors typically play a role. We can identify three major kinds of push and pull factors: economic, cultural, and environmental.

Economic Push and Pull Factors
Most people migrate for economic reasons. Because of economic restructuring, job prospects often vary from one country to another and within regions of the same country.

Cultural Push and Pull Factors
Forced international migration has historically occurred for two main cultural reasons: slavery and political instability. Large groups of people are no longer forced to migrate as slaves, but forced international migration persists because of political instability resulting from cultural diversity. Refugees are people who have been forced to migrate from their home country and cannot return for fear of persecution.

(82)

Political conditions can also operate as pull factors. People may be attracted to democratic countries that encourage individual choice in education, career, and place of residence. With the

27

election of democratic governments in Eastern Europe during the 1990s, Western Europe's political pull has disappeared as a migration factor. However, Western Europe pulls an increasing number of migrants from Eastern Europe for economic reasons.

Environmental Push and Pull Factors
People also migrate for environmental reasons, pulled toward physically attractive regions and pushed from hazardous ones. Attractive environments for migrants include mountains, seasides, and warm climates. Migrants are also pushed from their homes by adverse physical conditions. Water — either too much or too little — poses the most common environmental threat. Many people are forced to move by water-related disasters because they live in a vulnerable area, such as a floodplain. The **floodplain** of a river is the area subject to flooding during a specific number of years, based on historical trends.

(83)
Intervening Obstacles
Where migrants go is not always their desired destination. They may be blocked by an **intervening obstacle**. In the past, intervening obstacles were primarily environmental. Bodies of water long have been important intervening obstacles. However, today's migrant faces intervening obstacles created by local diversity in government and politics.

(84)
Distance of Migration
Ravenstein's theories made two main points about the distance that migrants travel to their home: Most migrants relocate a short distance and remain within the same country. Long-distance migrants to other countries head for major centers of economic activity.

Internal Migration
International migration is permanent movement from one country to another, whereas **internal migration** is permanent movement within the same country. International migrants are much less numerous than internal migrants. **Interregional migration** is movement from one region of a country to another, while **intraregional migration** is movement within one region.

International Migration
International migration is further divided into two types: **forced** and **voluntary**. Economic push and pull factors usually induce voluntary migration, and cultural factors normally compel forced migration.

Geographer Wilbur Zelinsky has identified a **migration transition**, which consists of changes in a society comparable to those in the demographic transition. A society in stage 1 has high daily or seasonal mobility in search of food. According to migration transition theory, societies in stages 3 and 4 are the destinations of the international migrants leaving the stage 2 countries in search of economic opportunities. Internal migration within countries in stages 3 and 4 of the demographic transition is intraregional, from cities to surrounding suburbs.

Characteristics of Migrants
Ravenstein noted distinctive gender and family-status patterns in his migration theories: Most long-distance migrants are male, and most long-distance migrants are adult individuals rather than families with children.

Gender of Migrants
Since the 1990s the gender pattern has reversed, and women now constitute about 55 percent of U.S. immigration. The increased female migration to the United States partly reflects the changing

role of women in Mexican society. Some Mexican women migrate to join husbands or brothers, but most are seeking jobs.

(85)
Family Status of Migrants
Ravenstein also believed that most long-distance migrants were young adults seeking work. For the most part, this pattern continues for the United States. With the increase in women migrating, more children are coming with their mothers.

Key Issue 2. Where Are Migrants Distributed?
- **Global migration patterns**
- **U.S. immigration patterns**
- **Impact of immigration on the United States**

About 9 percent of the world's people are international migrants. The country with by far the largest number is the United States.

Global Migration Patterns
At a global scale, Asia, Latin America, and Africa have net out-migration, whereas North America, Europe, and Oceania have net in-migration.

The United States has more foreign-born residents than any other country, approximately 40 million as of 2010, and growing annually by 1 million. Australia and Canada have higher rates of net in-migration. The highest rates can be found in petroleum-exporting countries in the Middle East, which attract immigrants from poorer neighboring countries to perform many of the dirty and dangerous functions in the oil fields.

(86)
U.S. Immigration Patterns
About 70 million people have migrated to the United States since 1820, including the 40 million alive in 2010. The United States has had three main eras in immigration, each drawing migrants from different regions.

Colonial Immigration from England and Africa
Immigration to the American colonies and the newly independent United States came from two sources: Europe and Africa. Most of the Africans were forced to migrate to the United States as slaves, whereas most Europeans were voluntary migrants — although harsh economic conditions and persecution in Europe blurred the distinction between forced and voluntary migration for many Europeans. From the first permanent English settlers to arrive at the Virginia colony of Jamestown in 1607 until 1840, a steady stream of Europeans (totaling 2 million) migrated to the American colonies and after 1776 the United States. Ninety percent of European immigrants prior to 1840 came from Great Britain. During the eighteenth century, about 400,000 Africans were shipped as slaves to the American colonies, and after importation of slaves was made illegal in 1808 by the United States another 250,000 were brought in.

(87)
Nineteenth-century Immigration from Europe
In the 500 years since Christopher Columbus sailed from Spain to the Western Hemisphere, 40 million Europeans migrated to the United States. Among them, Germany has sent the largest number of immigrants, 7.2 million. Migration from Europe to the United States peaked at several points during the nineteenth century.

During the 1840s and 1850s, annual immigration jumped to 200,000. Three-fourths of all U.S. immigrants during those two decades came from Ireland and Germany.

In the 1870s, emigration from Western Europe resumed following a temporary decline during the U.S. Civil War (1861–1865).

During the 1880s, immigration increased to a half million per year as Swedes and Norwegians joined Western Europeans in migrating to the United States.

Between 1900 and 1914, nearly a million people a year immigrated to the U.S., two-thirds of whom came from Southern and Eastern Europe (especially Italy, Russia, and Austria-Hungary). The shift coincided with the diffusion of the Industrial Revolution and rapid population growth.

(88)
Recent Immigration from Less Developed Regions
Immigration to the United States dropped sharply in the 1930s and 1940s, during the Great Depression and World War II, steadily increased beginning in the 1950s, and then surged to historically high levels during the 1980s.

More than three-fourths of the recent U.S. immigrants have originated in two regions:

Asia. The three leading sources of U.S. immigrants from Asia are China, India and the Philippines.

Latin America. Nearly one-half million immigrate to the United States annually from Latin America, more than twice as many as during the entire nineteenth century.

Impact of Immigration on the United States
The U.S. population has been built up through a combination of emigration from Africa and England primarily during the eighteenth century, from Europe primarily during the nineteenth century, and from Latin America and Asia primarily during the twentieth century. In this current century, the impact of immigration varies around the country.

Legacy of European Migration
The era of massive European migration ended with the start of World War I.

Europe's Demographic Transition. Rapid population growth in Europe fueled emigration. Application of new technologies, spawned by the Industrial Revolution, pushed much of Europe into stage 2 of the demographic transition. Migration to the United States served as a safety valve, draining off some of that increase.

Diffusion of European Culture. Europeans frequently imposed political domination on existing populations and injected their cultural values with little regard for local traditions. Economies in Africa and Asia became based on extracting resources for export to Europe, rather than on using those resources to build local industry. Many of today's conflicts in former European colonies result from past practices by European immigrants.

(90)
Unauthorized Immigration to the United States
Many people who cannot legally enter the United States are now immigrating illegally, called **unauthorized immigrants**. The Pew Hispanic Center estimated that there were 11.9 million in 2008 and around 59 percent of unauthorized immigrants came from Mexico, 22 percent came from elsewhere in Latin America, and 12 percent from Asia.

People are in the United States without authorization primarily because they wish to work but do not have permission to do so from the government. According to the Pew Hispanic Center's 2008 estimate, undocumented workers account for 5.4 percent of the total U.S. civilian labor force.

Americans are divided over whether undocumented migration helps or hurts the country.

Destinations of Immigrants Within the United States
Recent immigrants are not distributed uniformly through the United States. Individual states attract immigrants from different countries. **Chain migration** is the migration of people to a specific location because relatives or members of the same nationality previously migrated there.

Key Issue 3. Why Do Migrants Face Obstacles?
- **Immigration policies of host countries**
- **Cultural problems living in other countries**

The principal obstacle traditionally faced by migrants was the long, arduous, and expensive passage over land or sea. Today, the major obstacles faced by most immigrants are cultural: gaining permission to enter and hostile attitudes of citizens.

Immigration Policies of Host Countries
The United States uses a quota system to limit the number of people who can migrate. Other major recipients of immigrants permit guest workers but they cannot stay permanently.

U.S. Quota Laws
The era of unrestricted immigration to the United States ended when Congress passed the Quota Act in 1921 and the National Origins Act in 1924. Quota laws were designed to assure that most immigrants to the United States continued to be Europeans. Quotas for individual countries were eliminated in 1968 and replaced with hemispheric quotas. In 1978 the hemisphere quotas were replaced by a global quota of 290,000, including a maximum of 20,000 per country. The current law has a global quota of 620,000, with no more than 7 percent from one country, but numerous qualifications and exceptions can alter the limit considerably. Congress has set preferences to reunify families and admit skilled workers and exceptionally talented professionals. Other countries charge that by giving preference to skilled workers, the U.S. immigration policy now contributes to a **brain drain** which is a large-scale emigration by talented people.

Temporary Migration for Work
Prominent forms of temporary work migrants include **guest workers** in Europe and the Middle East and historically time-contract workers in Asia. (93) Guest workers serve a useful role in Western Europe because they take low-status and low-skilled jobs that local residents won't accept. Although relatively low paid by European standards, guest workers earn far more than they would at home. Most guest workers in Europe come from North Africa, the Middle East, Eastern Europe, and Asia. Millions of Asians migrated in the nineteenth century as time-contract laborers, recruited for a fixed period to work in mines or on plantations. More than 33 million ethnic Chinese currently live permanently in other countries, for the most part in Asia.

Distinguishing Between Economic Migrants and Refugees
It is sometimes difficult to distinguish between migrants seeking economic opportunities and refugees fleeing from government persecution. The distinction between economic migrants and refugees is important, because economic migrants are generally not admitted unless they possess special skills or have a close relative already there. However, refugees receive special priority in admission to other countries.

Emigrants from Cuba. The U.S. government regarded emigrants from Cuba as political refugees after the 1959 revolution that brought the Communist government of Fidel Castro to power. In the years immediately following the revolution, more than 600,000 Cubans were admitted to the United States. A second flood of Cuban emigrants reached the United States in 1980, when Fidel Castro suddenly decided to permit political prisoners, criminals, and mental patients to leave the country. More than 125,000 Cubans left within a few weeks to seek asylum in the U.S. in a migration stream known as the "Mariel Boatlift."

(94)
Emigrants from Haiti. Shortly after the 1980 Mariel Boatlift from Cuba, several thousand Haitians also sailed in small vessels for the United States. Claiming that they had migrated for economic advancement, rather than political asylum, U.S. immigration officials would not let the Haitian boat people stay. The Haitians brought a lawsuit. The government settled the case by agreeing to admit some of the Haitians. After a 1991 coup that replaced Haiti's elected president, Jean-Bertrand Aristide, thousands of Haitians fled their country. Although political persecution has subsided, many Haitians still try to migrate to the United States.

Emigrants from Vietnam. Thousands of people from Saigon (since re-named Ho Chi Minh City) evacuated after the Vietnam War ended in 1975. Thousands of other pro-U.S. South Vietnamese who were not politically prominent enough to get space on an American evacuation helicopter tried to leave by boat. A second surge of Vietnamese boat people began in the late 1980s. As memories of the Vietnam War faded, officials in other countries no longer considered Vietnamese boat people as refugees, but rather economic migrants. Vietnam remains a major source of immigrants to the United States, but the pull of economic opportunity in the United States is a greater incentive than the push of political persecution.

Cultural Challenges Faced While Living in Other Countries
For many immigrants, admission to another country does not end their problems. Politicians exploit immigrants as scapegoats for local economic problems.

U.S. Attitudes Toward Immigrants
Americans have always regarded new arrivals with suspicion but tempered their dislike during the nineteenth century because immigrants helped to settle the frontier and extend U.S. control across the continent. Opposition to immigration intensified when the majority of immigrants ceased to come from Northern and Western Europe. More recently, hostile citizens in California and other states have voted to deny undocumented immigrants access to most public services, such as schools, day-care centers, and health clinics.

Attitudes Toward Guest Workers
In Europe, many guest workers suffer from poor social conditions. Both guest workers and their host countries regard the arrangement as temporary. In reality, however, many guest workers remain indefinitely, especially if they are joined by other family members. Political parties that support restrictions on immigration have gained support in France, Germany, and other European countries, and attacks by local citizens on immigrants have increased. In the Middle East, petroleum-exporting countries fear that the increasing numbers of guest workers will spark political unrest and abandonment of traditional Islamic customs. As a result of lower economic growth rates, Middle Eastern and Western European countries have reduced the number of guest workers in recent years.

Key Issue 4. Why Do People Migrate within a Country?
- **Migration between regions of a country**
- **Migration within one region**

Internal migration for most people is less disruptive than international migration. Two main types of internal migration are interregional (between regions of a country) and intraregional (within a region).

Migration Between Regions of a Country

In the past, people migrated from one region to another in search of better farmland. Today, the principal type of interregional migration is from rural areas to urban areas.

Migration Between Regions Within the United States

An especially prominent example of large-scale internal migration is the opening of the American West. The U.S. Census Bureau computes the country's population center at the time of each census, and the changing location of the population center graphically demonstrates the march of the American people across the North American continent.

Colonial Settlement. When the first U.S. census was taken, in 1790, the population center was located in the Chesapeake Bay. This location reflects the fact that virtually all colonial-era settlements were near the Atlantic Coast.

Early Settlement in the Interior. Building of canals and other transportation improvements helped open the interior in the early 1800s. The Erie Canal allowed for inexpensive travel by boat between New York City and the Great Lakes. People moved into forested river valleys between the Appalachians and the Mississippi River.

Migration to California. The population center shifted more rapidly during the mid-nineteenth century, moving 400 miles west in 50 years. Pioneers passed over available agricultural lands to the west and kept going in search of gold in California beginning in the late 1840s. The tough sod of the Great Plains convinced early pioneers it was unsuitable for farming. Maps at the time labeled Great Plains as the Great American Desert.

Settlement of the Great Plains. The westward movement of the U.S. population center slowed in the late nineteenth and early twentieth centuries in part because large scale migration to the East Coast from Europe offset some of the migration to the West. Advances in agricultural technology (such as barbed wire, steel plows, and windmills) enabled people to cultivate the Great Plains. The expansion of the railroads also encouraged settlement of the Great Plains.

(97)

Recent Growth of the South. The population center resumed a more vigorous migration during the late twentieth century, moving across Illinois and into central Missouri by 2000. It has also moved southward by 75 miles since 1940 because of net migration into southern states.

Interregional migration has slowed considerably in the United States into the twenty-first century. Net migration between each pair of regions is now close to zero.

Migration Between Regions in Other Countries

As in the United States, long-distance interregional migration has been an important means of opening new regions for economic development in other large countries.

Russia. Soviet policy encouraged factory construction near raw materials rather than near existing population concentrations (see Chapter 11).

(98)

The collapse of the Soviet Union ended policies that encouraged interregional migration. In the transition to a market-based economy, Russian government officials no longer dictate "optimal" locations for factories.

Brazil. Most Brazilians live in a string of large cities near the Atlantic Coast. To increase the attractiveness of the interior, the government moved its capital in 1960 from Rio de Janeiro to a newly built city called Brasília, situated 600 miles inland.

Indonesia. Since 1969 the Indonesian government has paid for the migration of more than 5 million people, primarily from the island of Java, where nearly two-thirds of its people live, to less populated islands.

Europe. The principal flows of interregional migration in Europe are from east and south to west and north. This pattern reflects the relatively low incomes and bleak job prospects in eastern and southern Europe. In the twentieth century, wealthy Western European countries received many immigrants from their former colonies in Africa and Asia. Interregional migration flows can also be found within individual European countries, and the attractiveness of regions within Europe can change.

India. Indians require a permit to migrate — or even to visit — the State of Assam. The restrictions, which date from the British colonial era, are designed to protect the ethnic identity of Assamese.

(99)
Migration Within One Region
While interregional migration attracts considerable attention, far more people move within the same region, which is *intraregional* migration. In the United States, the principal intraregional migration is from cities to suburbs.

Migration from Rural to Urban Areas
Urbanization began in the 1800s in Europe and North America as a part of the Industrial Revolution. In recent years, urbanization has diffused to LDCs, especially in Asia.

Migration from Urban to Suburban Areas
Most intraregional migration in MDCs is from cities to surrounding suburbs. As a result of suburbanization, the territory occupied by urban areas has rapidly expanded.

Migration from Urban to Rural Areas
MDCs witnessed a new migration trend during the late twentieth century. More people in these regions immigrated into rural areas than emigrated out of them. Net migration from urban to rural areas is called **counterurbanization**.

(100)
Most counterurbanization represents genuine migration from cities and suburbs to small towns and rural communities. Like suburbanization, people move from urban to rural areas for lifestyle reasons.

Net in-migration into Rocky Mountain states has been offset by out migration from Great Plains states where the economy has been hurt by poor agricultural conditions. Future migration trends are unpredictable in more developed countries, because future economic conditions are difficult to forecast.

Key Terms

Brain drain (p.92)
Chain migration (p.90)
Circulation (p.80)
Counterurbanization (p.99)
Emigration (p.80)
Floodplain (p.82)
Forced migration (p.84)
Guest workers (p.93)
Immigration (p.80)
Internal migration (p.84)
International migration (p.84)
Interregional migration (p.84)

Intervening obstacle (p.83)
Intraregional migration (p.84)
Migration (p.80)
Migration transition (p.84)
Mobility (p.80)
Net migration (p.80)
Pull factor (p.81)
Push factor (p.81)
Quotas (p.92)
Refugees (p.81)
Unauthorized immigrants (p.90)
Voluntary migration (p.84)

Test Prep Questions

1) Migration and circulation are both forms of:
A) emigration
B) mobility
C) immigration
D) net migration

2) The desire to reunify with family living in another country would be considered:
A) an environmental push factor
B) a cultural pull factor
C) an economic push factor
D) an environmental pull factor

3) Which of the following is true of the characteristics of migrants since Ravenstein formulated his theories?
A) The percentage of men has increased.
B) The percentage of children has decreased.
C) The percentage of women has increased.
D) all of these

4) Which of the following regions has net in-migration?
A) Oceania
B) Asia
C) Latin America
D) Africa

5) Which European country has sent the largest number of immigrants to the United States?
A) Italy
B) Ireland
C) The United Kingdom
D) Germany

6) Which of the following countries is NOT one of the three leading sources of immigrants to the U.S. from Asia?
A) India
B) the Philippines
C) Japan
D) China

7) According to the Pew Hispanic Center estimates, how many unauthorized immigrants are thought to be residing in the U.S.?
A) 11.9 million
B) 3.2 million
C) 21 million
D) 5.7 million

8) Which of the following countries has NOT sent boats of refugees as part of their emigrants to the U.S.?
A) Cuba
B) Haiti
C) Vietnam
D) Mexico

9) How has the U.S. center of population changed, historically?
A) It has moved northward slightly.
B) It has moved to the west and the south.
C) It has moved dramatically to the south.
D) It has moved moderately to the east.

10) Which country relocated its capital in 1960 to the interior of the country from the coast in order to encourage interregional migration?
A) India
B) Russia
C) Brazil
D) Indonesia

Short Essay

1) What are the reasons that people migrate according to E. G. Ravenstein's "Laws"?

People migrate for Economic, cultural, and environmental push and pull factors.

People go to seek greater opportunity, avoid persecution, disaster, poverty, etc

2) Describe Zelinski's migration transition and identify the net migration from continent to continent.

Migration transition comparable to those in a demographic transition
stage 1 in high daily or seasonal mobility for food.
2 International migrants in search of economic opportunity
larger net migration is from asia to North america.

3) Explain the difficulty distinguishing between economic migrants and refugees, using Cubans, Haitians, and Vietnamese as examples.

All 3 of these countries are war torn poverish countries.
therefore it is difficult to tell if the push factors or economic
pull factors are the leading cause of the migration.

Chapter 4
Folk and Popular Culture

Key Issues
1. Where do folk and popular cultures originate and diffuse?
2. Why is folk culture clustered?
3. Why is popular culture widely distributed?
4. Why does globalization of popular culture cause problems?

(106)

In Chapter 1, *culture* was shown to combine three things: values, material artifacts, and political institutions. This chapter deals with the material artifacts of culture, the visible objects that a group possesses and leaves behind for the future. This chapter examines two facets of material culture: survival activities and leisure activities. Culture can be distinguished from habit and custom.

A **habit** is a repetitive act that a particular *individual* performs. A custom is a repetitive act of a group. A collection of social customs produces a group's material culture. Material culture falls into two basic categories that differ according to scale: folk and popular. **Folk culture** is traditionally practiced primarily by small, homogeneous groups living in isolated rural areas. **Popular culture** is found in large, heterogeneous societies.

(107)

Landscapes dominated by a collection of folk customs change relatively little over time. In contrast, popular culture is based on rapid, simultaneous global *connections*. Thus, folk culture is more likely to vary from place to place at a given time, whereas popular culture is more likely to vary from time to time at a given place.

In Earth's *globalization*, popular culture is becoming more dominant, threatening the survival of unique folk cultures. The disappearance of local folk customs reduces *local diversity* in the world and the intellectual stimulation that arises from differences in background. The dominance of popular culture can also threaten the quality of the environment.

Key Issue 1. Where Do Folk and Popular Cultures Originate and Diffuse?
- **Origin of folk and popular cultures**
- **Diffusion of folk and popular cultures**

Two basic factors help explain the spatial differences between popular and folk cultures: the process of origin and the pattern of diffusion.

Origin of Folk and Popular Cultures
A social custom originates at a hearth, a center of innovation. Folk customs often have anonymous hearths, originating from anonymous sources, at unknown dates, through unidentified originators. Popular culture is most often a product of MDCs, whose industrial technology permits the uniform reproduction of objects in large quantities.

(108)
Origin of Folk Music
Music exemplifies the differences in the origins of folk and popular culture. Folk songs are usually composed anonymously and transmitted orally. A song may be modified from one generation to the next as conditions change, but the content is often derived from events in daily life that are familiar to the majority of the people.

Origin of Popular Music

In contrast to folk music, popular music is written by specific individuals for the purpose of being sold to a large number of people.

Popular music as we know it today originated around 1900. To provide songs for music halls and vaudeville, a music industry was developed in a district of New York that became known as Tin Pan Alley. After World War II, Tin Pan Alley disappeared as recorded music became more important than printed songsheets.

The diffusion of American popular music worldwide began in earnest during World War II, when the Armed Forces Radio Network broadcast music to American soldiers. English became the international language for popular music.

Hip-hop is a more recent form of popular music that also originated in New York. Whereas Tin Pan Alley originated in Manhattan office buildings, hip-hop originated in the late 1970s in the South Bronx. Hip-hop demonstrates well the interplay between globalization and local diversity that is a prominent theme of this book. Lyrics make local references and represent a distinctive hometown scene. At the same time, hip-hop has diffused rapidly around the world through instruments of globalization.

(109)

Diffusion of Folk and Popular Cultures

The spread of popular culture typically follows the process of hierarchical diffusion from hearths or nodes of innovation. In contrast, folk culture is transmitted more slowly and on a smaller scale, primarily through migration (relocation diffusion).

The Amish: Relocation Diffusion of Folk Culture

Amish customs illustrate how relocation diffusion distributes folk culture. Although the Amish number only about one-quarter million, their folk culture remains visible on the landscape in at least 19 states. The Amish have distinctive clothing, farming, religious practices, and other customs. The distribution of Amish folk culture across a major portion of the U.S. landscape is explained by the diffusion of their culture through migration. In Europe, the Amish did not develop distinctive language, clothing, or farming practices and gradually merged with various Mennonite church groups. Several hundred Amish families migrated to North America in two waves. Living in rural and frontier settlements relatively isolated from other groups, Amish communities retained their traditional customs, even as other European immigrants to the United States adopted new ones. Amish communities from such diverse areas as southeastern Pennsylvania to east-central Iowa are relatively isolated from each other but share cultural traditions distinct from those of other Americans.

(110)

Sports: Hierarchical Diffusion of Popular Culture

In contrast with the diffusion of folk customs, organized sports provide examples of how popular culture is diffused. Many sports originated as isolated folk customs and were diffused like other folk culture, through the migration of individuals. The contemporary diffusion of organized sports, however, displays the characteristics of popular culture.

Folk Culture Origin of Soccer. Soccer is the world's most popular sport (it is called football outside North America). Its origin is obscure. Early football games resembled mob scenes. In the twelfth century the rules became standardized. Because football disrupted village life, King Henry II banned the game from England in the late twelfth century. It was not legalized again until 1603 by King James I. At this point, football was an English folk custom rather than a global popular custom.

Globalization of Soccer. The transformation of football from an English folk custom to global popular culture began in the 1800s. Sport became a subject that was taught in school. Increasing leisure time permitted people not only to view sporting events but to participate in them. With higher incomes, spectators paid to see first-class events.

(111)

Football was first played in continental Europe in the late 1870s by Dutch students who had been in Britain. British citizens further diffused the game throughout the worldwide British Empire. In the twentieth century, soccer, like other sports, was further diffused by new communication systems, especially radio and television.

Sports in Popular Culture. Each country has its own preferred sports. Cricket is popular primarily in Britain and former British colonies. Ice hockey prevails, logically, in colder climates. The most popular sports in China are martial arts, known as wushu, including archery, fencing, wrestling, and boxing. Baseball became popular in Japan after it was introduced by American soldiers after World War II. European colonists, primarily in Canada, picked up Lacrosse from the Iroquois and brought it to a handful of U.S. communities, especially Maryland, upstate New York, and Long Island.

Despite the diversity in distribution of sports across Earth's surface and the anonymous origin of some games, organized spectator sports today are part of popular culture.

Key Issue 2. Why Is Folk Culture Clustered?
- **Influence of physical environment**
- **Isolation promotes cultural diversity**

Folk culture typically has unknown or multiple origins among groups living in relative isolation. A combination of physical and cultural factors influences the distinctive distributions of folk culture.

Influence of the Physical Environment
Folk societies are particularly responsive to the environment because of their limited technology and the prevailing agricultural economy. Yet folk culture may ignore the environment. Broad differences in folk culture arise in part from physical conditions, and these conditions produce varied customs. Two necessities of daily life — food and shelter — demonstrate the influence of the environment on development of unique folk culture.

(112)
Food Preferences and the Environment
Folk food habits are embedded strongly in the environment. Inhabitants of a region must consider the soil, climate, terrain, vegetation, and other characteristics of the environment in deciding to produce particular foods.

In Europe, traditional preferences for quick-frying foods in Italy resulted in part from fuel shortages. In Northern Europe, an abundant wood supply encouraged the slow stewing and roasting of foods over fires, which also provided home heat in the colder climate. Soybeans, an excellent source of protein, are widely grown in Asia. In the raw state they are toxic and indigestible. Lengthy cooking renders them edible, but fuel is scarce in Asia. Asians derive foods from soybeans that do not require extensive cooking.

According to many folk customs, everything in nature carries a signature, or distinctive characteristic, based on its appearance and natural properties. People may desire or avoid certain foods in response to perceived beneficial or harmful natural traits. People refuse to eat particular plants or animals that are thought to embody negative forces in the environment. Such a restriction on behavior imposed by social custom is a **taboo**. Other social customs, such as sexual practices, carry prohibitions, but taboos are especially strong in the area of food.

(113)

Hindu taboos against consuming cows can be explained partly by environmental reasons. A large supply of oxen must be maintained in India, because every field has to be plowed at approximately the same time: when the monsoon rains arrive. But the taboo against consumption of meat among many people, including Muslims, Hindus, and Jews, cannot be explained primarily by environment factors. Social values must influence the choice of diet, because people in similar climates and with similar levels of income consume different foods. Religions sanctions have kept India's cow population large as a form of insurance against the loss of oxen and increasing population.

(114)

Folk Housing and the Environment. The house is a product of both cultural tradition and natural conditions. The type of building materials used to construct folk houses is influenced partly by what is available in the environment. The two most common building materials in the world are wood and brick; stone, grass, sod, and skins are also used. Even in areas that share similar climates and available building materials, folk housing can vary, because of minor differences in environmental features.

(115)
Isolation Promotes Cultural Diversity
Folk customs observed at a point in time vary widely from one place to another, even among nearby places.

Himalayan Art
In a study of artistic customs in the Himalaya Mountains, geographers P. Karan and Cotton Mather demonstrate that distinctive views of the physical environment emerge among neighboring cultural groups that are isolated. Each group reveals how their folk culture mirrors their religions and individual views of their environment.

Buddhists. In the northern region, Buddhists paint idealized divine figures, such as monks and saints. Some are depicted as terrifying or bizarre, perhaps reflecting the inhospitable environment.

Hindus. In the southern region, Hindus create scenes from everyday life and familiar local scenes, frequently representing the region's violent and extreme climatic conditions.

Muslims. In the western portion, Muslims show the region's beautiful plants and flowers because Islam prohibits displaying animate objects in art. In contrast with the Buddhist and Hindu regions, these paintings do not depict harsh climactic conditions.

Animists. Migrated to the eastern region, Animists paint symbols and designs that derive from their religion rather than from the local environment. The distribution of artistic subjects in the Himalayas shows how folk customs are influenced by cultural institutions like religion and by environmental processes such as climate, landforms, and vegetation.

Beliefs and Folk House Forms
The distinctive form of folk houses may derive primarily from religious values and other customary beliefs rather than from environmental factors.

Sacred Spaces. Houses may have sacred walls or corners. Sacred walls or corners are noted in China, parts of the Middle East, India, and Africa, among other places.

(116)
U.S. Folk Housing
Older houses in the United States display local folk-culture traditions. The style of pioneer homes reflected whatever upscale style was prevailing at the place on the East Coast from which they migrated.

Fred Kniffen identified three major hearths or nodes of folk house forms in the United States: New England, Middle Atlantic, and Lower Chesapeake.

Today, such distinctions are relatively difficult to observe in the United States. Rapid communication and transportation systems provide people throughout the country with knowledge of alternative styles. Furthermore, houses are usually mass-produced by construction companies.

(117)
Key Issue 3. Why Is Popular Culture Widely Distributed?
- **Diffusion of popular food, clothing, and housing**
- **Electronic diffusion of popular culture**

Popular culture varies more in time than in place. It diffuses rapidly across Earth to locations with a variety of physical conditions.

Diffusion of Popular Food, Clothing, and Housing
Some regional differences in food, clothing, and shelter persist in more developed countries, but difference is much less than in the past.

(118)
Popular Food Customs
People in MDCs are likely to have the income, time, and inclination to facilitate greater adoption of popular culture.

Regional Variations. Consumption of large quantities of alcoholic beverages and snack foods are characteristic of the food customs of popular societies. Americans choose particular beverages or snacks in part on the basis of preference for what is produced, grown, or imported locally. However, cultural backgrounds also affect the amount and types of alcohol and snack foods consumed.

Geographers cannot explain all the regional variations in food preferences.

Wine Production. The spatial distribution of wine production demonstrates that the environment plays a role in the distribution of popular as well as folk food customs.

(119)
Because of the unique product created by distinctive soil and climate characteristics, the world's finest wines are most frequently identified by their place of origin. Although grapes can be grown in a wide variety of locations, wine distribution is based principally on cultural values, both historical and contemporary. Wine production is discouraged in regions of the world dominated by religions other than Christianity.

Rapid Diffusion of Clothing Styles
Individual clothing habits reveal how popular culture can be distributed across the landscape with little regard for distinctive physical features. In MDCs, clothing habits generally reflect occupations rather than particular environments.

A second influence on clothing in MDCs is higher income. Improved communications have permitted the rapid diffusion of clothing styles from one region of Earth to another. Until recently, a year could elapse from the time an original dress was displayed to the time that inexpensive reproductions were available in the stores. Now the time lag is only a few weeks. The globalization of clothing styles has involved increasing awareness by North Americans and Europeans of the variety of folk costumes around the world. The continued use of folk costumes in some parts of the globe may persist not because of distinctive environmental conditions or traditional cultural values but to preserve past memories or to attract tourists.

(120)
Jeans. An important symbol of the diffusion of western popular culture is jeans, which became a prized possession for young people throughout the world. Jeans became an obsession and a status symbol among youth in the former Soviet Union, when the Communist government prevented their import. The scarcity of high-quality jeans was just one of many consumer problems that were important motives in the dismantling of Communist governments in Eastern Europe around 1990. Ironically, as access to Levi's increased around the world, American consumers turned away from the brand.

Popular Housing Styles
Housing built in the United States since the 1940s demonstrates how popular customs vary more in time than in place.

In contrast with folk housing that is characteristic of the early 1800s, newer housing in the United States has been built to reflect rapidly changing fashion concerning the most suitable house form. In the years immediately after World War II, most U.S. houses were built in a *modern style*. Since the 1960s, styles that architects call *neo-eclectic* have predominated.

Modern House Styles (1945–1960). Specific types of modern-style houses were popular at different times:

- **Minimal traditional:** Dominant in the late 1940s and early 1950s; small modest homes built to house young families and veterans returning from World War II.

- **Ranch house:** replaced minimal traditional in the 50s and 60s; took up a large lot that encourages the sprawl of urban areas.

- **Split level:** Popular variant of the ranch between the 50s and 70s; lower level contained the newly invented "family" room where the television was placed.

- **Contemporary:** Especially popular between the 50s and 70s for architect designed houses; frequently had flat or low-pitched roofs.

- **Shed:** Popular in the late 60s; characterized by high pitched roof.

(122)
Neo-eclectic House Styles (Since 1960). In the late 1960s, *neo-eclectic* styles became popular and by the 1970s had surpassed modern styles in vogue.

- **Mansard:** The first popular neo-eclectic style, in the late 60s and early 70s; shingle-covered second story walls sloped inward and merged with the roofline.

- **Neo-Tudor:** Popular in the 70s; characterized by steep-pitched front-facing gables and half-timbered detailing.

- **Neo-French:** By early 1980 was the most fashionable style for new houses; dormer windows and high-hipped roofs.

- **Neo-colonial:** An adaptation of English colonial houses, continuously popular but never dominant.

Electronic Diffusion of Popular Culture

Watching television is an especially significant popular custom for two reasons. First, it is the most popular leisure activity in MDCs throughout the world. Second, television is the most important mechanism by which knowledge of popular culture, such as professional sports, is rapidly diffused across Earth. In the twenty-first century, other electronic media have become important transmitters of popular culture.

Diffusion of Television

Television technology was developed simultaneously in the United Kingdom, France, Germany, Japan, and the Soviet Union, as well as the United States, but in the early years of broadcasting the United States held a near monopoly. Through the second half of the twentieth century, television diffused from the United States, first to Europe and other MDCs, then to LDCs. In 1954 the United States had 86 percent of the world's TV sets. In 1970, however, the share of the world's sets in the United States had declined to one-fourth. Still, in 1970, half of the countries in the world, including most of those in Africa and Asia, had little if any TV broadcasting. By 2005, international differences in TV ownership had diminished, although had not disappeared altogether.

Diffusion of the Internet

The diffusion of Internet service is following the pattern established by television a generation earlier, but at a more rapid pace. In 1995, there were 40 million Internet users and Internet service had not yet reached most countries.

Between 1995 and 2000, Internet usage increased rapidly in the United States, from 9 percent to 44 percent of the population. But the worldwide increase was much greater in the rest of the world, from 40 million users to 361 million.

In 2008, Internet usage further diffused rapidly. World usage more than quadrupled in 8 years to 1.6 billion. U.S. usage increased to 74 percent, although the share of the world's Internet users found in the U.S. declined to 14 percent.

The diffusion of television from the United States to the rest of the world took a half-century, whereas the diffusion of the Internet has taken only a decade.

(125)
Diffusion of Facebook

Facebook, founded in 2004 by Harvard University students, has begun to diffuse rapidly. In 2009, five years after its founding, Facebook had 200 million active users. As with television and the Internet, the U.S. had far more Facebook users than any other country. In the years ahead, Facebook will either diffuse to other parts of the world or it will be overtaken by other social networking programs.

(125)
Key Issue 4. Why Does Globalization of Popular Culture Cause Problems?
* **Threat to folk culture**
* **Environmental impact of popular culture**

The international diffusion of popular culture has led to two issues, both of which can be understood from geographic perspectives. First, the diffusion of popular culture may threaten the survival of traditional folk culture in many countries. Second, popular culture may be less responsive to the diversity of local environments and consequently may generate adverse environmental impacts.

Threat to Folk Culture
When people turn from folk to popular culture, they may also turn away from the society's traditional values.

Loss of Traditional Values
One example of the symbolic importance of folk culture is clothing. In African and Asian countries today, there is a contrast between the clothes of rural farm workers and of urban business and government leaders. Leaders of African and Asian countries have traveled to MDCs and experienced the sense of social status attached to clothes, such as men's business suits. Back home, executives and officials may wear Western business suits as a symbol of authority and leadership.

(126)
Wearing clothes typical of MDCs is controversial in some Middle Eastern countries. Fundamentalist Muslims may oppose the widespread adoption of Western clothes, especially by women living in cities. Women are urged to abandon skirts and blouses in favor of the traditional *chador*, a combination head covering and veil.

Beyond clothing, global diffusion of popular culture may threaten the subservience of women to men that is embedded in some folk customs. However, contact with popular culture also has brought negative impacts for women in LDCs. Prostitution has increased in some LDCs to serve men from MDCs traveling on "sex tours." International prostitution is encouraged in some countries as a major source of foreign currency.

Threat of Foreign Media Imperialism
Leaders of some LDCs consider the dominance of popular customs by MDCs as a threat to their independence. The threat is posed primarily by the media, especially news-gathering organizations and television.

Western Control of Media. Leaders of many LDCs view the spread of television as a new method of economic and cultural imperialism on the part of the more developed countries, especially the United States. Less developed countries fear the effects of the news-gathering capability of the media even more than their entertainment function. The news media in most LDCs are dominated by the government, which typically runs the radio and TV service as well as the domestic news-gathering agency. In many regions of the world the only reliable and unbiased news accounts come from the BBC World Service shortwave radio newscasts. Many African and Asian government officials criticize the Western concept of freedom of the press. They argue that the American news organizations reflect American values and do not provide a balanced, accurate view of other countries.

(128)
Satellites. In recent years, changing technology — especially the diffusion of small satellite dishes — has made television a force for political change rather than stability. A number of governments

in Asia have tried to prevent consumers from obtaining satellite dishes by its citizens, although foreigners and upscale hotels were allowed to keep them. Governments have had little success in shutting down satellite technology.

Environmental Impact of Popular Culture

Popular culture is less likely than folk culture to be distributed with consideration for physical features. In a global economy and culture, popular culture appears increasingly uniform.

Modifying Nature

Popular culture can significantly modify or control the environment. It may be imposed on the environment rather than springing forth from it, as with many folk customs.

Diffusion of Golf. Because of their large size (80 hectares, or 200 acres) golf courses provide a prominent example of imposing popular culture on the environment. Golf courses are designed partially in response to local physical conditions. Yet, like other popular customs, golf courses remake the environment.

(129)

Uniform Landscapes

The distribution of popular culture around the world tends to produce more uniform landscapes. In fact, promoters of popular culture want a uniform appearance to generate "product recognition" and greater consumption. The diffusion of fast-food restaurants is a good example of such uniformity. The success of fast-food restaurants depends on large-scale mobility. Uniformity in the appearance of the landscape is promoted by a wide variety of other popular structures in North America, such as gas stations, supermarkets, and motels. These structures are designed so that both local residents and visitors immediately recognize the purpose of the building, even if not the name of the company.

Negative Environmental Impact

The diffusion of some popular customs can adversely impact environmental quality in two ways: depletion of scarce natural resources and pollution of the landscape.

Increased Demand for Natural Resources. Diffusion of some popular customs increases demand for raw materials.

(130)

Increased demand for some products can strain the capacity of the environment, such as with increased meat consumption. With a large percentage of the world's population undernourished, some question inefficient use of grain to feed animals for eventual human consumption.

Pollution. Popular culture also can pollute the environment. Folk culture, like popular culture, can also cause environmental damage, especially when natural processes are ignored. A widespread belief exists that indigenous peoples of the Western Hemisphere practiced more "natural," ecologically sensitive agriculture before the arrival of Columbus and other Europeans. Geographers increasingly question this. Very high rates of soil erosion have been documented in Central America from the practice of folk culture.

The MDCs that produce endless supplies for popular culture have created the technological capacity both to create large-scale environmental damage and to control it. However, a commitment of time and money must be made to control the damage.

Key Terms

Custom (p.106)   Popular culture (p.106)
Folk culture (p.106)   Taboo (p.112)
Habit (p.106)   Terroir (p. 114)

Test Prep Questions

1) Which of the following characteristics is associated with groups that practice folk culture?
A) urban
B) isolated
C) large
D) heterogeneous

2) What two factors explain the spatial differences between folk and popular culture?
A) origin and diffusion
B) distribution and pattern
C) origin and distribution
D) diffusion and pattern

3) The spread of popular culture typically follows the process of_____ from hearths or nodes of
   innovation. In contrast, folk culture is transmitted through_____.
A) relocation diffusion/hierarchical diffusion
B) relocation diffusion/stimulus diffusion
C) contagious diffusion/relocation diffusion
D) hierarchical diffusion/relocation diffusion

4) Which of the following statements about the Amish is true?
A) Because Amish communities are isolated from each other, they share few cultural traditions.
B) While relatively small in population, the Amish are widely dispersed.
C) In Europe, the Amish retained distinct cultural characteristics from other Mennonite groups.
D) Amish culture spreads primarily through hierarchical diffusion.

5) Which of the following statements about soccer is false?
A) It was outlawed in England by Henry VIII.
B) It diffused to Europe by Dutch students who been to England.
C) It was diffused by the British Empire rather than radio and television.
D) It began as an English folk custom.

6) In the Himalayas, which of the following groups is forbidden by religion to depict animate objects in
   their art?
A) Muslims
B) Hindus
C) Buddhists
D) Animists

7) Which of the following is NOT a hearth of U.S. folk housing form?
A) New England
B) Middle Atlantic
C) Lower Chesapeake
D) Southern Coastal

8) What U.S. popular housing style was popular in the late 60s and characterized by a high pitched roof?
A) shed
B) split level
C) ranch
D) contemporary

9) Which of the following is NOT a way in which popular culture generally threatens folk culture?
A) threatening loss of folk clothing styles in favor of western attire
B) threatening military intervention to force popular culture on folk societies
C) threatening subservience of women embedded in some folk customs
D) threatening dominance of the news media in LDCs by MDCs

10) Which of the following is NOT an environmental impact of popular culture?
A) uniformity of the landscape
B) increased demand for resources
C) increase in efficiency in use of grain
D) increase in pollution to the environment

Short Essay

1) Explain the relationship between folk culture and the physical environment and provide examples.
_____
_____
_____
_____
_____
_____
_____
_____
_____

2) Compare and contrast folk housing styles with popular housing styles in the United States.
_____
_____
_____
_____
_____
_____
_____
_____
_____

3) What are the ways in which popular culture can have a negative impact on the environment?

_____

_____

_____

_____

_____

_____

_____

_____

Chapter 5
Language

Key Issues
1. Where are English-language speakers distributed?
2. Why is English related to other languages?
3. Where are other language families distributed?
4. Why do people preserve local languages?

(136)

Language is a system of communication through speech. Many languages also have a **literary tradition**, or a system of written communication. The lack of written records makes it difficult to document the distribution of many languages. Many countries designate at least one language as their **official language**. A country with more than one official language may require all public documents to be in all languages.

We start our study of the geographic elements of cultural values with language in part because it is the means through which other cultural values, such as religion and ethnicity, are communicated. The study of language follows logically from migration, because the contemporary distribution of languages around the world results largely from past migrations of peoples.

The final section of the chapter discusses contradictory trends of *scale* in language. On the one hand, English has achieved an unprecedented *globalization*. On the other hand, people are trying to preserve *local diversity* in language. The global distribution of languages results from a combination of two geographic processes — interaction and isolation. The interplay between interaction and isolation helps to explain the *regions* of individual languages and entire language families.

(137)
Key Issue 1. Where Are English-Language Speakers Distributed?
- **Origin and diffusion of English**
- **Dialects of English**

A language originates at a particular place and diffuses to other locations through the migration of its speakers.

Origin and Diffusion of English
English is the first language of 328 million people and is spoken fluently by another one-half to one billion people. It is an official language in 57 countries, more than any other language, and is the predominant language in two more (Australia and the United States).

English Colonies
The contemporary distribution of English speakers around the world exists because the people of England migrated with their language when they established colonies during the past four centuries.

English first diffused west from England to North America in the seventeenth century. Similarly, the British took control of Ireland in the seventeenth century, South Asia in the mid-eighteenth century, the South Pacific in the late eighteenth and early nineteenth centuries, and southern Africa in the late nineteenth century. More recently, the United States has been responsible for diffusing English to several places, most notably the Philippines.

Origin of English in England

The British Isles had been inhabited for thousands of years, but we know nothing of their early languages, until tribes called the Celts arrived around 2000 B.C., speaking languages we call Celtic. Then, around A.D. 450, tribes from mainland Europe invaded, pushing the Celts into the remote northern and western parts of Britain.

(138)

German Invasion. The invading tribes were the Angles, Jutes, and Saxons. All three were Germanic tribes — the Jutes from Northern Denmark, the Angles from Southern Denmark, and the Saxons from Northwestern Germany. Today, English people and others who trace their cultural heritage back to England are called Anglo-Saxons, after the two larger tribes. England comes from Angles' land. In Old English, Angles was spelled Engles. The Angles came from a corner, or angle, of Germany known as Schleswig-Holstein.

Other peoples subsequently invaded England and added to the basic English. Although defeated in their effort to conquer the islands, many Vikings remained in the country to enrich the language with new words.

Norman Invasion. English is different from German today primarily because England was conquered by the Normans in 1066. The Normans, who came from present-day Normandy in France, spoke French, which they established as England's official language for the next 300 years. The leaders of England spoke French, however the majority of the people continued to speak English.

England lost control of Normandy in 1204 and entered a long period of conflict with France. Parliament enacted the Statute of Pleading in 1362 to change the official language of court business from French to English. During the 300-year period that French was the official language of England, the Germanic language used by the common people and the French used by the leaders mingled to form a new language.

(139)

Dialects of English

A **dialect** is a regional variation of a language distinguished by distinctive vocabulary, spelling, and pronunciation. The distribution of dialects is documented through the study of particular words. A word-usage boundary, known as an **isogloss**, can be constructed for each word. English has an especially large number of dialects. In a language with multiple dialects, one dialect may be recognized as the **standard language**, which is a dialect that is well established and widely recognized as the most acceptable for government, business, education, and mass communication. One particular dialect of English, the one associated with upper-class Britons living in the London area, is recognized in much of the English-speaking world as the standard form of British speech, known as **British Received Pronunciation (BRP).**

Dialects in England

English originated with three invading groups who settled in different parts of Britain. The language each spoke was the basis of distinct regional dialects of Old English. Following the Norman invasion of 1066, by the time English again became the country's dominant language, five major regional dialects had emerged.

(140)

From a collection of local dialects, the dialect used by upper-class residents in the capital city of London and the two important university cities of Cambridge and Oxford became the standard language. The diffusion of this dialect was encouraged by the introduction of the printing press to England in 1476.

Grammar books and dictionaries printed in the eighteenth century established rules for spelling and grammar that were based on the London dialect. Strong regional differences persist in the United Kingdom, especially in rural areas. They can be grouped into three main ones: Northern, Midland, and Southern. The main dialects can be subdivided; distinctive southwestern and southeastern accents occur within the Southern dialect.

(141)
Differences between British and American English

The earliest colonists were most responsible for the dominant language patterns that exist today in the English-speaking part of the Western Hemisphere. U.S. English differs from that of England in three significant ways:

- **Vocabulary.** The vocabulary is different because settlers in America encountered many new objects and experiences, which were given names borrowed from Native Americans. As new inventions appeared, they acquired different names on either side of the Atlantic.

- **Spelling**. Spelling diverged because of a strong national feeling in the United States for an independent identity. Noah Webster, the creator of the first comprehensive American dictionary and grammar books, was not just a documenter of usage, he had an agenda. Webster argued that spelling and grammar reforms would help establish a national language, reduce cultural dependence on England, and inspire national pride.

- **Pronunciation.** Interaction between British and U.S. speakers was largely confined to exchange of letters and other printed matter rather than direct speech. Surprisingly, pronunciation has changed more in England than in the United States. People in the United States do not speak "proper" English because when the colonists left England "proper" English was not what it is today.

(142)
Dialects in the United States

Major differences in U.S. dialects originated because of differences in dialects among the original settlers.

Settlement in the East. The original American settlements can be grouped into three areas:

- **New England**. Two-thirds of the colonists were Puritans from East Anglia in southeastern England.

- **Southeastern**. About half of the settlers came from southeast England, although they represented a diversity of social-class backgrounds.

- **Middle Atlantic.** These immigrants were more diverse. Early settlers of Pennsylvania were Quakers from the north of England, and Scots and Irish settled there also, as well as New Jersey and Delaware. German, Dutch, and Swedish settlers also settled this area.

Current Dialect Differences in the East. Today, major dialect differences within the United States continue to exist, primarily on the East Coast. Two important isoglosses separate the eastern United States into three major dialect regions, known as Northern, Midland, and Southern. Some words are commonly used within one of the three major dialect areas but rarely in the other two. In most instances, these words relate to rural life, food, and objects from daily activities. Many words that were once regionally distinctive are now national in distribution. Mass media, especially television and radio, influence the adoption of the same words throughout the country.

Pronunciation Differences. Regional pronunciation differences are more familiar to us than word differences, although it is harder to draw precise isoglosses for them. The *southern dialect* includes making such words as *half* and *mine* into two syllables and pronouncing *Tuesday* and *due* with a /y/ sound. The *New England accent* is well known for dropping the /r/ sound, shared with speakers from the south of England. Residents of Boston maintained especially close ties to the important ports of southern England. Compared to other colonists, New Englanders received more exposure to changes in pronunciation that occurred in Britain during the eighteenth century.

(143)

The New England and southern accents sound unusual to the majority of Americans because the standard pronunciation throughout the American West comes from the Middle Atlantic states rather than the New England and Southern regions. This pattern occurred because most western settlers came from the Middle Atlantic states.

Key Issue 2. Why Is English Related to Other Languages?
- **Indo-European branches**
- **Origin and diffusion of Indo-European**

English is part of the Indo-European language family. A **language family** is a collection of languages related through a common ancestor that existed long before recorded history.

Indo-European Branches
Within a language family, a **language branch** is a collection of languages related through a common ancestor that existed several thousand years ago.

Indo-European is divided into eight branches. Four of the branches — Indo-Iranian, Romance, Germanic, and Balto-Slavic—are spoken by large numbers of people. The four less extensively used Indo-European language branches are Albanian, Armenian, Greek, and Celtic.

(144)
Germanic Branch of Indo-European
A **language group** is a collection of languages within a branch that share a common origin in the relatively recent past. English and German are both languages in the West Germanic group. The Germanic language branch also includes North Germanic languages, spoken in Scandinavia. The four Scandinavian language s— Swedish, Danish, Norwegian, and Icelandic — all derive from Old Norse.

Indo-Iranian Branch of Indo-European
The branch of the Indo-European language family with the most speakers is Indo-Iranian, more than 100 individual languages are divided into an eastern group (Indic) and a western group (Iranian).

(145)
Indic (Eastern) Group of Indo-Iranian Language Branch. The most widely used languages in India, as well as in the neighboring countries of Pakistan and Bangladesh, belong to the Indic group of the Indo-Iranian branch of Indo-European. *Ethnologue* identifies 438 languages spoken in India. The official language is Hindi, an Indo-European Language. Originally a variety of Hindustani spoken in the area of New Delhi, Hindi grew into a national language in the nineteenth century when the British encouraged its use in government. Hindi is spoken many different ways — and

therefore could be regarded as a collection of many individual languages — but there is only one official way to write the language, using a script called Devanagari.

Urdu is spoken very much like Hindi but Urdu is written with the Arabic alphabet, a legacy of the fact that most Pakistanis are Muslims, and their holiest book (the Quran) is written in Arabic.

Iranian (Western) Group of Indo-Iranian Language Branch. Indo-Iranian languages are also spoken in Iran and neighboring countries.

(146)
These form a separate group from Indic. The major Iranian group languages include Persian (sometimes called Farsi) in Iran, Pathan in eastern Afghanistan and western Pakistan, and Kurdish, used by the Kurds of western Iran, northern Iraq, and eastern Turkey. These languages are written in the Arabic alphabet.

Balto-Slavic Branch of Indo-European
Slavic was once a single language, but differences developed in the seventh century A.D. when several groups of Slavs migrated from Asia to different areas of Eastern Europe.

East Slavic and Baltic Groups of Balto-Slavic Language Branch. The most widely used Slavic languages are the eastern ones, primarily Russian. With the demise of the Soviet Union, the newly independent republics adopted official languages other than Russian, although Russian remains the language for communications among officials in the countries that were formerly part of the Soviet Union. After Russian, Ukrainian and Belarusian are the two most important East Slavic languages.

West and South Slavic Groups of Balto-Slavic Language Branch. The most spoken West Slavic language is Polish, followed by Czech and Slovak. The latter two are quite similar, and speakers of one can understand the other. The most important South Slavic language is the one spoken in Bosnia and Herzegovina, Croatia, Montenegro, and Serbia. Bosnians and Croats write in the Roman alphabet, whereas Montenegrins and Serbs use the Cyrillic alphabet.

When these countries were all part of Yugoslavia the language was called Serbo-Croatian. This name now offends Bosnians and Croatians. The names Bosnian, Croatian, and Serbian are preferred by people in these countries, to demonstrate that each language is unique, even though linguists consider them one.

In general, differences among all Slavic languages are relatively small. However, because language is a major element in a people's cultural identity, relatively small differences among Slavic as well as other languages are being preserved and even accentuated in recent independence movements.

Romance Branch of Indo-European
The Romance language branch evolved from the Latin language spoken by the Romans 2,000 years ago. The four most widely used contemporary Romance languages are Spanish, Portuguese, French, and Italian. Physical boundaries such as mountains are strong intervening obstacles, creating barriers to communication between people living on opposite sides. The fifth most important Romance language, Romanian, is the principal language of Romania and Moldova.

(147)
Two other official Romance languages are Romansh and Catalán. Sardinian was once the official language of Sardinia. In addition to these official languages, several other Romance languages have individual literary traditions. In Italy, Ladin (not Latin) and Friulian are dialects of Rhaeto-Romanic. Ladino — a mixture of Spanish, Greek, Turkish, and Hebrew — is spoken by 100,000 Sephardic Jews, most of whom now live in Israel.

Origin and Diffusion of Romance Languages. As the conquering Roman armies occupied the provinces of this vast empire, they brought the Latin language with them.

The languages spoken by the natives of the provinces were either extinguished or suppressed. Latin used in each province was based on that spoken by the Roman army at the time of occupation. Each province also integrated words spoken in the area. The Latin that people in the provinces learned was not the standard literary form but a spoken form, known as **Vulgar Latin**, from the Latin word referring to "the masses" of the populace.

(148)
By the eighth century, regions of the former empire had been isolated from each other long enough for distinct languages to evolve

Romance Language Dialects. Distinct Romance languages did not suddenly appear. They evolved over time. The creation of standard national languages, such as French and Spanish, was relatively recent. The dialect of the Île-de-France region, known as Francien, became the standard form of French because the region included Paris. The most important surviving dialect difference within France is between the north and the south. The northern dialect, *langue d'oïl* and the southern *langue d'òc* provide insight into how languages evolve. These terms derive from different ways in which the word for "yes" was said. Spain, like France, contained many dialects during the Middle Ages. In the fifteenth century, when the Kingdom of Castile and Léon merged with the Kingdom of Aragón, Castilian became the official language for the entire country. Spanish and Portuguese have achieved worldwide importance because of the colonial activities of their European speakers. Approximately 90 percent of the speakers of these two languages live outside Europe. Spanish is the official language of 18 Latin American states, while Portuguese is spoken in Brazil. The division of Central and South America into Portuguese- and Spanish-speaking regions is the result of a 1493 decision by Pope Alexander VI. The Portuguese and Spanish languages spoken in the Western Hemisphere differ somewhat from their European versions.

(149)
Distinguishing Between Dialects and Languages. Difficulties arise in determining whether two languages are distinct or whether they are merely two dialects of the same language.

• Galician, spoken in Spain and Portugal, is classified as a dialect whereas Catalan is considered a language although it differs as much from Spanish as Galician does from Portuguese.

• Moldova, the official language of Moldova, is generally classified as a dialect of Romanian.

• Flemish, the official Language of Northern Belgium, is generally considered a dialect of Dutch.

Distinguishing individual languages from dialects is difficult, because many speakers choose to regard their languages as distinct. Romance languages spoken in some former colonies can be classified as different languages because they differ substantially from the original introduced by European colonizers. A **creole or creolized language** is defined as a language that results from the mixing of the colonizer's language with the indigenous language. A creolized language forms when the colonized group makes some changes, such as simplifying the grammar. The word creole derives from a word in several Romance languages for a slave who is born in the master's house.

Origin and Diffusion of Indo-European
If Germanic, Romance, Balto-Slavic, and Indo-Iranian are all part of the same language family, then they must be descended from a single common ancestral language. The existence of a single ancestor — called Proto-Indo-European — cannot be proved with certainty, because it would have

existed thousands of years before the invention of writing or recorded history. The evidence that Proto-Indo-European once existed is "internal." Individual Indo-European languages share common root words for winter and snow but not for ocean. Therefore, linguists conclude that original Proto-Indo-European speakers probably lived in a cold climate, or one that had a winter season, but did not come in contact with oceans.

(150)
Not surprisingly, scholars disagree on where and when the first speakers of Proto-Indo-European lived.

Nomadic Warrior Thesis. One influential hypothesis, espoused by Marija Gimbutas, is that the first Proto-Indo-European speakers were the Kurgan people, whose homeland was in the steppes near the border between present-day Russia and Kazakhstan. Between 3500 and 2500 B.C., Kurgan warriors, using their domesticated horses as weapons, conquered much of Europe and South Asia.

Sedentary Farmer Thesis. Archaeologist Colin Renfrew argues that they lived 2,000 years before the Kurgans, in eastern Anatolia, part of present-day Turkey. Biologist Russell D. Gray supports the Renfrew position but dates the first speakers even earlier, at around 6700 B.C. The Indo-Iranian branch originated either directly through migration from Anatolia, or indirectly by way of Russia north of the Black and Caspian seas. Renfrew argues that Indo-European diffused with agricultural practices rather than by military conquest. After many generations of complete isolation, individual groups evolved increasingly distinct languages.

(151)
Key Issue 3. Where Are Other Language Families Distributed?
- **Classification of languages**
- **Distribution of language families**

The several thousand spoken languages can be organized logically into a small number of language families. Larger language families can be further divided into language branches and language groups.

Classification of Languages
About 46 percent of all people speak a language in the Indo-European family. About 21 percent speak a language in the *Sino-Tibetan* family. An *Afro-Asiatic* language, such as Arabic, is spoken by 6 percent, mostly in the Middle East. In Southeast Asia, *Austronesian* languages are spoken by 6 percent. The *Niger-Congo* family languages are spoken by 6 percent, mostly in Africa. The language in the *Dravidian* family is spoken by 4 percent, mostly in India. *Altaic* family languages are spoken by 2 percent, mostly in Asia. *Japanese,* a separate language family, is spoken by 2 percent. The remaining 5 percent of the world's people speak a language belonging to one of 100 smaller families.

Distribution of Language Families
Nearly half the people in the world speak an Indo-European language. The second-largest family is Sino-Tibetan, spoken by one-fifth of the world. Another half-dozen families account for the remainder.

Sino-Tibetan Family
The Sino-Tibetan family encompasses languages spoken in the People's Republic of China as well as several smaller countries in Southeast Asia. There is no single Chinese language. Spoken by approximately three-fourths of the Chinese people, Mandarin is by a wide margin the most used language in the world.

Other Sinitic branch languages are spoken by tens of millions of people in China. The Chinese government is imposing Mandarin countrywide. The relatively small number of languages in China compared to India is a source of national unity. Unity is also fostered by a consistent written form for all Chinese languages. Although the words are pronounced differently in each language, they are written the same way. The structure of Chinese languages is quite different from Indo-European. They are based on 420 one-syllable words. This number far exceeds the possible one-syllable sounds that humans can make, so Chinese languages use each sound to denote more than one thing. The listener must infer the meaning from the context in the sentence and the tone of voice the speaker uses. In addition, two one-syllable words can be combined.

(152)
The other distinctive characteristic of the Chinese languages is the method of writing with a collection of thousands of characters. Some represent sounds. Most are **ideograms**, which represent ideas or concepts, not specific pronunciations.

Other East and Southeast Asian Language Families
Austronesian. Speakers are mostly in Indonesia, which has an extremely large number of languages and dialects. 722 languages are actively used, the largest being Javanese. The people of Madagascar speak Malagasy, which belongs to this family, and is strong evidence of migration perhaps 2,000 years ago.

Austro-Asiactic. Based in Southeast Asia; Vietnamese, the most spoken tongue, is written with the Roman alphabet with diacritical marks, a system devised by Roman Catholic missionaries in the seventh century.

Tai Kadai. Once classified as a branch of Sino Tibetan, principal languages are spoken in Thailand and neighboring portions of China.

Japanese. Written in part with Chinese ideograms and two systems of phonetic symbols, one of which is used for foreign terms.

Korean. May be related to the Altaic languages of Central Asia or to Japanese, but usually classified as a separate language family. Written not in ideograms but in a system known as hankul. More than half the vocabulary derives from Chinese words.

(154)
Languages of the Middle East and Central Asia
Major language families include Afro-Asiatic and Altaic. Uralic languages were one classified with Altaic.

Afro-Asiatic. Arabic is the major language, an official language in two-dozen countries of the Middle East and one of six official languages of the United Nations. The family also includes Hebrew.

Altaic. Present distribution covers an 8,000-kilometer (5,000-mile) band of Asia. Turkish, by far the most widely used, was once written with Arabic letters, but in 1928 the Turkish government, led by Kemal Ataturk, ordered that the language be written with the Roman alphabet instead in order to modernize the economy and culture of Turkey through increased communications with European countries. With the dissolution of the Soviet Union in the early 1990s, Altaic languages became official in several newly independent countries, including Azerbaijan, Kazakhstan, Kyrgyzstan, Turkmenistan, and Uzbekistan.

(155)

Uralic. Every European country is dominated by Indo-European speakers, except for three: Estonia, Finland, and Hungary. The Estonians, Finns, and Hungarians speak languages that belong to the Uralic family, first used 7,000 years ago by people living in the Ural Mountains north of the Kurgan homeland.

(156)

African Language Families

No one knows the precise number of languages spoken in Africa, and scholars disagree on classifying the known ones into families. More than 1,000 distinct languages and several thousand named dialects have been documented. In northern Africa, Arabic dominates, although in a variety of dialects. In sub-Saharan Africa, languages grow far more complex.

Niger-Congo. More than 95 percent of the people in sub-Saharan Africa speak languages of the Niger-Congo family. One of these languages — Swahili — is the first language of only 800,000 people, and an official language of only one country (Tanzania), but it is spoken as a second language by approximately 30 million Africans. Its vocabulary has strong Arabic influences. Swahili is one of the few African languages with an extensive literature.

Nilo-Saharan. These languages are spoken by a few million people in north-central Africa, immediately north of the Niger-Congo language region. Despite fewer speakers, the Nilo-Saharan family is divided into six branches.

Khoisan. A distinctive characteristic of the Khoisan is the use of clicking sounds. Whites in southern Africa derisively and onomatopoeically named the most important Khoisan language Hottentot.

Key Issue 4. Why Do People Preserve Local Languages?
- **Preserving language diversity**
- **Global dominance of English**

The distribution of a language is a measure of the fate of an ethnic group. As in other cultural traits, language displays the two competing geographic trends of globalization and local diversity.

Preserving Language Diversity

Thousands of languages are **extinct languages**, once in use — even in the recent past — but no longer spoken or read in daily activities by anyone in the world. The eastern Amazon region of Peru in the sixteenth century had more than 500 languages. (157) Only 92 survive today and 14 of these face immediate extinction, because fewer than 100 speakers remain.

Gothic was widely spoken in Eastern and Northern Europe in the third century A.D. The last speakers of Gothic lived in the Crimea in Russia in the sixteenth century. Many Gothic people switched to speaking the Latin language after their conversion to Christianity.

Some endangered languages are being preserved. Nonetheless, linguists expect that only about 300 languages are clearly safe from extinction.

Hebrew: Reviving Extinct Languages

Hebrew is a rare case of an extinct language that has been revived. Hebrew diminished in use in the fourth century B.C. and was thereafter retained only for Jewish religious services. The effort was initiated by Eliezer Ben-Yehuda, credited with the invention of 4,000 new Hebrew words — related when possible to ancient ones — and the creation of the first modern Hebrew dictionary.

Celtic: Preserving Endangered Languages

Two thousand years ago Celtic languages were spoken in much of present-day Germany, France, and northern Italy, as well as in the British Isles. Today Celtic languages survive only in remoter parts of Scotland, Wales, and Ireland, and on the Brittany peninsula of France.

The Celtic language branch is divided into Goidelic (Gaelic) and Brythonic groups. Two Goidelic languages survive: Irish Gaelic and Scottish Gaelic.

Over time, speakers of Brythonic (also called Cymric or Britannic) fled westward to Wales, southwestward to Cornwall, or southward across the English Channel to the Brittany peninsula of France.

Irish Gaelic. Irish is spoken by 350,000 people on a daily basis and 1.5 million say they can speak it.

Scottish Gaelic. In Scotland 59,000, or 1 percent of the population, speak Scottish Gaelic. Gaelic was carried from Ireland back to Scotland about 1,500 years ago.

Brythonic (Welsh). Welsh remained dominant in Wales until the nineteenth century, when many English speakers migrated there. A 2004 survey found 22 percent of the population spoke Welsh, and in some isolated communities in the northwest two-thirds speak it.

(159)
Cornish. Cornish became extinct in 1777, with the death of the language's last known native speaker, Dolly Pentreath. An English historian recorded as much of her speech as possible so that future generations could study the Cornish language.

Breton. In Brittany — like Cornwall, an isolated peninsula that juts out into the Atlantic Ocean — 250,000 people still speak Breton.

The Celtic languages declined because the Celts lost most of the territory they once controlled to speakers of other languages. In the 1300s, the Irish were forbidden to speak their own language in the presence of their English masters.

Recent efforts have prevented the disappearance of Celtic languages. Britain's 1988 Education Act made Welsh language training a compulsory subject in all schools in Wales. An Irish-language TV station began broadcasting in 1996. A few hundred people have now become fluent in the formerly extinct Cornish language, which was revived in the 1920s. Faced with the diffusion of alternatives used by people with greater political and economic strength, speakers of Celtic and other languages must work hard to preserve their linguistic cultural identity.

Multilingual States

Difficulties can arise at the boundary between two languages. The boundary between the Romance and Germanic branches runs through the middle of Belgium and Switzerland. Belgium has had more difficulty than Switzerland in reconciling the interests of the different language speakers.

Southern Belgians (known as Walloons) speak French, whereas northern Belgians (known as Flemings) speak a dialect of the Germanic language of Dutch, called Flemish.

(160)
Historically, the Walloons dominated Belgium's economy and politics, so French was the official state language. In response to pressure from Flemish speakers, Belgium was divided into two independent regions, Flanders and Wallonia. For many in Flanders, regional autonomy is not

enough and they want to see Belgium divided into two countries, which would make Flanders one of Europe's richest, and Wallonia one of Europe's poorest.

In contrast, Switzerland peacefully exists with multiple languages. The key is a decentralized government. Switzerland has four official languages: German, French, Italian, and Romansh. The Swiss have institutionalized cultural diversity by creating a form of government that places considerable power in small communities.

Isolated Languages
An **isolated language** is a language unrelated to any other and therefore not attached to any language family. Isolated languages arise through lack of interaction with speakers of other languages.

(161)
A Pre-Indo-European Survivor: Basque. The best example of an isolated language in Europe is Basque. It is now the first language of 666,000 people in the Pyrenees Mountains of northern Spain and southwestern France.

(162)
An Unchanging Language: Icelandic. Unlike Basque, Icelandic is related to other languages. Icelandic's significance is that over the past thousand years it has changed less than any other in the Germanic branch.

Global Dominance of English
One of the most fundamental needs in a global society is a common language for communication. Increasingly in the modern world, the language of international communication is English.

English: An Example of a Lingua Franca
A language of international communication is known as a **lingua franca**.

A group that learns English or another lingua franca may learn a simplified form, called a **pidgin language**. Two groups construct a pidgin language by learning a few of the grammar rules and words of a lingua franca, while mixing in some elements of their own languages. Other than English, modern lingua franca languages include Swahili in East Africa, Hindustani in South Asia, and Russian in the former Soviet Union.

Expansion Diffusion of English
In the past, a lingua franca achieved widespread distribution through migration and conquest. In recent centuries, use of English spread around the world primarily through the British Empire. In contrast, the current growth in use of English is an example of expansion diffusion, rather than through the relocation of people. Unlike most examples of expansion diffusion, recent changes in English have percolated up from common usage and ethnic dialects rather than directed down to the masses by elite people. Examples include dialects spoken by African-Americans and residents of Appalachia. African-American slaves preserved a distinctive dialect in part to communicate in a code not understood by their white masters.

In the twentieth century, living in racially segregated neighborhoods within northern cities and attending segregated schools, many blacks preserved their distinctive dialect. That dialect has been termed Ebonics, a combination of ebony and phonics. The American Speech, Language, and Hearing Association has classified Ebonics as a distinct dialect, with a recognized vocabulary, grammar, and word meaning.

(163)

Natives of Appalachian communities, such as in rural West Virginia, also have a distinctive dialect. Use of Ebonics is controversial within the African-American community. Similarly, speaking an Appalachian dialect produces both pride and problems.

Diffusion to Other Languages

English words have become increasingly integrated into other languages. Many French speakers regard the invasion of English words with alarm, but Spanish speakers may find the mixing of the two languages stimulating.

(164)

Franglais. The French are particularly upset with the increasing worldwide domination of English, especially the invasion of their language by English words. French is an official language in 26 countries and for hundreds of years served as the lingua franca for international diplomats. The widespread use of English in the French language is called **franglais**, a combination of *français* and *anglais*, the French words for French and English. Protection of the French language is even more extreme in Quebec, which is completely surrounded by English-speaking provinces and U.S. states.

Spanglish. English is diffusing into the Spanish language spoken by 34 million Hispanics in the United States, creating **Spanglish**.

For example, shorts (pants) becomes chores, and vacuum cleaner becomes bacuncliner. In other cases, awkward Spanish words or phrases are dropped in favor of English words, such using *taipear* instead of *escribir a maquina* for *to type*. Spanglish is a richer integration of English with Spanish than the mere borrowing of English words. New words have been invented in Spanglish that do not exist in English but would be useful if they did. Spanglish has become especially widespread in popular culture, as evidenced in song lyrics, television, and magazines aimed at young Hispanic women, but it has also been adopted by writers of serious literature.

Denglish. The diffusion of English words into German is called **Denglish**. For many Germans, wishing someone "happy birthday" sounds more melodic than the German *Herzlichen Gluuuckwunsch zum Geburtstag*. English has diffused into other languages as well. The Japanese, for example, refer to *beisboru* (baseball), *naifu* (knife), and *sutoroberi keki* (strawberry cake).

Key Terms

British Received Pronunciation (BRP) (p.139)
Creole or creolized language (p.149)
Denglish (p. 164)
Dialect (p.139)
Ebonics (p.162)
Extinct language (p.156)
Franglais (p.164)
Ideograms (p.152)
Isogloss (p.139)
Isolated language (p.160)

Language (p.136)
Language branch (p.143)
Language family (p.143)
Language group (p.144)
Lingua franca (p.162)
Literary tradition (p.136)
Official language (p.136)
Pidgin language (p.162)
Spanglish (p.164)
Standard language (p.139)
Vulgar Latin (p.147)

Test Prep Questions

1) Which of the following groups did NOT significantly impact the development of English?
A) the Normans
B) the Celts
C) the Germanic invaders
D) the Vikings

2) What is NOT a city where the standard dialect of British English, BRP, originated?
A) Birmingham
B) Oxford
C) Cambridge
D) London

3) Which of the following is NOT one of the three major dialect regions of the U.S.?
A) Northern
B) Midwestern
C) Southern
D) Midlands

4) What is the language group that English belongs to?
A) Indo-European
B) Germanic
C) West Germanic
D) Low Germanic

5) Which branch if the Indo-European language family has the most speakers?
A) Germanic
B) Romance
C) Balto-Slavic
D) Indo-Iranian

6) Which of the following is NOT a Romance language?
A) Italian
B) German
C) French
D) Romanian

7) Which of the following European countries do NOT speak languages that belong to the Indo-European language family?
A) Estonia
B) Finland
C) Hungary
D) all of these

8) Which Celtic language went extinct in 1777 but has since been revived?
A) Breton
B) Cornish
C) Welsh
D) Irish Gaelic

9) Which of the following is a good example of an isolated language?
A) Hebrew
B) Denglish
C) Icelandic
D) Basque

10) Which of these languages is NOT a modern example of a lingua franca?
A) Mandarin Chinese
B) Swahili
C) Russian
D) Hindustani

Short Essay

1) Explain the ways in which American English and British English differ, citing examples.

_____

_____

_____

_____

_____

_____

_____

2) Identify and explain the two competing hypotheses about the origin and diffusion of the Proto-Indo-European language.

_____

_____

_____

_____

_____

_____

_____

3) Identify the two small European countries through which the boundary between the Germanic and Romance language branches runs and compare them in terms of their respective abilities to function effectively as multilingual states.

_____

_____

_____

_____

_____

_____

_____

Chapter 6
Religion

Key Issues
1. Where are religions distributed?
2. Why do religions have different distributions?
3. Why do religions organize space in distinctive patterns?
4. Why do territorial conflicts arise among religious groups?

(170)

Religion interests geographers because it is essential for understanding how humans occupy Earth. Geographers, though, are not theologians, so they stay focused on those elements of religions that are geographically significant. Geographers study spatial *connections* in religion: the distinctive place of origin, the extent of diffusion, the processes by which religions diffused, and practices and beliefs that lead some to have more widespread distributions.

Geographers find the tension in *scale* between *globalization* and *local diversity* especially acute in religion for a number of reasons. People care deeply about their religion; some religions are *designed* to appeal to people throughout the world, whereas other religions appeal primarily to people in geographically limited areas; religious values are important in how people identify themselves, (and) the ways they organize the landscape; adopting a global religion usually requires turning away from a traditional local religion; and while migrants typically learn the language of the new location, they retain their religion.

This chapter starts by describing the distribution of major religions, and then explains why some religions have diffused widely, whereas others have not. The third section of the chapter discusses religion's strong imprint on the physical environment. Unfortunately, intense identification with one religion can lead adherents into conflicts discussed in the fourth key issue of the chapter.

Key Issue 1. Where Are Religions Distributed?
- **Universalizing religions**
- **Ethnic religions**

Geographers distinguish two types of religions: universalizing and ethnic.

Universalizing religions attempt to be global, to appeal to all people. An **ethnic religion** appeals primarily to one group of people living in one place.

(171)
Universalizing Religions
About 58 percent of the world's population adheres to a universalizing religion, 26 percent to an ethnic religion, and 16 percent to no religion. The three main universalizing religions are Christianity, Islam, and Buddhism. Each is divided into branches, denominations, and sects. A **branch** is a large and fundamental division within a religion. A **denomination** is a division of a branch that unites a number of local congregations. A **sect** is a relatively small group that has broken away from an established denomination.

Christianity. Christianity has about 2 billion adherents, far more than any other world religion, and has the most widespread distribution.

Branches of Christianity. Christianity has three major branches: Roman Catholic, Protestant, and Orthodox. Within Europe, Roman Catholicism is the dominant Christian branch in the southwest and east, Protestantism in the northwest, and Orthodoxy in the east and southeast. The regions of Roman Catholic and Protestant majorities frequently have sharp boundaries, even when they run through the middle of countries.

The Orthodox branch of Christianity is a collection of 14 self-governing churches in Eastern Europe and the Middle East. More than 40 percent of all Eastern Orthodox Christians belong to the Russian Orthodox Church, established in the sixteenth century. Nine of the other 13 self-governing churches were established in the nineteenth or twentieth century. The largest of these 9, the Romanian church, includes 20 percent of all Orthodox Christians.

The remaining 4 of the 14 churches — Constantinople, Alexandria, Antioch, and Jerusalem — trace their origins to the earliest days of Christianity. They have a combined membership of about 3 percent of all Orthodox Christians.

(172)
Christianity in the Western Hemisphere. The overwhelming percentage of people living in the Western Hemisphere — about 90 percent — are Christian. Roman Catholics comprise 95 percent of Christians in Latin America, compared with 40 percent in North America. Within North America, Roman Catholics are clustered in the southwestern and northeastern United States and the Canadian province of Québec. Protestants comprise 40 percent of Christians in North America. Baptists have the largest number of adherents in the U.S. Baptists are highly clustered in the southeast, whereas Lutherans are in the upper Midwest. Other Christian denominations are more evenly distributed around the country.

Smaller Branches of Christianity. Several other Christian churches developed independent of the three main branches. Two small Christian churches survive in northeast Africa: the Coptic Church of Egypt and the Ethiopian Church.

(173)
The Armenian Church originated in Antioch, Syria, and was important in diffusing Christianity to South and East Asia between the seventh and thirteenth centuries. The Armenian Church, like other small sects, plays a significant role in regional conflicts. The Maronites, (clustered in Lebanon) are another example of a small Christian sect that plays a disproportionately prominent role in political unrest. In the U.S., members of The Church of Jesus Christ of Latter Day Saints (Mormons) regard their church as a branch of Christianity separate from other branches.

Islam. Islam, the religion of 1.3 billion people, is the predominant religion of the Middle East from North Africa to Central Asia. Half of the world's Muslims live in four countries outside the Middle East: Indonesia, Pakistan, Bangladesh, and India.

(174)
Branches of Islam. Islam is divided into two important branches: Sunni (from the Arabic word for orthodox) and Shiite (from the Arabic word for sectarian, sometimes written Shia in English). Sunnis comprise 83 percent of Muslims and are the largest branch in most Muslim countries. Sixteen percent of Muslims are Shiites, clustered in a handful of countries. Shiites comprise nearly 90 percent of the population in Iran and more than half the population in Iraq.

(175)
Islam in North America and Europe. The Muslim population of North America and Europe has increased rapidly in recent years. Estimates of the number of Muslims in North America vary widely, from 1 to 5 million but it has increased from only a few hundred thousand in 1990. In Europe, France has the largest Muslim population, a legacy of immigration from former colonies in North Africa. Islam also has a presence in the United States through the Nation of Islam, also

known as Black Muslims, founded in Detroit in 1930 and led for more than 40 years by Elijah Muhammad, who called himself "the messenger of Allah." Since Muhammad's death, in 1975, his son Wallace D. Muhammad led the Black Muslims closer to the principles of orthodox Islam, and the organizations name was changed to the American Muslim Mission.

Buddhism. Buddhism, the third of the world's major universalizing religions, has 350 million adherents, especially in China and Southeast Asia.

(176)
Like the other two universalizing religions, Buddhism split into more than one branch. The three main branches are Mahayana, Theravada, and Tantrayana.

An accurate count of Buddhists is especially difficult, because only a few people participate in Buddhist institutions. Buddhism differs in significant respects from the Western concept of a formal religious system. Christianity and Islam both require exclusive adherence. Most Buddhists in China and Japan, in particular, believe at the same time in an ethnic religion.

Other Universalizing Religions. Sikhism and Bahá'í are the two universalizing religions other than Christianity, Islam, and Buddhism with the largest numbers of adherents. Sikhism's first guru (religious teacher or enlightener) was Nanak (A.D. 1469–1538), who lived in a village near the city of Lahore, in present-day Pakistan. The Bahá'í religion is even more recent than Sikhism. It grew out of the Bábi faith, which was founded in Shíráz, Iran, in 1844 by Siyyid 'Ali Muhammad, known as the Báb (Persian for gateway).

Ethnic Religions
The ethnic religion with by far the largest number of followers is Hinduism. With 900 million adherents, Hinduism is the world's third-largest religion, behind Christianity and Islam. Ethnic religions in Asia and Africa comprise most of the remainder.

Hinduism. Ethnic religions typically have much more clustered distributions than do universalizing religions. Ninety-seven percent of Hindus are concentrated in one country, India, and most of the remainder can be found in India's neighbor, Nepal.

(177)
The appropriate form of worship for any two individuals may not be the same. Hinduism does not have a central authority or a single holy book. The largest number of adherents — an estimated 70 percent — worships the god Vishnu, a loving god incarnated as Krishna. An estimated 26 percent adhere to Siva, a protective and destructive god. Shaktism is a form of worship dedicated to the female consorts of Vishnu and Siva.

Other Ethnic Religions
Several hundred million people practice ethnic religions in East Asia, especially in China and Japan. Buddhism does not compete for adherents with Confucianism, Daoism, and other ethnic religions in China, because many Chinese accept the teachings of both universalizing and ethnic religions.

Confucianism. Confucius (551–479 B.C.) was a philosopher and teacher in the Chinese province of Lu. Confucianism prescribed a series of ethical principles for the orderly conduct of daily life in China.

Daoism (Taoism). Lao-Zi (604–531? B.C., also spelled Lao Tse), a contemporary of Confucius, organized Daoism. Daoists seek dao (or tao), which means the way or path. Dao cannot be comprehended by reason and knowledge, because not everything is knowable. Daoism split into many sects, some acting like secret societies, and followers embraced elements of magic.

(178)
Shintoism. Since ancient times, Shintoism has been the distinctive ethnic religion of Japan. Ancient Shintoists considered forces of nature to be divine, especially the Sun and Moon, as well as rivers, trees, rocks, mountains, and certain animals. Gradually, deceased emperors and other ancestors became more important deities for Shintoists than natural features. Shintoism still thrives in Japan, although no longer as the official state religion.

(194)
Judaism. Around one-third of the world's 14 million Jews live in the United States, one-third in Israel, and one third in the rest of the world.

Judaism plays a more substantial role in Western civilization than its number of adherents would suggest, because two of the three main universalizing religions — Christianity and Islam — find some of their roots in Judaism. It was the first recorded religion to espouse **monotheism**, belief that there is only one God. Judaism offered a sharp contrast to the **polytheism** practiced by neighboring people, who worshiped a collection of gods. The name Judaism derives from Judah, one of the patriarch Jacob's 12 sons; Israel is another biblical name for Jacob.

Ethnic African Religions. Approximately 100 million Africans, 12 percent of the population, follow traditional ethnic religions, sometimes called **animism**. African animist religions are apparently based on monotheistic concepts, although below the supreme god there is a hierarchy of divinities, assistants to god or personifications of natural phenomena, such as trees or rivers. Some atlases and textbooks persist in classifying Africa as predominantly animist, even though the actual percentage is small and declining. Africa is now 46 percent Christian and another 40 percent are Muslims. The growth in the two universalizing religions at the expense of ethnic religions reflects fundamental geographical differences between the two types of religions.

Key Issue 2. Why Do Religions Have Different Distributions?
- **Origin of religions**
- **Diffusion of religions**
- **Holy places**
- **The calendar**

We can identify several major geographical differences between universalizing and ethnic religions: locations where the religions originated, processes by which they diffused to other regions, types of places considered holy, calendar dates identified as important holidays, and attitudes toward modifying the physical environment.

Origin of Religions
Universalizing religions have precise places of origin, based on events in the life of a man. Ethnic religions have unknown or unclear origins, not tied to single historical individuals.

(179)
Origin of Universalizing Religions. Each of the three universalizing religions can be traced to the actions and teachings of a man who lived since the start of recorded history. Specific events also led to the division of the universalizing religions into branches.

Origin of Christianity. Christianity was founded upon the teachings of Jesus, who was born in Bethlehem between 8 and 4 B.C. and died on a cross in Jerusalem about A.D. 30.

Christians believe that Jesus died to atone for human sins, that he was raised from the dead by God, and that his Resurrection from the dead provides people with hope for salvation. Roman Catholics accept the teachings of the Bible, as well as the interpretation of those teachings by the Church hierarchy, headed by the Pope. Orthodoxy comprises the faith and practices of a collection of churches that arose in the eastern part of the Roman Empire. The split between the Roman and Eastern churches dates to the fifth century, as a result of rivalry between the Pope of Rome and the Patriarchy of Constantinople. Protestantism originated with the principles of the Reformation in the sixteenth century.

Origin of Islam. Islam traces its origin to the same narrative as Judaism and Christianity. All three religions consider Adam to have been the first man and Abraham to have been one of his descendants.

Jews and Christians trace their story through Abraham's original wife and son, Sarah and Isaac. Muslims trace their story through his second wife and son, Hagar and Ishmael. One of Ishmael's descendants, Muhammad, became the Prophet of Islam. Muhammad was born in Makkah about A.D. 570.

(180)
Differences between the two main branches — Shiites and Sunnis — go back to the earliest days of Islam and basically reflect disagreement over the line of succession in Islamic leadership.

Origin of Buddhism. The founder of Buddhism, Siddhartha Gautama, was born about 563 B.C. in present-day Nepal, near the border with India. The son of a lord, he led a privileged existence sheltered from life's hardships. At age 29 Gautama left his palace and lived in a forest for the next six years, thinking and experimenting with forms of meditation. Gautama emerged as the Buddha, the "awakened or enlightened one," and spent 45 years preaching his views across India. While the Theravadists emphasize Buddha's life of self-help and years of solitary introspection, Mahayanists emphasize Buddha's later years of teaching and helping others.

(181)
Origin of Other Universalizing Religions. Sikhism and Bahá'í were founded more recently than the three large universalizing religions. The founder of Sikhism, Guru Nanak, traveled widely through South Asia around 500 years ago preaching his new faith, and many people became his Sikhs, which is the Hindi word for disciples. When it was established in Iran during the nineteenth century, Bahá'í provoked strong opposition from Shiite Muslims. The Báb was executed in 1850, as were 20,000 of his followers.

Origin of Hinduism, an Ethnic Religion. Unlike the universalizing religions, Hinduism did not originate with a specific founder. Hinduism existed prior to recorded history. Aryan tribes from Central Asia invaded India about 1400 B.C. and brought their religion. Centuries of intermingling with the Dravidians already living in the area modified their religious beliefs.

Diffusion of Religions
The three universalizing religions diffused from specific hearths, or places of origin, to other regions of the world. In contrast, ethnic religions typically remain clustered in one location.

Diffusion of Universalizing Religions. The hearths of the three largest universalizing religions are in Asia (Christianity and Islam in Southwest Asia, Buddhism in South Asia). Today these three together have several billion adherents distributed across wide areas of the world.

(182)
Diffusion of Christianity. Christianity's diffusion has been rather clearly recorded. Consequently, geographers can examine its diffusion by reconstructing patterns of communications, interaction, and migration. Christianity first diffused from its hearth in Palestine through relocation diffusion. **Missionaries** carried the teachings of Jesus along the Roman Empire's protected sea routes and excellent road network. People in commercial towns and military settlements that were directly linked by the communications network received the message first. Christianity also spread widely through contagious diffusion — daily contact between believers in the towns and nonbelievers in the surrounding countryside. **Pagan**, the word for a follower of a polytheistic religion in ancient times, derives from the Latin word for *countryside*. The dominance of Christianity was assured during the fourth century through hierarchical diffusion. Emperor Constantine embraced it in A.D. 313, and Emperor Theodosius proclaimed it the empire's official religion in 380. In subsequent centuries, Christianity further diffused into Eastern Europe through conversion of kings or other elite figures.

Migration and missionary activity since 1500 has extended Christianity to other regions, through permanent resettlement of Europeans, by conversion of indigenous populations, and by intermarriage. In recent decades Christianity has further diffused to Africa, where it is now the most widely practiced religion. Latin Americans are predominantly Roman Catholic, colonized by the Spanish and Portuguese. Canada (except Québec) and the United States have Protestant majorities because colonists came primarily from Protestant England. Followers of the Church of Jesus Christ of Latter Day Saints, popularly known as Mormons, originated at Fayette, New York, and then eventually migrated to the sparsely inhabited Salt Lake Valley in the present-day state of Utah.

(183)
Diffusion of Islam. Muhammad's successors organized followers into armies that extended the region of Muslim control over an extensive area of Africa, Asia, and Europe.

Islam diffused well beyond its hearth through relocation diffusion of missionaries to portions of sub-Saharan Africa and Southeast Asia. Spatially isolated from the Islamic core region, Indonesia is predominantly Muslim, because Arab traders brought the religion there in the thirteenth century.

Diffusion of Buddhism. Buddhism did not diffuse rapidly from its point of origin in northeastern India. Most responsible for the spread of Buddhism was Asoka, emperor of the Magadhan Empire from about 273 to 232 B.C. About 257 B.C., at the height of the Magadhan Empire's power, Asoka became a Buddhist and thereafter attempted to put into practice Buddha's social principles. In the first century A.D., merchants along the trading routes from northeastern India introduced Buddhism to China. Chinese rulers allowed their people to become Buddhist monks during the fourth century A.D. Buddhism further diffused from China to Korea in the fourth century and from Korea to Japan two centuries later. During the same era, Buddhism lost its original base of support in India.

(184)
Diffusion of Other Universalizing Religions. The Bahá'í religion diffused to other regions in the late nineteenth and early twentieth centuries and then spread rapidly during the late twentieth century, when a temple was constructed in every continent. Sikhism remained relatively clustered in the Punjab, where the religion originated. In 1802 they created an independent state in the Punjab. But when the British government created the independent states of India and Pakistan in 1947, it divided the Punjab between the two instead of giving the Sikhs a separate country.

Lack of Diffusion of Ethnic Religions. Most ethnic religions have limited, if any, diffusion. These religions lack missionaries. Diffusion of universalizing religions, especially Christianity and Islam, typically comes at the expense of ethnic religions.

Mingling of Ethnic and Universalizing Religions. Universalizing religions may supplant ethnic religions or mingle with them. Equatorial Guinea, a former Spanish colony, is mostly Roman Catholic, whereas Namibia, a former German colony, is heavily Lutheran. Elsewhere, traditional African religious ideas and practices have been merged with Christianity. In East Asia, Buddhism is the universalizing religion that has most mingled with ethnic religions, such as Shintoism in Japan.

The current situation in Japan offers a strong caution to anyone attempting to document the number of adherents of any religion. About 90 percent of Japanese say they are Shintos and about 70 percent say they are Buddhists. Ethnic religions can diffuse if adherents migrate to new locations for economic reasons and are not forced to adopt a strongly entrenched universalizing religion. The religious diversity of Mauritius is a function of the country's history of immigration. Mauritius was uninhabited until 1638, so it had no traditional ethnic religion. Hinduism on Mauritius traces back to the Indian immigrants, Islam to the African immigrants, and Christianity to the European immigrants.

(185)
Judaism, an Exception. Only since the creation of the state of Israel in 1948 has a significant percentage of the world's Jews lived in their Eastern Mediterranean homeland.

The Romans forced the Jewish diaspora, (from the Greek word for dispersion) after crushing an attempt by the Jews to rebel against Roman rule. Jews lived among other nationalities, retaining separate religious practices but adopting other cultural characteristics of the host country, such as language. Other nationalities often persecuted the Jews living in their midst. Historically, the Jews of many European countries were forced to live in a **ghetto**, a city neighborhood set up by law to be inhabited only by Jews. During World War II the Nazis systematically rounded up European Jews and exterminated them. Many of the survivors migrated to Israel. Today about 10 percent of the world's 14 million Jews live in Europe, compared to 90 percent a century ago.

Holy Places
Religions may elevate particular places to a holy position. An ethnic religion's holy places derive from the distinctive physical environment of its hearth, such as mountains, rivers, or rock formations. A universalizing religion endows with holiness cities and other places associated with the founder's life. Making a **pilgrimage** to these holy places is incorporated into the rituals of some universalizing and ethnic religions.

Holy Places in Universalizing Religions. Buddhism and Islam are the universalizing religions that place the most emphasis on identifying shrines.

Buddhist Shrines. Eight places are holy to Buddhists because they were the locations of important events in Buddha's life.

(186)
Holy Places in Islam. The holiest locations in Islam are in cities associated with the life of the Prophet Muhammad. The holiest city for Muslims is Makkah (Mecca), the birthplace of Muhammad.

The second most holy geographic location in Islam is Madinah (Medina). Muhammad's tomb is at Madinah, inside Islam's second mosque. Every healthy Muslim who has adequate financial resources is expected to undertake a pilgrimage, called a *hajj*, to Makkah (Mecca).

Holy Places in Sikhism. Sikhism's most holy structure, the Darbar Sahib, or Golden Temple, was built at Amritsar, during the seventh century. Militant Sikhs used the Golden Temple as a base for launching attacks in support of greater autonomy during the 1980s.

(187)
Holy Places in Ethnic Religions. Ethnic religions are closely tied to the physical geography of a particular place. Pilgrimages are undertaken to view these physical features.

Holy Places in Hinduism. As an ethnic religion of India, Hinduism is closely tied to the physical geography of India.

The natural features most likely to rank among the holiest shrines in India are riverbanks or coastlines. Hindus consider a pilgrimage, known as a tirtha, to be an act of purification. Hindus believe that they achieve purification by bathing in holy rivers. The Ganges is the holiest river in India because it is supposed to spring forth from the hair of Siva. Recent improvements in transportation have increased the accessibility of shrines.

(188)
Cosmogony in Ethnic Religions. Ethnic religions differ from universalizing religions in their understanding of relationships between human beings and nature. These differences derive from distinctive concepts of **cosmogony**, which is a set of religious beliefs concerning the origin of the universe. For example, Chinese ethnic religions, such as Confucianism and Daoism, believe that the universe is made up of two forces, yin and yang, which exist in everything.

The universalizing religions that originated in Southwest Asia, notably Christianity and Islam, consider that God created the universe, including Earth's physical environment and human beings. A religious person can serve God by cultivating the land, draining wetlands, clearing forests, building new settlements, and otherwise making productive use of natural features that God created. In the name of God, some people have sought mastery over nature, not merely independence from it.

Christians are more likely to consider natural disasters to be preventable and may take steps to overcome the problem by modifying the environment. However, some Christians regard natural disasters as punishment for human sins. Ethnic religions do not attempt to transform the environment to the same extent. Environmental hazards may be accepted as normal and unavoidable.

The Calendar
Universalizing and ethnic religions have different approaches to the calendar. An ethnic religion typically has holidays based on the distinctive physical geography of the homeland. In universalizing religions, major holidays relate to events in the life of the founder rather than to the changing seasons of one particular place.

The Calendar in Ethnic Religions. A prominent feature of ethnic religions is celebration of the seasons. Rituals are performed to pray for favorable environmental conditions or to give thanks for past success.

(189)

The Jewish Calendar. Judaism is classified as an ethnic religion in part because its major holidays are based on events in the agricultural calendar of the religion's homeland in present-day Israel. The reinterpretation of natural holidays in the light of historical events has been especially important for Jews in the United States, Western Europe, and other regions who are unfamiliar with the agricultural calendar of the Middle East. Israel uses a lunar, rather than a solar, calendar. The appearance of the new Moon marks the new month in Judaism and Islam and is a holiday for both religions. The lunar month is only about 29 days long, so a lunar year of about 350 days quickly becomes out of step with the agricultural seasons. The Jewish calendar solves the problem by adding an extra month 7 out of every 19 years.

The Solstice. The **solstice** has special significance in some ethnic religions. A major holiday in some pagan religions is the winter solstice, the shortest day and longest night of the year. Stonehenge is a prominent remnant of a pagan structure apparently aligned so the Sun rises between two stones on the solstice.

(190)

The Calendar in Universalizing Religions. The principal purpose of the holidays in universalizing religions is to commemorate events in the founder's life. Christians associate their holidays with seasonal variations, but climate and the agricultural cycle are not central to the liturgy and rituals.

Islamic and Bahá'í calendars. Islam, like Judaism, uses a lunar calendar. Islam as a universalizing religion retains a strict lunar calendar. As a result of using a lunar calendar, Muslim holidays arrive in different seasons from generation to generation. The Bahá'ís use a calendar in which the year is divided into 19 months of 19 days each, with the addition of four intercalary days (five in leap years). The year begins on the first day of spring.

Christian, Buddhist, and Sikh Holidays. Christians commemorate the resurrection of Jesus on Easter, observed on the first Sunday after the first full Moon following the spring equinox in late March. But not all Christians observe Easter on the same day, because Eastern Orthodox churches use the Julian calendar. Christians may relate Easter to the agricultural cycle, but that relationship differs with where they live. Northern Europeans and North Americans associate Christmas, the birthday of Jesus, with winter conditions. But for Christians in the Southern Hemisphere, December 25 is the height of the summer, with warm days and abundant sunlight.

All Buddhists celebrate as major holidays Buddha's birth, Enlightenment, and death. However, Buddhists do not all observe them on the same days. The major holidays in Sikhism are the births and deaths of the religion's 10 gurus. Commemorating historical events distinguishes Sikhism as a universalizing religion, in contrast to India's ethnic religion, Hinduism, which glorifies the physical geography of India.

(191)

Key Issue 3. Why Do Religions Organize Space in Distinctive Patterns?
- **Places of worship**
- **Sacred space**
- **Administration of space**

Geographers study the major impact on the landscape made by all religions, regardless of whether they are universalizing or ethnic. The distribution of religious elements on the landscape reflects the importance of religion in people's values.

Places of Worship
Church, basilica, mosque, temple, pagoda, and synagogue are familiar names that identify places of worship in various religions. Some religions require a relatively large number of elaborate structures, whereas others have more modest needs.

Christian Churches
The Christian landscape is dominated by a high density of churches. The word *church* derives from a Greek term meaning *lord*, *master*, and *power*. *Church* also refers to a gathering of believers, as well as the building where the gathering occurs. The church building plays a more critical role in Christianity than in other religions, in part because the structure is an expression of religious principles, an environment in the image of God, and because attendance at a collective service of worship is considered extremely important. The prominence of churches on the landscape also stems from their style of construction and location. Since Christianity split into many denominations, no single style of church construction has dominated.

Places of Worship in Other Religions. Unlike Christianity, other major religions do not consider their important buildings a sanctified place of worship.

Muslim Mosques. Unlike a church, a *mosque* is not viewed as a sanctified place but rather as a location for the community to gather together for worship. The mosque is organized around a central courtyard, and a distinctive feature of the mosque is the minaret, a tower where a man known as a muzzan summons people to worship.

Hindu Temples. In Asian ethnic and universalizing religions, important religious functions are likely to take place at home within the family. The Hindu temple serves as a home to one or more gods, although a particular god may have more than one temple. Because congregational worship is not part of Hinduism, the temple does not need a large closed interior space filled with seats. The site of the temple may also contain a pool for ritual baths.

(192)
Buddhist and Shintoist Pagodas. The pagoda is a prominent and visually attractive element of the Buddhist and Shintoist landscapes. Pagodas contain relics that Buddhists believe to be a portion of Buddha's body or clothing. Pagodas are not designed for congregational worship.

Bahá'í Houses of Worship. Bahá'ís built seven Houses of Worship dispersed to different continents to dramatize Bahá'í as a universalizing religion, open to adherents of all religions. Services include reciting the scriptures of various religions.

Sacred Space
The impact of religion is clearly seen at several scales. How each religion distributes its elements on the landscape depends on its beliefs.

Disposing of the Dead. A prominent example of religiously inspired arrangement of land at a smaller scale is burial practices.

Burial. Christians, Muslims, and Jews usually bury their dead in a specially designated area called a *cemetery*. After Christianity became legal, Christians buried their dead in the yard around the church. As these burial places became overcrowded, separate burial grounds had to be established. The remains of the dead are customarily aligned in some traditional direction. In congested urban areas, Christians and Muslims have traditionally used cemeteries as public open space. Traditional burial practices in China have removed as much as 10 percent of the land from productive agriculture. Cremation is encouraged instead.

(193)

Other Methods of Disposing of Bodies. Not all faiths bury their dead. Hindus generally practice cremation rather than burial. Cremation was the principal form of disposing of bodies in Europe before Christianity. Motivation for cremation may have originated from unwillingness on the part of nomads to leave their dead behind. Cremation could also free the soul from the body. To strip away unclean portions of the body, Parsis (Zoroastrians) expose the dead to scavenging birds and animals. Tibetan Buddhists also practice exposure for some dead, with cremation reserved for the most exalted priests. Disposal of bodies at sea is used in some parts of Micronesia, but the practice is much less common than in the past.

Religious Settlements. Buildings for worship and burial places are smaller-scale manifestations of religion on the landscape, but there are larger-scale examples: entire settlements. A utopian settlement is an ideal community built around a religious way of life. By 1858 some 130 different utopian settlements had begun in the United States.

Most utopian communities declined in importance or disappeared altogether. Although most colonial settlements were not planned primarily for religious purposes, religious principles affected many of the designs. New England settlers placed the church at the most prominent location in the center of the settlement.

(194)

Religious Place Names. Roman Catholic immigrants frequently have given religious place names, or toponyms, to their settlements in the New World, particularly in Québec and the U.S. Southwest.

Administration of Space

Followers of a universalizing religion must be connected so as to assure communication and consistency of doctrine. Ethnic religions tend not to have organized, central authorities.

Hierarchical Religions. A hierarchical religion has a well-defined geographic structure and organizes territory into local administrative units.

Latter-Day Saints. Latter-Day Saints (Mormons) exercise strong organization of the landscape. The highest authority in the Church frequently redraws ward and stake boundaries in rapidly growing areas to reflect the ideal population standards.

Roman Catholic Hierarchy. The Roman Catholic Church has organized much of Earth's inhabited land into an administrative structure, ultimately accountable to the Pope in Rome. Reporting to the Pope are *archbishops*. Each archbishop heads a *province*, which is a group of several *dioceses*. The archbishop also is bishop of one diocese. Reporting to each archbishop are *bishops*. Each bishop administers a diocese, of which there are several thousand. A diocese in turn is spatially divided into parishes, each headed by a priest, who reports to the bishop.

(195)

Locally Autonomous Religions. Some universalizing religions are highly **autonomous religions**, or self-sufficient, and interaction among communities is confined to little more than loose cooperation and shared ideas. Islam and some Protestant denominations are good examples.

Local Autonomy in Islam. Islam has neither a religious hierarchy nor a formal territorial organization. Strong unity within the Islamic world is maintained by a relatively high degree of communication and migration, such as the pilgrimage to Makkah. In addition, uniformity is fostered by Islamic doctrine, which offers more explicit commands than other religions.

Protestant Denominations. Protestant Christian denominations vary in geographic structure from extremely autonomous to somewhat hierarchical. The Episcopalian, Lutheran, and most Methodist churches have hierarchical structures, somewhat comparable to the Roman Catholic Church. Extremely autonomous denominations such as Baptists and United Church of Christ are organized into self-governing congregations. Presbyterian churches represent an intermediate degree of autonomy.

Ethnic Religions. Judaism and Hinduism also have no centralized structure of religious control.

Key Issue 4. Why Do Territorial Conflicts Arise among Religious Groups?
- **Religion vs. government policies**
- **Religion vs. religion**

The twentieth century was a century of global conflict. The threat of global conflict has receded in the twenty-first century, but local conflicts have increased in areas of cultural diversity. The element of cultural diversity that has led to conflict in many localities is religion.

(213)
Religion vs. Government Policies. The role of religion in organizing Earth's surface has diminished in some societies, owing to political and economic change. Yet in recent years, religious principles have become increasingly important in the political organization of countries, especially where a branch of Christianity or Islam is the prevailing religion.

Religion vs. Social Change. Participation in the global economy and culture can expose local residents to values and beliefs originating in MDCs. North Americans and Western Europeans may not view economic development as incompatible with religious values, but many religious adherents in LDCs do, especially where Christianity is not the predominant religion.

Taliban vs. Western Values. Once in control of Afghanistan's government in the late 1990s, the Taliban imposed very strict laws inspired by Islamic values as the Taliban interpreted them. Islamic scholars criticized the Taliban as poorly educated in Islamic law and history and for misreading the Quran. A U.S.-led coalition overthrew the Taliban in 2001 and replaced it with a democratically elected government. However, the Taliban was able to regroup and resume its fight to regain control of Afghanistan.

Hinduism vs. Social Equality. Hinduism has been strongly challenged since the 1800s, when British colonial administrators introduced their social and moral concepts to India. The most vulnerable aspect of the Hindu religion was its rigid **caste** system. British administrators and Christian missionaries pointed out the shortcomings of the caste system, such as neglect of the untouchables' health and economic problems. The Indian government legally abolished the untouchable caste, and the people formerly in that caste now have equal rights with other Indians.

Religion vs. Communism. Organized religion was challenged in the twentieth century by the rise of communism in Eastern Europe and Asia.

Orthodox Christianity and Islam vs. the Soviet Union. In 1721, Czar Peter the Great made the Russian Orthodox Church a part of the Russian government. Following the 1917 Bolshevik revolution, which overthrew the czar, the Communist government of the Soviet Union pursued antireligious programs.

(197)

People's religious beliefs could not be destroyed overnight, but the role of organized religion in Soviet life was reduced. With religious organizations prevented from conducting social and cultural work, religion dwindled in daily life. The end of Communist rule in the late twentieth century brought a religious revival in Eastern Europe, especially where Roman Catholicism is the most prevalent branch. Property confiscated by the Communist governments reverted to Church ownership, and attendance at church services increased. Central Asian countries that were former parts of the Soviet Union are struggling to determine the extent to which laws should be rewritten to conform to Islamic custom rather than to the secular tradition inherited from the Soviet Union.

Buddhism vs. Southeast Asian Countries. In Southeast Asia, Buddhists were hurt by the long Vietnam War. Neither antagonist was particularly sympathetic to Buddhists. The current Communist governments in Southeast Asia have discouraged religious activities and permitted monuments to decay. These countries do not have the funds necessary to restore the structures.

Religion vs. Religion

Conflicts are most likely to occur at a boundary between two religious groups. Contributing to more intense religious conflict has been a resurgence of religious **fundamentalism**, which is a literal interpretation and a strict and intense adherence to basic principles of a religion. In a world increasingly dominated by a global culture and economy, it is one of the most important ways that a group maintains a distinctive cultural identity. Two long-standing conflicts involving religious groups are in Northern Ireland and the Middle East.

Religious Wars in Ireland. The most troublesome religious boundary in Western Europe lies on the island of Eire (Ireland). The Republic of Ireland, which occupies five-sixths of the island, is 87 percent Roman Catholic, but the island's northern one-sixth, which is part of the United Kingdom rather than Ireland, is about 46 percent Protestant and 40 percent Roman Catholic. Ireland became a self-governing dominion within the British Empire in 1921. Complete independence was declared in 1937, and a republic was created in 1949. When most of Ireland became independent, a majority in six northern counties voted to remain in the United Kingdom.

(199)

Demonstrations by Roman Catholics protesting discrimination began in 1968. Since then, more than 3,000 have been killed in Northern Ireland — both Protestants and Roman Catholics. A small number of Roman Catholics in both Northern Ireland and the Republic of Ireland joined the Irish Republican Army (IRA), a militant organization dedicated to achieving Irish national unity by whatever means available, including violence. Similarly, a scattering of Protestants created extremist organizations to fight the IRA, including the Ulster Defense Force (UDF). As long as most Protestants are firmly committed to remaining in the United Kingdom and most Roman Catholics are equally committed to union with the Republic of Ireland, peaceful settlement appears difficult.

Religious Wars in the Middle East. Jews, Christians, and Muslims have fought for 2,000 years to control the same small strip of land in the Eastern Mediterranean.

- Judaism, as an ethnic religion, makes a special claim to the territory it calls the Promised Land. The religion's customs and rituals acquired meaning from the agricultural life of the ancient Hebrew tribe. After the Romans gained control of the area they dispersed the Jews from Palestine.

- Islam became the most widely practiced religion in Palestine after the Muslim army conquered it. Muslims regard Jerusalem as their third holiest city, after Makkah and Madinah, because it is thought to be the place from which Muhammad ascended to heaven.

- • Christianity considers Palestine the Holy Land and Jerusalem the Holy City because the major events in Jesus' life, death, and Resurrection were concentrated there.

Crusades between Christians and Muslims. In the seventh century, Muslims captured most of the Middle East. The Arab army moved west across North Africa and invaded Europe at Gibraltar in AD 711 and crossed the Pyrenees Mountains a few years later. Its initial advance in Europe was halted by the Franks. The Arab army continued to control portions of present-day Spain until 1492. To the east, the Arab army captured Eastern Orthodox Christianity's most important city, Constantinople (present-day Istanbul in Turkey), in 1453 and advanced a few years later into Southeast Europe, as far north as present-day Bosnia and Herzegovina. The recent civil war in that country is a legacy of the fifteenth-century Muslim invasion. To recapture the Holy Land from its Muslim conquerors, European Christians launched a series of military campaigns, known as Crusades.

Jews vs. Muslims in Palestine. The Muslim Ottoman Empire controlled Palestine between 1516 and 1917. After World War I, Great Britain took over Palestine under a mandate from the League of Nations. The British allowed some Jews to return to Palestine, but immigration was restricted again during the 1930s in response to intense pressure by Arabs in the region. As violence initiated by both Jewish and Muslim settlers escalated after World War II, the British announced their intention to withdraw from Palestine. The United Nations voted to partition Palestine into two independent states. Jerusalem was to be an international city, open to all religions, and run by the United Nations. When the British withdrew in 1948, Jews declared an independent state of Israel within the boundaries prescribed by the U.N. resolution. The next day its neighboring Arab Muslim states declared war. The combatants signed an armistice in 1949 that divided control of Jerusalem. Israel won three more wars with its neighbors, in 1956, 1967, and 1973. During the 1967 Six-Day War, Israel captured the entire city of Jerusalem and other territories from its neighbors.

(200)
Conflict over the Holy Land: Palestinian Perspective. After the 1973 war, Egypt and Jordan renounced their territorial claims and recognized the Palestinians as the legitimate rulers of these territories. Five groups of people consider themselves Palestinians:
- • People living in the territories captured by Israel in 1967
- • Citizens of Israel who are Muslims
- • People who fled from the West Bank or Gaza after the 1967 War
- • Citizens of other countries, especially those in the Middle East, who identify themselves as Palestinians.

After capturing the West Bank from Jordan in 1967, Israel permitted Jewish settlers to construct more than 100 settlements in the territory. Jewish settlers comprise about 10 percent of the West Bank population and Palestinians see their immigration as a hostile act. Some Palestinians, especially those aligned with the Fatah Party, are willing to recognize the State of Israel with its Jewish majority in exchange for return of all territory taken by Israel in the 1967 war. Other Palestinians, especially those aligned with the Hamas Party, do not recognize the right of Israel to exist and want to continue fighting for control of the entire territory between the Jordan River and the Mediterranean Sea. The United States, European countries, and Israel consider Hamas to be a terrorist organization.

(201)
Conflict over the Holy Land: Israeli Perspective. Israel sees itself as a very small country with a Jewish majority, surrounded by a region of hostile Muslim Arabs. Israel considers two elements of the local landscape especially meaningful. First, the country's major population centers are quite

close to international borders, making them vulnerable to surprise attack. The second geographical problem from Israel's perspective derives from local landforms.

(203)
The partition of Palestine in 1947 allocated most of the coastal plain to Israel, while Jordan took most of the hills between the coastal plain and the Jordan River, called the West Bank (of the Jordan River). Farther north, Syria controlled the highlands east of the valley, known as the Golan Heights. Between 1948 and 1967 Jordan and Syria used the hills as staging areas to attack Israeli settlements on the adjacent coastal plain and in the Jordan River valley. During the 1967 War, Israel captured these highlands to stop attacks on the lowland population concentrations.

Israeli Jews are divided between those who wish to retain some of the occupied territories and those who wish to make compromises with the Palestinians. Peace will be difficult to achieve because Israelis have no intention of giving up control of the Old City of Jerusalem, and Palestinians have no intention of giving up their claim to it.

Key Terms

Animism (p.178)
Autonomous religion (p.195)
Branch (p.171)
Caste (p.196)
Cosmogony (p.188)
Denomination (p.171)
Ethnic religion (p.170)
Fundamentalism (p.197)
Ghetto (p.185)

Hierarchical religion (p.194)
Missionary (p.182)
Monotheism (p.178)
Pagan (p.182)
Pilgrimage (p.185)
Polytheism (p.178)
Sect (p.171)
Solstice (p.189)
Universalizing religion (p.170)

Test Prep Questions

1) Which of the following is NOT a universalizing religion?
A) Islam
B) Christianity
C) Hinduism
D) Buddhism

2) Which of the following is NOT a branch of Christianity?
A) Lutheranism
B) Orthodoxy
C) Roman Catholicism
D) Protestantism

3) What was the first major religion known to espouse monotheism?
A) Islam
B) Christianity
C) Hinduism
D) Judaism

4) Which of the following religions does NOT trace its origins to the patriarch Abraham?
A) Judaism
B) Islam
C) Hinduism
D) Christianity

5) Where are the hearths of the three largest universalizing religions all located?
A) Asia
B) Europe
C) Africa
D) North America

6) What do Hindus consider to be the holiest river?
A) the Indus
B) the Ganges
C) the Tigres
D) the Nile

7) In which religion is burial of the dead NOT widely practiced?
A) Islam
B) Christianity
C) Judaism
D) Hinduism

8) Which of the following Protestant denominations is the MOST autonomous?
A) Baptist
B) Lutheran
C) Presbyterian
D) Episcopalian

9) Which of the following is NOT a conflict based upon religion?
A) Christianity/Islam vs. the former Soviet Union
B) The Taliban in Afghanistan vs. western values
C) Protestants vs. Catholics in North America
D) Hinduism vs. social equality

10) Which of the following territories was NOT captured by Israel during the 1967 War?
A) The Golan Heights
B) The Mediterranean lowlands
C) The Gaza Strip
D) The West Bank

Short Essay

1) Identify the three major universalizing religions on Earth and accurately describe their origins.

_____

_____

_____

_____

_____

_____
_____
_____
_____
_____

2) Describe the differences between universalizing religions and ethnic religions with respect to how they identify holy places, citing examples.

_____
_____
_____
_____
_____
_____
_____
_____
_____

3) Compare the Palestinian perspective with the Israeli perspective regarding the conflict over the Holy Land.

_____
_____
_____
_____
_____
_____
_____

Chapter 7
Ethnicity

Key Issues
1. Where are ethnicities distributed?
2. Why have ethnicities been transformed into nationalities?
3. Why do ethnicities clash?
4. What is ethnic cleansing?

(208)

Ethnicity is identity with a group of people who share the cultural traditions of a particular homeland or hearth. Ethnicity comes from the Greek word *ethnikos*, which means *national*. It is distinct from **race**, which is identity with a group of people who share a biological ancestor. Geographers are interested in *where* ethnicities are distributed across *space*, like other elements of culture. Like other cultural elements, ethnic identity derives from the interplay of *connections* with other groups and isolation from them. Ethnicity is an especially important cultural element of *local diversity* because our ethnic identity is immutable. The study of ethnicity lacks the tension in *scale* between preservation of local diversity and *globalization* observed in other cultural elements.

No ethnicity is attempting or even aspiring to achieve global dominance. In the face of globalization ethnicity stands as the strongest bulwark for the preservation of local diversity.

Key Issue 1. Where Are Ethnicities Distributed?
- **Distribution of ethnicities in the United States**
- **Differentiating ethnicity and race**

This section of the chapter examines the clustering of ethnicities within countries, and the next key issue looks at ethnicities at the national scale.

Distribution of Ethnicities in the United States
The two most numerous ethnicities in the United States are African Americans, about 15 percent, and Hispanics or Latinos, about 13 percent. In addition, about 4 percent of the population are Asian American, and 1 percent is American Indian.

(209)
Clustering of Ethnicities
Clustering of ethnicities can occur at two scales, particular regions of the country, and particular neighborhoods within cities.

Regional Concentrations of Ethnicities. On a regional scale, ethnicities have distinctive distributions within the United States:
- **Hispanic or Latino/Latina.** Clustered in the four southwestern states, California is home to one-third of all Hispanics. *Hispanic* or *Hispanic American* is a term that the U.S. government chose in 1973 because it was an inoffensive label that could be applied to all people from Spanish-speaking countries. Some Americans of Latin-American descent have adopted the term Latino instead. Most Hispanics identify with a more specific ethnic or national origin.
- **African Americans.** Clustered in the Southeast, they comprise between one-fourth to more than one-third in many southern states, yet, 9 states have fewer than 1 percent African Americans.

- **Asian Americans.** Clustered in the west and over 40 percent of the population of Hawaii, one-half of all Asian Americans live in California. Chinese account for one-fourth of Asian Americans, Indians and Filipinos one-fifth each, and Korean and Vietnamese one-tenth each.
- **American Indians and Alaska Natives.** Within the 48 continental United States, American Indians are most numerous in the Southwest and the Plains states.

(210)

Concentration of Ethnicities in Cities. African Americans and Hispanics are highly clustered in urban areas. Their distinctive distribution is especially noticeable at the levels of states and neighborhoods. For example, at the state level, African Americans comprise 85 percent of the population in the city of Detroit and only 7 percent in the rest of Michigan. The distribution of Hispanics is similar to that of African Americans in large northern cities. In the states with the largest Hispanic populations — California and Texas — the distribution is mixed. The clustering of ethnicities is especially pronounced at the scale of neighborhoods within cities. During the twentieth century, the children and grandchildren of European immigrants moved out of most of the original inner-city neighborhoods. For descendants of European immigrants, ethnic identity is more likely to be retained through religion, food, and other cultural traditions rather than through location of residence. Ethnic concentrations in U.S. cities increasingly consist of African Americans who migrate from the South, or immigrants from Latin America and Asia. In Los Angeles, which contains large percentages of African Americans, Hispanics, and Asian Americans, the major ethnic groups are clustered in different areas.

(211)

African American Migration Patterns
Three major migration flows have shaped African-American distribution within the United States: forced migration from Africa in the eighteenth century; immigration from the South to northern cities during the first half of the twentieth century; and immigration from inner-city ghettos to other urban neighborhoods in the second half of the twentieth century.

Forced Migration from Africa. The first Africans brought to the American colonies as slaves arrived in 1619. During the eighteenth century, the British shipped about 400,000 Africans to the 13 colonies. In 1808, the United States banned bringing in slaves, but an estimated 250,000 were illegally imported during the next half century. Slavery was widespread during the time of the Romans but was replaced in Europe by a feudal system, in which laborers were bound to the land and not free to migrate elsewhere. Although slavery was rare in Europe, Europeans were responsible for diffusing the practice to the Western Hemisphere. The forced migration began when people living along the east and west coasts of Africa, taking advantage of their superior weapons, captured members of other groups living farther inland and sold the captives to Europeans. (212) Fewer than 5 percent of the slaves ended up in the United States. At the height of the eighteenth-century slave demand, a number of European countries adopted the **triangular slave trade**. Some ships added another step, making a rectangular trading pattern, in which molasses was carried from the Caribbean to the North American colonies, and rum from the colonies to Europe.

In the 13 colonies that later formed the United States, most of the large plantations in need of labor were located in the South, primarily those growing cotton as well as tobacco. Attitudes toward slavery dominated U.S. politics during the nineteenth century.

The Civil War (1861–1865) was fought to prevent 11 pro-slavery southern states from seceding from the Union. Freed as slaves, most African Americans remained in the rural South during the late nineteenth century working as sharecroppers. A **sharecropper** works fields rented from a landowner and pays the rent by turning over to the landowner a share of the crops. The sharecropper system burdened poor African Americans with high interest rates and heavy debts. Instead of growing food that they could eat, sharecroppers were forced by landowners to plant extensive areas of crops such as cotton that could be sold for cash.

Immigration to the North. Sharecropping declined in the early twentieth century as farm machinery and decline in cotton reduced demand for labor. At the same time sharecroppers were being pushed off the farms, they were being pulled to the prospect of jobs in the booming industrial cities of the North. African Americans migrated out of the South along the major two-lane long-distance U.S. roads that had been paved and signposted in the early decades of the twentieth century. Southern African Americans migrated north and west in two main waves, the first in the 1910s and 1920s before and after World War I and the second in the 1940s and 1950s before and after World War II.

(213)
Expansion of the Ghetto. When they reached the big cities, African-American immigrants clustered in the one or two neighborhoods where the small numbers who had arrived in the nineteenth century were already living. These areas became known as ghettos, after the term for neighborhoods in which Jews were forced to live in the Middle Ages. African Americans moved from the tight ghettos into immediately adjacent neighborhoods during the 1950s and 1960s.

Differentiating Ethnicity and Race

Race and ethnicity are often confused. In the United States, consider three prominent ethnic groups — Asian Americans, African Americans, and Hispanic Americans. All three ethnicities display distinct cultural traditions that originate at particular hearths, but the three are regarded in different ways:

- Asian as a race and Asian American as an ethnicity encompass basically the same group.
- African American and black are different groups. Some American blacks trace their cultural heritage to regions other than Africa, including Latin America, Asia, or Pacific islands.
- The term African American identifies a group with an extensive cultural tradition, whereas black in principle denotes nothing more than dark skin.
- Hispanic or Latino is not considered a race.

The traits that characterize race are those that can be transmitted genetically from parents to children: lactose intolerance, for example. Biological features are so highly variable among members of a race that any prejudged classification is meaningless. The degree of isolation needed to keep biological features distinct genetically vanished when the first human crossed a river or climbed a hill. At worst, biological classification by race is the basis for **racism**, which is the belief that race is the primary determinant of human traits and capacities and that racial differences produce an inherent superiority of a particular race.

Race in the United States

Every 10 years the U.S. Bureau of the Census asks people to classify themselves according to races with which they most closely identify. The 2000 census permitted people to check more than 1 of 14 categories listed, and 2 percent of Americans did.

"Separate but Equal" Doctrine. A distinctive feature of race relations in the United States has been the strong discouragement of spatial interaction — in the past through legal means, today through cultural preferences or discrimination. In 1896, the U.S. Supreme Court upheld a Louisiana law that required black and white passengers to ride in separate railway cars, in Plessy v. Ferguson. Once the Supreme Court permitted "separate but equal" treatment of the races, southern states enacted a comprehensive set of laws to segregate blacks from whites as much as possible. These were called "Jim Crow" laws. Throughout the country, not just in the South, house deeds contained restrictive covenants that prevented the owners from selling to blacks, as well as to Roman Catholics or Jews in some places.

"White Flight." Segregation laws were eliminated during the 1950s and 1960s. The landmark Supreme Court decision, *Brown v. Board of Education* of Topeka, Kansas, in 1954, found that having separate schools for blacks and whites was unconstitutional. A year later, the Supreme Court further ruled that schools had to be desegregated "with all deliberate speed." Rather than integrate, whites fled. The expansion of the black ghettos in American cities was made possible by "white flight."

Detroit provides a clear example. White flight was encouraged by unscrupulous real estate practices, especially **blockbusting**. The National Advisory Commission on Civil Disorders wrote in 1968 that U.S. cities were divided into two separate and unequal societies. Four decades later, despite serious efforts to integrate and equalize the two, segregation and inequality persist.

Division by Race in South Africa

Discrimination by race reached its peak in the late twentieth century in South Africa. **Apartheid** was the physical separation of different races into different geographic areas. Although South Africa's apartheid laws were repealed during the 1990s, it will take many years for it to erase the impact of past policies.

In South Africa, under apartheid, a newborn baby was classified as being one of four races: black, white, colored (mixed white and black), or Asian. Under apartheid, each of the four races had a different legal status. The apartheid system was created by descendants of whites who arrived in South Africa from Holland in 1652. They were known either as *Boers*, from the Dutch word for *farmer*, or *Afrikaners*, from the word "Afrikaans," the name of their language, which is a dialect of Dutch. The British controlled South Africa's government until 1948, when the Afrikaner-dominated Nationalist Party won elections. The Afrikaners gained power at a time when colonial rule was being replaced in the rest of Africa by a collection of independent states run by the local black population. The Nationalist Party created the apartheid laws in the next few years to perpetuate white dominance of the country. To ensure further geographic isolation of different races, the South African government designated 10 so-called *homelands* for blacks.

(217)

In 1991, the white-dominated government of South Africa repealed the apartheid laws. The African National Congress was legalized, and its leader, Nelson Mandela, was released from jail after more than 27 years. In April 1994, Mandela was overwhelmingly elected the country's first black president. Whites were guaranteed representation in the government during a five-year transition period, until 1999. Now that South Africa's apartheid laws have been dismantled and the country is governed by its black majority, other countries have reestablished economic and cultural ties. However, the legacy of apartheid will linger for many years. Average income among white South Africans is about 10 times higher than for blacks.

Key Issue 2. Why Have Ethnicities Been Transformed into Nationalities?
- **Rise of nationalities**
- **Multinational states**
- **Revival of ethnic identity**

Ethnicity and race are distinct from nationality, another term commonly used to describe a group of people with shared traits. **Nationality** is identity with a group of people who share legal attachment and personal allegiance to a particular country.

Rise of Nationalities

In the United States, nationality is generally kept reasonably distinct from ethnicity and race in common usage:

- Nationality identifies citizens of the U.S., including those born in the country and those who immigrated and became citizens.
- Ethnicity identifies groups with distinct ancestry and cultural traditions.
- Race distinguishes people of color from whites.

The United States forged a nation in the late eighteenth century out of a collection of ethnic groups. To be an American meant believing in the "unalienable rights" of "life, liberty, and the pursuit of happiness." In Canada, the Québécois are clearly distinct from other Canadians in language, religion, and other cultural traditions. But do the Québécois form a distinct ethnicity within the Canadian nationality or a second nationality separate altogether from Anglo-Canadian? The distinction is critical. Outside North America, distinctions between ethnicity and nationality are even muddier. Confusion between ethnicity and nationality can lead to violent conflicts.

Nation-States

A **nation-state** is a state whose territory corresponds to that occupied by a particular ethnicity that has been transformed into a nationality. The concept that ethnicities have the right to govern themselves is known as **self-determination**.

Denmark: There Are No Perfect Nation-States. Denmark is a fairly good example of a European nation-state. The territory occupied by the Danish ethnicity closely corresponds to the state of Denmark. But even Denmark is not a perfect example of a nation-state. The country's southern boundary with Germany does not divide Danish and German nationalities precisely. Denmark controls two territories in the Atlantic Ocean that do not share Danish cultural characteristics — the Faeroe Islands and Greenland. In 1979, Greenlanders received more authority to control their own domestic affairs. One decision was to change all place names in Greenland from Danish to the local Inuit language.

Nation-States in Europe. Ethnicities were transformed into nationalities throughout Europe during the nineteenth century. Most of Western Europe was made up of nation-states by the early twentieth century.

(219)

Germany did not emerge as a nation-state until 1871, more recently than its neighbors. During the 1930s, German National Socialists (Nazis) claimed that all German-speaking parts of Europe constituted one nationality and should be unified into one state. Other European powers did not attempt to stop the Germans from taking over Austria and the German-speaking portion of Czechoslovakia. Not until the Germans invaded Poland (not a German-speaking country) in 1939 did England and France try to stop them. After it was defeated in World War II, Germany was divided into two countries until the end of communist rule in 1990.

Nationalism

A nationality, once established, must hold the loyalty of its citizens to survive. **Nationalism** typically promotes a sense of national consciousness that exalts one nation above all others.

States foster nationalism by promoting symbols of the nation-state, such as flags and songs. Nationalism can have a negative impact. The sense of unity within a nation-state is sometimes achieved through the creation of negative images of other nation-states. Nationalism is an important example of a **centripetal force**, which is an attitude that tends to unify people and enhance support for a state. (The word centripetal means "directed toward the center." It is the opposite of centrifugal, which means to spread out from the center.)

Multinational States

In some **multi-ethnic states**, ethnicities all contribute cultural features to the formation of a single nationality. The United States has numerous ethnic groups, all of whom consider themselves as belonging to the American nationality. Other multi-ethnic states, known as **multinational states**, contain two ethnic groups with traditions of self-determination that agree to coexist peacefully by recognizing each other as distinct nationalities. (220) One example of a multinational state is the United Kingdom, which contains four main nationalities — England, Scotland, Wales, and Northern Ireland. Today, the strongest element of national identity comes from sports. The four nationalities all have their own national soccer teams and compete separately in major international tournaments. Given the history of English conquest, the other nationalities typically root against England when it is playing teams from other countries.

Former Soviet Union: The Largest Multinational State
The Soviet Union was an especially prominent example of a multinational state until its collapse in the early 1990s. The 15 republics that once constituted the Soviet Union are now independent countries. When the Soviet Union existed, its 15 republics were based on the 15 largest ethnicities. Less numerous ethnicities were not given the same level of recognition. With the breakup a number of these less numerous ethnicities are now divided among more than one state. The 15 newly independent states consist of five groups; 3 Baltic, 3 European, 5 Central Asian, 3 Caucasus, and Russia.

Reasonably good examples of nation-states have been carved out of the Baltic, European, and some Central Asian states but not in any of the small Caucasus states, and Russia is an especially prominent example of a state with major difficulties in keeping all of its ethnicities contented.

New Baltic Nation-States. Estonia, Latvia, and Lithuania had been independent countries between 1918 and 1940. Of the three Baltic states, Lithuania most closely fits the definition of a nation-state, because 83 percent of its population is ethnic Lithuanian. These three small neighboring Baltic countries have clear cultural differences and distinct historical traditions.

(221)
New European Nation-States. To some extent, the former Soviet republics of Belarus, Moldova, and Ukraine now qualify as nation-states. The ethnic distinctions among Belarusians, Ukrainians, and Russians are somewhat blurred. Belarusians and Ukrainians became distinct ethnicities because they were isolated from the main body of Eastern Slavs — the Russians — during the thirteenth and fourteenth centuries. The situation is different in Moldova. Moldovans are ethnically indistinguishable from Romanians, and Moldova (then called Moldavia) was part of Romania until the Soviet Union seized it in 1940. In 1992, many Moldovans pushed for reunification with Romania. But it was not to be that simple. The Soviet government increased the size of Moldova by about 10 percent, transferring from Ukraine a sliver of land on the east bank of the Dniester (River). Inhabitants of this area are Ukrainian and Russian. They oppose Moldova's reunification with Romania.

New Central Asian States. The five states in Central Asia carved out of the former Soviet Union display varying degrees of conformance to the principles of nation-state. Together the five provide an important reminder that multinational states can be more peaceful than nation-states.

In Turkmenistan and Uzbekistan, the leading ethnic group has an overwhelming majority — 85 percent Turkmen and 80 percent Uzbek, respectively. Kyrgyzstan is 69 percent Kyrgyz, 15 percent Uzbek, and 9 percent Russian. The Kyrgyz — also Muslims who speak an Altaic language — resent the Russians for seizing the best farmland. In principle, Kazakhstan, twice as large as the other four Central Asian countries combined, is a recipe for ethnic conflict. The country is divided almost evenly between Kazakhs and Russians. Kazakhstan has been peaceful, in part because it has a somewhat less depressed economy than its neighbors. In contrast, Tajikistan — 79 percent Tajik, 15 percent Uzbek, and only 1 percent Russian — would appear to be a stable country, but it suffers from a civil war among the Tajik people. The civil war has been between Tajiks who are former Communists and an unusual alliance of Muslim fundamentalists and Western-oriented intellectuals.

Russia: Now the Largest Multinational State

Russia officially recognizes the existence of 39 nationalities, many of which are eager for independence. Russia's ethnicities are clustered in two principal locations. Some are located along borders with neighboring states. Overall, 20 percent of the country's population is non-Russian. Other ethnicities are clustered in the center of Russia. Most of these groups were conquered by the Russians in the sixteenth century. Independence movements are flourishing, because Russia is less willing to suppress these movements forcibly than the Soviet Union had once been. Particularly troublesome are the Chechens, a group of Sunni Muslims who speak a Caucasian language and practice distinctive social customs. Chechnya was brought under Russian control in the nineteenth century only after a 50-year fight. When the Soviet Union broke up, the Chechens declared their independence. Russia fought hard to prevent Chechnya from gaining independence because it feared that other ethnicities would follow suit. Chechnya was also important to Russia because the region contained deposits of petroleum.

(222)

Turmoil in the Caucasus

The Caucasus region gets its name from the mountains that separate Russia from Azerbaijan and Georgia. The region is home to several ethnicities. Each ethnicity has a long-standing and complex set of grievances against others in the region. Every ethnicity in the Caucasus has the same aspiration: to carve out a sovereign nation-state.

Azerbaijan. Azeris (or Azerbaijanis) trace their roots to Turkish invaders in the eighth and ninth centuries. An 1828 treaty allocated northern Azeri territory to Russia and southern Azeri territory to Persia (now Iran). More than 7 million Azeris now live in Azerbaijan, 91 percent of the country's total population. Another 16 million Azeris are clustered in northwestern Iran. Azeris hold positions of responsibility in Iran's government and economy, but Iran restricts teaching of the Azeri language.

(223)

Armenians. More than 3,000 years ago Armenians controlled an independent kingdom in the Caucasus. During the late nineteenth and early twentieth centuries, hundreds of thousands of Armenians were killed in a series of massacres organized by the Turks. Others were forced to migrate to Russia. After World War I the allies created an independent state of Armenia, but it was soon swallowed by its neighbors. Turkey and the Soviet Union divided Armenia. The Soviet portion became an independent country in 1991. More than 90 percent of the population in Armenia is Armenian, making it the most ethnically homogeneous country in the region. Armenians and Azeris have been at war with each other since 1988 over the boundaries between the two nationalities.

Georgians. The population of Georgia is more diverse than that in Armenia and Azerbaijan. Georgia's cultural diversity has been a source of unrest, especially among the Ossetians and Abkhazians. During the 1990s, the Abkhazians fought for control of the northwestern portion of Georgia and have declared independence. In 2008, the Ossetians declared the South Ossetia portion of Georgia independent. Only Russia and a handful of other countries recognize the independence of Abkazia and South Ossetia, although the two operate as if they were independent.

Revival of Ethnic Identity

Europeans thought that ethnicity had been left behind as an insignificant relic, such as wearing quaint costumes to amuse tourists. Until they lost power around 1990, Communist leaders in Eastern Europe and the former Soviet Union used centripetal forces, such as the Russian language, to discourage ethnicities from expressing their cultural uniqueness

Rebirth of Nationalism in Eastern Europe
In the twenty-first century, ethnic identity has once again become more important than nationality, even in much of Europe. In Eastern Europe, the breakup of the Soviet Union and Yugoslavia has given more numerous ethnicities the opportunity to organize nation-states. But the less numerous ethnicities still find themselves existing as minorities in multinational states, or divided among more than one of the new states. Especially severe problems have occurred in the Balkans. The Soviet Union, Yugoslavia, and Czechoslovakia were dismantled largely because minority ethnicities opposed the long-standing dominance of the most numerous ones in each country. The relatively close coincidence between the boundaries of the Slovene ethnic group and the country of Slovenia has promoted the country's relative peace and stability, compared to other former Yugoslavian republics.

(224)
Key Issue 3. Why Do Ethnicities Clash?
• **Ethnic competition to dominate nationality**
• **Dividing ethnicities among more than one state**

Ethnic Competition to Dominate Nationality
Sub-Saharan Africa has been a region especially plagued by conflicts among ethnic groups competing to become dominant within the various countries. The Horn of Africa and central Africa are the two areas where conflicts have been particularly complex and brutal.

Ethnic Competition in the Horn of Africa
The Horn of Africa encompasses the countries of Djibouti, Ethiopia, Eritrea, and Somalia. Especially severe problems have been found in Ethiopia, Eritrea, and Somalia, as well as the neighboring country of Sudan.

Ethiopia and Eritrea. Eritrea, located along the Red Sea, became an Italian colony in 1890. Ethiopia, an independent country for more than 2,000 years, was captured by Italy during the 1930s. After World War II, Ethiopia regained its independence, and the United Nations awarded Eritrea to Ethiopia. Ethiopia dissolved the Eritrean legislature and banned the use of Tigrinya, Eritrea's major local language. The Eritreans rebelled, beginning a 30-year fight for independence (1961–1991). In 1991, Eritrean rebels defeated the Ethiopian army, and in 1993 Eritrea became an independent state. But war between Ethiopia and Eritrea flared up again in 1998 because of disputes over the location of the border. Ethiopia defeated Eritrea in 2000 and took possession of the disputed areas.

Even with the loss of Eritrea, Ethiopia remained a complex multi-ethnic state. From the late nineteenth century until the 1990s, Ethiopia was controlled by the Amharas, who are Christians. After the government defeat in the early 1990s, power passed to a combination of ethnic groups.

(225)
Sudan. In Sudan, several civil wars have raged since the 1980s between Arab Muslim-dominated government forces in the north.
• South: Black Christians and animist ethnicities resisted government attempts to convert the country from a multiethnic society to one nationality ties to Muslim traditions
• West: Black Muslim ethnic groups in the Darfur region of western Sudan fought against the government beginning in 2003. The U.S. considers the mass murders and rape of civilians conducted by Sudanese troops to be genocide.
• East: Ethnicities along the eastern front fought the government between 2004 and 2006 with support from Eritrea over the disbursement of profits from oil.

Somalia. On the surface, Somalia should face fewer ethnic divisions than its neighbors in the Horn of Africa. Somalis are overwhelmingly Sunni Muslims and speak Somali. Somalia's 9 million inhabitants are divided among six major ethnic groups known as clans, each of which is divided into subclans. Traditionally, the major clans occupied different portions of Somalia. In 1991 a dictatorship that ran the government collapsed, and various clans and subclans claimed control over portions of the country. The United States sent several thousand troops to Somalia in 1992, after an estimated 300,000 people died from famine and from warfare between clans. After peace talks among the clans collapsed in 1994, U.S. troops withdrew. Islamist militias took control of much of Somalia between 2004 and subsequently withdrew, but have since returned and again control much of the country.

Ethnic Competition in Lebanon

Lebanon has been severely damaged by fighting among ethnicities since the 1970s. Lebanon is divided between around 60 percent Muslim and 39 percent Christian.

(226)

When Lebanon became independent in 1943, the constitution required that each religion be represented in the Chamber of Deputies according to its percentage in the 1932 census. By unwritten convention, the president of Lebanon was a Maronite Christian, the premier a Sunni Muslim, the speaker of the Chamber of Deputies a Shiite Muslim, and the foreign minister a Greek Orthodox Christian. Other cabinet members and civil servants were similarly apportioned among the various faiths. Lebanon's religious groups have tended to live in different regions of the country. Maronites are concentrated in the west central part, Sunnis in the northwest, and Shiites in the south and east. During a civil war between 1975 and 1990, each religious group formed a private army or militia to guard its territory. When the governmental system was created, Christians constituted a majority and controlled the country's main businesses, but as the Muslims became the majority, they demanded political and economic equality.

Israel and the United States sent troops into Lebanon at various points in failed efforts to restore peace. The United States pulled out in 1983. Lebanon was left under the control of Syria, which had a historical claim over the territory until it too was forced to withdraw its troops in 2005.

India and Pakistan

Newly independent countries were often created to separate two ethnicities. However, two ethnicities can rarely be segregated completely.

Dividing Ethnicities in South Asia

When the British ended their colonial rule of the Indian subcontinent in 1947, they divided the colony into two irregularly shaped countries: India and Pakistan. (226) The basis for separating West and East Pakistan from India was ethnicity. Antagonism between the two religious groups was so great that the British decided to place the Hindus and Muslims in separate states. The partition of South Asia into two states resulted in massive migration, because the two boundaries did not correspond precisely to the territory inhabited by the two ethnicities. Hindus in Pakistan and Muslims in India were killed attempting to reach the other side of the new border by people from the rival religion. Pakistan and India never agreed on the location of the boundary separating the two countries in the northern region of Kashmir. Since 1972 the two countries have maintained a "line of control" through the region. Muslims, who comprise a majority in both portions, have fought a guerrilla war to secure reunification of Kashmir, either as part of Pakistan or as an independent country. India's religious unrest is further complicated by the presence of 25 million Sikhs, who have long resented that they were not given their own independent country when India was partitioned. Sikhs comprise a majority in the Indian state of Punjab. Sikh extremists have fought for more control over the Punjab or even complete independence from India.

Sinhalese and Tamil in Sri Lanka. Sri Lanka (formerly Ceylon), an island country of 20 million inhabitants off the Indian coast, is inhabited by two principal ethnicities known as the Sinhalese and the Tamils. Sinhalese, who comprise 82 percent of Sri Lanka's population, migrated from northern

India in the fifth century B.C., occupying the southern portion of the island. Sinhalese are Buddhists who speak an Indo-European language. Tamils — 14 percent of Sri Lanka's population — migrated across the narrow 80-kilometer-wide (50-mile) Palk Strait from India beginning in the third century B.C. and occupied the northern part of the island. Tamils are Hindus, and the Tamil language is in the Dravidian family. The dispute between Sri Lanka's two ethnicities extends back more than 2,000 years but was suppressed during 300 years of European control. Since independence in 1948, Sinhalese have dominated. Tamils have received support, from Tamils living in other countries, for a rebellion that began in 1983. The long war between the ethnicities ended in 2009 with the defeat of the Tamil, who fear that their military defeat jeopardizes their ethnic identity again.

(229)
Key Issue 4. What Is Ethnic Cleansing?
- **Ethnic cleansing in Europe**
- **Ethnic cleansing in Central Africa**

Throughout history, ethnic groups have been forced to flee from other ethnic groups' more powerful armies. **Ethnic cleansing** is a process in which a more powerful ethnic group forcibly removes a less powerful one in order to create an ethnically homogeneous region.

Ethnic Cleansing in Europe
The largest forced migration came during World War II. Especially notorious was the deportation by the German Nazis of millions of Jews, Gypsies, and other ethnic groups to the infamous concentration camps, where they exterminated most of them. The scale of forced migration during (and after) World War II has not been repeated, but in recent years ethnic cleansing in Europe has occurred in portions of former Yugoslavia, especially Bosnia and Herzegovina and Kosovo.

Ethnic cleansing in former Yugoslavia is part of a complex pattern of ethnic diversity in the region of southeastern Europe known as the Balkan Peninsula. The Balkans includes Albania, Bulgaria, Greece, and Romania, as well as several countries that once comprised Yugoslavia.

Creation of Multi-ethnic Yugoslavia
The Balkan Peninsula, a complex assemblage of ethnicities, has long been a hotbed of unrest. Northern portions were incorporated into the Austria-Hungary Empire, whereas southern portions were ruled by the Ottomans. In June 1914 the heir to the throne of Austro-Hungary was assassinated in Sarajevo by a Serb who sought independence for Bosnia. The incident sparked World War I. After World War I, the allies created a new country, Yugoslavia, to unite several Balkan ethnicities that spoke similar South Slavic languages. The prefix "Yugo" in the country's name derives from the Slavic word for "south."

(230)
Under the long leadership of Josip Broz Tito, who governed Yugoslavia from 1953 until his death in 1980, Yugoslavs liked to repeat a refrain that roughly translates as follows: "Yugoslavia has seven neighbors, six republics, five nationalities, four languages, three religions, two alphabets, and one dinar." The refrain concluded that Yugoslavia had one dinar, the national unit of currency. Despite cultural diversity, according to the refrain, common economic interests kept Yugoslavia's nationalities unified.

(231)
Destruction of Multi-Ethnic Yugoslavia
Rivalries among ethnicities resurfaced in Yugoslavia during the 1980s after Tito's death, leading to the breakup of the country. When Yugoslavia's republics were transformed from local government units into five separate countries, ethnicities fought to redefine the boundaries.

Ethnic Cleansing in Bosnia. The creation of a viable country proved especially difficult in the case of Bosnia and Herzegovina. Rather than live in an independent multi-ethnic country with a Muslim plurality, Bosnia and Herzegovina's Serbs and Croats fought to unite the portions of the republic that they inhabited with Serbia and Croatia, respectively. Ethnic cleansing by Bosnian Serbs against Bosnian Muslims was especially severe, because much of the territory inhabited by Bosnian Serbs was separated from Serbia by areas with Bosnian Muslim majorities. Accords reached in Dayton, Ohio, in 1996 divided Bosnia and Herzegovina into three regions, one each dominated by the Bosnian Croats, Muslims, and Serbs. Bosnian Muslims, one-half of the population before the ethnic cleansing, got one-fourth of the land.

(232)
Ethnic Cleansing in Kosovo. After the breakup of Yugoslavia, Serbia remained a multi-ethnic country. Particularly troubling was the province of Kosovo, where ethnic Albanians comprised 90 percent of the population. Serbia had an historical claim to Kosovo, having controlled it between the twelfth and fourteenth centuries. Serbia was given control of Kosovo when Yugoslavia was created in the early twentieth century.

With the breakup of Yugoslavia, Serbia took direct control of Kosovo and launched a campaign of ethnic cleansing of the Albanian majority. Outraged by the ethnic cleansing, the United States and Western European countries, operating through the North Atlantic Treaty Organization (NATO), launched an air attack against Serbia. The bombing campaign ended when Serbia agreed to withdraw all of its soldiers and police from Kosovo. Kosovo declared its independence from Serbia in 2008. Around 60 countries, including the United States, recognize Kosovo as an independent country, but Serbia and Russia oppose it.

Balkanization. A century ago, the term **Balkanized** was widely used to describe a small geographic area that could not successfully be organized into one or more stable states because it was inhabited by many ethnicities with complex, long-standing antagonisms toward each other. **Balkanization** directly led to World War I. After two world wars and the rise and fall of communism during the twentieth century, the Balkans have once again become Balkanized in the twenty-first century. If peace comes to the Balkans, it will be because, in a tragic way, ethnic cleansing "worked." Millions of people were rounded up and killed or forced to migrate. Ethnic homogeneity may be the price of peace in areas that once were multi-ethnic.

Ethnic Cleansing in Central Africa
Ethnic conflict is widespread in Africa largely because the present day boundaries of states do not match the boundaries of ethnic groups.

(233)
Long-standing conflicts between two ethnic groups, the Hutus and Tutsis, lie at the heart of a series of wars in central Africa. The Hutus were settled farmers. The Tutsi were cattle herders who migrated from the Rift Valley of western Kenya beginning 400 years ago. The Tutsi took control of the kingdom of Rwanda and turned the Hutu into their serfs. Belgian colonial administrators permitted a few Tutsis to attend university and hold governmental positions, excluding the Hutu altogether. Shortly before Rwanda gained its independence in 1962, Hutus killed or ethnically cleansed most of the Tutsis out of fear that the Tutsis would seize control of the newly independent country. Those fears were realized in 1994 after the airplane carrying the presidents of Rwanda and Burundi was shot

down, probably by a Tutsi. Descendents of the ethnically cleansed Tutsis, most of whom lived in neighboring Uganda, poured back into Rwanda, defeated the Hutu army, and killed half a million Hutus. Three million of the country's 7 million Hutus fled to Zaire, Tanzania, Uganda, and Burundi. The conflict between Hutus and Tutsis spilled into neighboring countries of central Africa, especially the Democratic Republic of Congo. Congo is thought to have had the world's deadliest war since the end of World War II in 1945.

Tutsis were instrumental in the successful overthrow of the Congo's longtime president, Joseph Mobutu, in 1997, replacing him with Laurent Kabila. But Tutsis soon split with Kabila and led a rebellion that gained control of the eastern half of the Congo. Armies from Angola, Namibia, Zimbabwe, and other neighboring countries came to Kabila's aid. Kabila was assassinated in 2001 and succeeded by his son, who negotiated an accord with rebels the following year.

Key Terms

Apartheid (p. 215)
Balkanization (p. 232)
Balkanized (p. 232)
Blockbusting (p. 215)
Centripetal force (p. 219)
Ethnic cleansing (p. 229)
Ethnicity (p. 208)
Multi-ethnic state (p. 219)
Multinational state (p. 219)

Nationalism (p. 219)
Nationality (p. 217)
Nation-state (p. 217)
Race (p. 208)
Racism (p. 214)
Racist (p. 214)
Self-determination (p. 217)
Sharecropper (p. 212)
Triangular slave trade (p. 212)

Test Prep Questions

1) Which of the following is NOT a migration flow that has shaped the distribution of African Americans in the United States
A) forced migration from Africa to the South
B) migration from northern cities to the rural countryside
C) migration from the South to northern cities
D) migration from inner city neighborhoods to other urban neighborhoods

2) Why is Denmark not a perfect example of a nation-state?
A) Denmark rules Greenland, and thus has ethnic minorities.
B) Most Danes live in Denmark.
C) Most of the people who live in Denmark are Danes.
D) Most Danes speak Danish.

3) What is the name of the region in the Caucasus country of Georgia that declared independence from that state?
A) Chechnya
B) South Ossetia
C) Azerbaijan
D) Armenia

4) Which of the following countries did NOT dissolve because of internal ethnic disputes?
A) The Soviet Union
B) Czechoslovakia
C) Yugoslavia
D) Hungary

5) With what neighboring nation has Ethiopia had the most hostile relations?
A) Sudan
B) Kenya
C) Eritrea
D) Somalia

6) What is the basis for ethnicity in Somalia?
A) clan or subclan membership
B) religious affiliation
C) race
D) language

7) What is the underlying reason for the enduring animosity between Pakistan and India?
A) Sikh separatists in northern India wish to join Pakistan.
B) Hindus and Muslims don't get along.
C) The border between Jammu and Kashmir was never agreed upon.
D) all of these

8) On the island of Sri Lanka, and ethnic conflict ended in 2009 between what two groups?
A) Dravidian language speakers and Indo-European language speakers
B) Tamils and Sinhalese
C) Buddhists and Hindus
D) all of these

9) After the breakup of Yugoslavia, in what territory did Serbia wage a campaign of ethnic cleansing against an ethnic Albanian majority?
A) Kosovo
B) Bosnia and Herzegovina
C) Montenegro
D) Croatia

10) In the Early 1960s, the Hutus killed and ethnically cleansed the Tutsis, only to have their descendents come back and do the same to them in 1994 in what Central African country?
A) Burundi
B) Uganda
C) Rwanda
D) Democratic Republic of Congo

Short Essay

1) Contrast the geographic distribution of African Americans, Hispanics and Asians in the United States and account for the factors that explain those distributions.

_____

_____

_____

_____

_____

_____

_____

_____

_____

_____

2) Describe the basis of the ethnic tensions in the Caucasus region.

_____

_____

_____

_____

_____

_____

_____

_____

3) Explain why India has ethnic problems in its northern territories.

_____

_____

_____

_____

_____

_____

_____

_____

Chapter 8
Political Geography

Key Issues
1. Where are states located?
2. Why do boundaries between states cause problems?
3. Why do states cooperate with each other?
4. Why has terrorism increased?

(240)

With the end of the Cold War in the 1990s, the global political landscape changed fundamentally. Geographic concepts help us to understand this changing political organization of Earth's surface. We can also use geographic methods to examine the causes of political change. Boundary lines are not painted on Earth, but they might as well be, for these national divisions are very real. To many, national boundaries are more meaningful than natural features. In the post–Cold War era, the familiar division of the world into countries or states is crumbling. Between the mid-1940s and the late 1980s two superpowers — the United States and the Soviet Union — essentially "ruled" the world. But the United States is less dominant in the political landscape of the twenty-first century, and the Soviet Union no longer exists. Today globalization means more connections among states. Power is exercised through connections among states created primarily for economic cooperation. Despite (or perhaps because of) greater global political cooperation, local diversity has increased in political affairs, as individual cultural groups demand more control over the territory they inhabit.

Key Issue 1. Where Are States Located?
- **Problems of defining states**
- **Development of the state concept**

As recently as the 1940s, the world contained only about 50 countries, compared to 192 members of the United Nations as of 2009.

(241)
Problems of Defining States
A state is an area organized into a political unit and ruled by an established government that has control over its internal and foreign affairs. The term country is a synonym for state. There is some disagreement about the actual number of sovereign states. Among places that test the definition of a state are Korea, China, and Western Sahara (Sahrawi Republic).

Korea: One State or Two?
A colony of Japan for many years, Korea was divided into two occupation zones by the United States and former Soviet Union after they defeated Japan in World War II. Both Korean governments are committed to reuniting the country into one sovereign state. Meanwhile, in 1992, North Korea and South Korea were admitted to the United Nations as separate countries.

China and Taiwan: One State or Two?
Most other governments in the world consider China and Taiwan as two separate and sovereign states. According to China's government officials, Taiwan is not a separate sovereign state but is a part of China. This confusing situation arose from a civil war. After losing, nationalist leaders in 1949 fled to Taiwan, 200 kilometers (120 miles) off the Chinese coast and proclaimed that they were still the legitimate rulers of the entire country of China. Taiwan's president announced in 1999 that Taiwan would also regard itself as a sovereign independent state.

The United States continued to regard the Nationalists as the official government of China until 1971, when U.S. policy finally changed and the United Nations voted to transfer China's seat from the Nationalists to the Communists.

Western Sahara (Sahrawi Republic)

The Sahrawi Arab Democratic Republic, also known as Western Sahara, is considered a sovereign state by most African countries. Morocco, however, claims Spain controlled the territory until withdrawing in 1976, whereupon an independent republic was declared by the Polisario Front and recognized by most African countries. Morocco controls most of the populated area, but the Polisario Front operates in the vast, sparsely populated deserts.

Polar Regions: Many Claims

Antarctica is the only large landmass on Earth's surface that is not part of a state. Several states claim portions of Antarctica, and some are conflicting. The United States, Russia, and a number of other states do not recognize the claims of any country to Antarctica. The Antarctic Treaty, signed in 1959, provides a legal framework for managing Antarctica. As for the Arctic, the 1982 United Nations Convention on the Law of the Sea permitted countries to submit claims inside the Arctic Circle, which is thought to be rich in energy resources, by 2009.

Varying Size of States

The land area occupied by the states of the world varies considerably. The largest state is Russia, which encompasses 11 percent of the world's entire land area. Other states with more than 5 million square kilometers (2 million square miles) include China, Canada, United States, Brazil, and Australia. At the other extreme are about two dozen **microstates**, which are states with very small land areas. The smallest microstate in the United Nations — Monaco — encompasses only 1.5 square kilometers (0.6 square miles). Many of these microstates are islands, which explains both their small size and sovereignty.

(243)

Development of the State Concept

The concept of dividing the world into a collection of independent states is recent. Prior to the 1800s, Earth's surface was organized in other ways, such as city-states, empires, and tribes. Much of Earth's surface consisted of unorganized territory.

Ancient and Medieval States. The development of states can be traced to the ancient Middle East, in an area known as the Fertile Crescent. The modern movement to divide the world into states originated in Europe.

Ancient States. Situated at the crossroads of Europe, Asia, and Africa, the Fertile Crescent was a center for land and sea communications in ancient times. The first states to evolve in Mesopotamia were known as city-states. A **city-state** is a sovereign state that comprises a town and the surrounding countryside. Mesopotamia was organized into a succession of empires by the Sumerians, Assyrians, Babylonians, and Persians. Meanwhile, the state of Egypt emerged as a separate empire at the western end of the Fertile Crescent in a long, narrow region along the banks of the Nile River. Egypt's empire lasted from approximately 3000 B.C. until the fourth century B.C.

Early European States. Political unity in the ancient world reached its height with the establishment of the Roman Empire, which controlled most of Europe, North Africa, and Southwest Asia, from modern-day Spain to Iran and from Egypt to England.

The Roman Empire collapsed in the fifth century A.D. after a series of attacks by people living on its frontiers, and because of internal disputes. The European portion of the Roman Empire was fragmented into a large number of estates. Beginning about the year 1100, a handful of powerful kings emerged as rulers over large numbers of estates. The consolidation formed the basis for the development of such modern Western European states as England, France, and Spain. Central Europe remained fragmented until the nineteenth century.

Colonies
A **colony** is a territory that is legally tied to a sovereign state rather than being completely independent.

(244)
Colonialism. European states came to control much of the world through **colonialism**. European states established colonies for three basic reasons: to promote Christianity, to provide resources, and to indicate relative power. The three motives can be summarized as God, gold, and glory. The colonial era began in the 1400s. The European states eventually lost most of their Western Hemisphere colonies, then turned their attention to Africa and Asia. The European colonization of Africa and Asia is often called **imperialism**, which is control of territory already occupied and organized by an indigenous society. Colonialism, in contrast, is control of uninhabited or sparsely inhabited land.

The British assembled by far the largest colonial empire, with colonies on every continent. France had the second-largest overseas territory, primarily in West Africa and Southeast Asia.

France attempted to assimilate its colonies into French culture. The British created different government structures and policies for various territories of their empire. Most African and Asian colonies became independent after World War II.

(246)
The Few Remaining Colonies. At one time, colonies were widespread over Earth's surface, but today only a handful remains.

(247)
Most are islands in the Pacific Ocean or Caribbean Sea. The most populous remaining colony is Puerto Rico, which is a Commonwealth of the United States. Its 4 million residents are citizens of the United States. The world's least populated colony is Pitcairn Island settled in 1790 by British mutineers.

Key Issue 2. Where Are Boundaries Drawn between States?
- **Shapes of states**
- **Types of boundaries**
- **Boundaries inside states**

A state is separated from its neighbors by a **boundary**, an invisible line marking the extent of a state's territory. Boundaries interest geographers because the process of selecting their location is frequently difficult.

Shapes of States
The shape of a state affects the potential for communications and conflict with neighbors, can influence the ease or difficulty of internal administration, and can affect social unity.

Five Basic Shapes
Countries have one of five basic shapes: compact, prorupted, elongated, fragmented, and perforated.

Compact States: Efficient. In a **compact state**, the distance from the center to any boundary does not vary significantly. Compactness is a beneficial characteristic for most smaller states, because good communications can be more easily established to all regions.

Prorupted States: Access or Disruption. An otherwise compact state with a large projecting extension is a **prorupted state**. Proruptions are created for two principal reasons. First, a proruption can provide a state with access to a resource, such as water. Second, proruptions can separate two states that otherwise would share a boundary.

Elongated States: Potential Isolation. There are a handful of elongated states, or states with a long and narrow shape. Chile, Malawi, Italy, and Gambia are examples. A less extreme example of an elongated state is Italy. Elongated states may suffer from poor internal communications.

(248)
Perforated States: South Africa. A state that completely surrounds another one is a **perforated state**. The one good example of a perforated state is South Africa, which completely surrounds the state of Lesotho.

Fragmented States: Problematic. A **fragmented state** includes several discontinuous pieces of territory. There are two kinds of fragmented states: those with areas separated by water, and those separated by an intervening state.

A difficult type of fragmentation occurs if the two pieces of territory are separated by another state. Picture the difficulty of communicating between Alaska and the lower 48 states if Canada were not a friendly neighbor. Perhaps the most intractable fragmentation results from a tiny strip of land in India called Tin Bigha, only 178 meters (about 600 feet) by 85 meters (about 300 feet). For most of the twentieth century, Panama was a fragmented state divided in two parts by the Canal, built in 1914 by the United States.

Landlocked States
Landlocked states lack a direct outlet to the sea; they are most common in Africa, where 14 out of 54 states have no direct ocean access. The prevalence of landlocked states in Africa is a remnant of the colonial era, when Britain and France controlled extensive regions.

Direct access to an ocean is critical to states because it facilitates international trade. To send and receive goods by sea, a landlocked state must arrange to use another country's seaport.

(250)
Types of Boundaries
Boundaries are of two types: physical and cultural. Neither type of boundary is better or more "natural," and many boundaries are a combination of both types.

Physical Boundaries
Important physical features on Earth's surface can make good boundaries because they are easily seen, both on a map and on the ground. Three types of physical elements serve as boundaries between states: mountains, deserts, and water.

Desert Boundaries. Like mountains, deserts are hard to cross and sparsely inhabited. Desert boundaries are common in Africa and Asia.

Mountain Boundaries. Mountains can be effective boundaries if they are difficult to cross because they are rather permanent and usually are sparsely inhabited. Mountains do not always provide for the amicable separation of neighbors. Argentina and Chile agreed to be divided by the crest of the Andes Mountains but could not decide on the precise location of the crest.

(251)

Water Boundaries. Rivers, lakes, and oceans are the physical features most commonly used as boundaries. Water boundaries are especially common in East Africa. Water boundaries may seem to be set permanently, but the precise position of the water may change over time. Rivers, in particular, can slowly change their course. Ocean boundaries also cause problems because states generally claim that the boundary lies not at the coastline but out at sea. The reasons are for defense and for control of valuable fishing industries.

Cultural Boundaries

Two types of cultural boundaries are common: geometric and ethnic. Geometric boundaries are simply straight lines drawn on a map. Other boundaries coincide with differences in ethnicity, especially language and religion.

Geometric Boundaries. Part of the northern U.S. boundary with Canada is a straight line (more precisely, an arc) along 49° north latitude, established in 1846 by a treaty between the United States and Great Britain, which still controlled Canada. The United States and Canada share an additional geometric boundary between Alaska and the Yukon Territory along the north-south arc of 14° west longitude.

(252)

The boundary between Chad and Libya is a straight line drawn across the desert in 1899 by the French and British. Subsequent actions by European countries created confusion over the boundary.

Religious Boundaries. Religious differences often coincide with boundaries between states, but in only a few cases has religion been used to select the actual boundary line. The most notable example was in South Asia, when the British partitioned India into two states on the basis of religion. Religion was also used to some extent to draw the boundary between two states on the island of Eire (Ireland).

Language Boundaries. Language is an important cultural characteristic for drawing boundaries, especially in Europe. In the nineteenth century, Italy and Germany emerged as states that unified the speakers of particular languages.

The movement to identify nationalities on the basis of language spread throughout Europe in the twentieth century. After World War I, the Versailles Peace Conference redrew the map of Europe. The geographer Isaiah Bowman played a major role in the decisions. Language was the most important criterion used to create new states and to adjust the boundaries of existing ones. The conference was particularly concerned with Eastern and Southern Europe, regions long troubled by political instability and conflict. The nation-states created at the Versailles conference lasted with minor adjustment through most of the twentieth century. However, during the 1990s, the map of Europe drawn at Versailles in 1919 collapsed.

Cyprus' "Green Line" Boundary

Cyprus, the third-largest island in the Mediterranean Sea, contains two nationalities: Greek and Turkish. When Cyprus gained independence from Britain in 1960, its constitution guaranteed the

Turkish minority a substantial share of elected offices and control over its own education, religion, and culture. But Cyprus has never peacefully integrated the Greek and Turkish nationalities. In 1974, several Greek Cypriot military officers who favored unification of Cyprus with Greece seized control of the government. Turkey invaded Cyprus to protect the Turkish Cypriot minority. The Turkish sector declared itself the independent Turkish Republic of Northern Cyprus in 1983, but only Turkey recognizes it as a separate state. A wall was constructed and a buffer zone patrolled by the UN was delineated across the entire island, geographically isolating the two nationalities. The European Union agreed to accept the entire island of Cyprus as a member in 2004.

Frontiers

Historically, frontiers rather than boundaries separated states. A **frontier** is a zone where no state exercises complete political control. A frontier is a tangible geographic area, whereas a boundary is an infinitely thin, invisible, imaginary line.

A frontier area is either uninhabited or sparsely settled by a few isolated pioneers seeking to live outside organized society. Almost universally, frontiers between states have been replaced by boundaries. The only regions of the world that still have frontiers rather than boundaries are Antarctica and the Arabian Peninsula.

(254)

Boundaries Inside States

Within countries, local government boundaries are sometimes drawn to separate different nationalities or ethnicities. They are also drawn sometimes to provide advantage to a political party.

Unitary and Federal States

In the face of increasing demands by ethnicities for more self-determination, states have restructured their governments to transfer some authority from the national government to local government units.

The governments of states are organized according to one of two approaches: the unitary system or the federal system. The **unitary state** places most power in the hands of central government officials, whereas the **federal state** allocates strong power to units of local government within the country.

In principle, the unitary government system works best in nation-states characterized by few internal cultural differences and a strong sense of national unity. Unitary states are especially common in Europe. In a federal state, such as the United States, local governments possess more authority to adopt their own laws. Multinational states may adopt a federal system of government to empower different nationalities, especially if they live in separate regions of the country.

The federal system is also more suitable for very large states because the national capital may be too remote to provide effective control over isolated regions. The size of the state is not always an accurate predictor of the form of government. Some multinational states have adopted unitary systems, so that the values of one nationality can be imposed on others.

Trend Toward Federal Government

In recent years there has been a strong global trend toward federal government.

France: Curbing a Unitary Government. A good example of a nation-state, France has a long tradition of unitary government in which a very strong national government dominates local government decisions. Their basic local government unit is the *département*. A second tier of

102

local government in France is the *commune*. The French government has granted additional legal powers to the departments and communes in recent years. In addition, 22 regional councils that previously held minimal authority have been converted into full-fledged local government units.

Poland: A New Federal Government. Poland switched from a unitary to a federal system after control of the national government was wrested from the Communists. Under the Communists' unitary system, local governments held no legal authority. In 1999, Poland adopted a three-tier system of local government with provinces, counties, and municipalities. The transition to a federal system of government proved difficult in Poland and other Eastern European countries. The first task for many newly elected councilors was to attend a training course in how to govern.

Electoral Geography

The boundaries separating legislative districts within the United States and other countries are redrawn periodically to ensure that each district has approximately the same population. Boundaries must be redrawn because migration inevitably results in some districts gaining population, whereas others are losing. The job of redrawing boundaries in most European countries is entrusted to independent commissions, but in most U.S. states, the job of redrawing boundaries is entrusted to the state legislature. The process of redrawing legislative boundaries for the purpose of benefiting the party in power is called **gerrymandering**. The term gerrymandering was named for Elbridge Gerry (1744–1814), governor of Massachusetts (1810–12) and vice president of the United States (1813–14).

Gerrymandering takes three forms. "Wasted vote" spreads opposition supporters across many districts but in the minority. "Excess vote" concentrates opposition supporters into a few districts. "Stacked vote" links distant areas of like-minded voters through oddly shaped boundaries. "Stacked vote" gerrymandering has been especially attractive to create districts inclined to elect ethnic minorities.

(257)
Key Issue 3. Why Do States Cooperate with Each Other?
- **Political and military cooperation**
- **Economic cooperation**

Chapter 7 illustrated examples of threats to the survival of states from the trend toward local diversity. The inability to accommodate the diverse aspirations of ethnicities has led to the breakup of states into smaller ones. The future of the world's current collection of sovereign states is also threatened by the trend toward globalization. States are willingly transferring authority to regional organizations, established primarily for economic cooperation.

Political and Military Cooperation

During the Cold War era (late 1940s until early 1990s) global and regional organizations were established primarily to prevent a third world war and to prevent countries from attack.

The United Nations

The most important global organization is the United Nations. When established in 1945, the United Nations comprised 49 states, but membership grew to 189 in 2006, making it a truly global institution. The number of countries in the United Nations has increased rapidly on three occasions: 1955, 1960, and the early 1990s. The United Nations replaced an earlier organization known as the League of Nations, established after World War I, which was never an effective peacekeeping organization.

UN members can vote to establish a peacekeeping force and request states to contribute military forces. The UN is playing an important role in trying to separate warring groups in a number of regions, however, any one of the five permanent members of the Security Council could veto the operation. Because it must rely on individual countries to supply troops, the United Nations often lacks enough troops to keep peace effectively. Despite its shortcomings, the United Nations represents a forum where, for the first time in history, virtually all states of the world can meet and vote on issues without resorting to war.

Regional Military Alliances
In addition to joining the United Nations, many states joined regional military alliances after World War II.

Era of Two Superpowers. During the Cold War era, the United States and the Soviet Union were the world's two superpowers. Before then, the world typically contained more than two superpowers. During the Napoleonic Wars in the early 1800s, Europe boasted eight major powers. Before the outbreak of World War I in the early twentieth century, eight great powers again existed. When a large number of states ranked as great powers were of approximately equal strength, major powers joined together to form temporary alliances. A condition of roughly equal strength between opposing alliances is known as a **balance of power**. In contrast, the post–World War II balance of power was bipolar between the United States and the Soviet Union.

(258)
Other states lost the ability to tip the scales significantly in favor of one or the other superpower. They were relegated to a new role, that of ally or satellite. Both superpowers repeatedly demonstrated that they would use military force if necessary to prevent an ally from becoming too independent.

Military Cooperation in Europe. After World War II, most European states joined one of two military alliances dominated by the superpowers: the North Atlantic Treaty Organization (NATO) or the Warsaw Pact. NATO and the Warsaw Pact were designed to maintain a bipolar balance of power in Europe. In a Europe no longer dominated by military confrontation between two blocs, the Warsaw Pact was disbanded, and the number of troops under NATO command was sharply reduced. NATO expanded its membership to include former Warsaw Pact countries.

Other Regional Organizations
- **The Organization on Security and Cooperation in Europe (OSCE).** It has 56 members, including the United States, Canada, and Russia, as well as most European countries. Although the OSCE does not directly command armed forces, it can call upon member states to supply troops if necessary.
- **The Organization of American States (OAS).** All 35 states are in the western hemisphere. Cuba is a member but was suspended from most activities in 1962. The OAS promotes social, cultural, political, and economic links among member states.
- **The African Union (AU).** Established in 2002. The AU replaced an earlier organization called the Organization of African Unity, founded in 1963, primarily to seek the end of colonialism and apartheid in Africa.
- **The Commonwealth.** It includes the United Kingdom and 52 other states that were once British colonies. Commonwealth members seek economic and cultural cooperation.

(259)
Economic Cooperation
The era of a bipolar balance of power formally ended when the Soviet Union was disbanded in 1992. The world has returned to the pattern of more than two superpowers. But the contemporary

pattern of global power displays two key differences: 1. The most important elements of state power are increasingly economic rather than military; 2. The leading superpower in the 1990s is not a single state but is an economic union of European states.

With the decline in the military-oriented alliances, European states increasingly have turned to economic cooperation. Western Europe's most important economic organization is the European Union (formerly known as the European Economic Community, the Common Market, and the European Community). The European Union has expanded from six countries during the 1950s to 27 countries during the first decade of the twenty-first century. A European Parliament is elected by the people in each of member states simultaneously. Several states have begun negotiations or have been designated potential candidates to join.

In 1949, the seven Eastern European states in the Warsaw Pact formed an organization for economic cooperation, the Council for Mutual Economic Assistance (COMECON). Cuba, Mongolia, and Vietnam were also members. Like the Warsaw Pact, COMECON disbanded in the early 1990s.

The European Union has taken on more importance in recent years, as member states seek greater economic and political cooperation. It has removed most barriers to free trade. The introduction of the euro as the common currency in 12 European Union countries has eliminated many differences in prices, interest rates, and other economic policies within the region. The effect of these actions has been to turn to Western Europe into the world's wealthiest market.

(260)
Key Issue 4. Why Has Terrorism Increased?
- **Terrorism by individuals and organizations**
- **State support for terrorism**

Terrorism is the systematic use of violence by a group in order to intimidate a population or coerce a government into granting its demands. Terrorists consider violence necessary to bring widespread publicity to goals and grievances that are not being addressed through peaceful means.

Terrorism by Individuals and Organizations
The term *terror* (from the Latin "to frighten") was first applied to the period of the French Revolution between March 1793 and July 1794 known as the Reign of Terror. In modern times, terrorism has been applied to actions by groups operating outside government rather than by official government agencies, although some governments provide military and financial support for terrorists. Terrorism differs from assassinations and other acts of political violence because terrorist attacks are aimed at ordinary people rather than military targets or political leaders. Average individuals are unintended victims rather than principal targets in most conflicts, whereas a terrorist considers all citizens responsible for the actions being opposed, so therefore equally justified as victims. Distinguishing terrorism from other acts of political violence can be difficult.

Terrorism against Americans
The United States suffered several terrorist attacks during the late twentieth century. In 1988, a terrorist bomb destroyed a Pan Am flight over Lockerbie, Scotland; in 1993 a car bomb killed six and injured 1,000 in the underground garage at the World Trade Center in New York; in 1995, 168 people were killed in Oklahoma City by a car bomb in the Alfred P. Murrah Federal Building; in 1996, a truck bomb at an apartment complex in Saudi Arabia killed 19 U.S. soldiers; in 1998, bombings at U.S. embassies in Kenya and Tanzania killed 190 and wounded nearly 5,000; in 2000, the USS Cole was bombed in the port of Aden, Yemen, killing 17 Americans.

With the exception of the Oklahoma City bombing, Americans generally paid little attention to the attacks and had only a vague notion of who had committed them. It took the attack on the World Trade Center and Pentagon on September 11, 2001, for most Americans to feel threatened by terrorism. Some of the terrorists during the 1990s were American citizens operating alone or with a handful of others. (261) Theodore J. Kaczynski, known as the Unabomber, was convicted of killing 3 people and injuring 23 others by sending bombs through the mail during a 17-year period. His targets were mainly academics in technological disciplines and executives in businesses whose actions he considered to be adversely affecting the environment. Timothy J. McVeigh was convicted and executed for the Oklahoma City bombing. McVeigh claimed his terrorist act was provoked by rage against the U.S. government for such actions as the Federal Bureau of Investigation's 51-day siege of the Branch Davidian religious compound near Waco, Texas, culminating with an attack on April 19, 1993, that resulted in 80 deaths.

Al-Qaeda. Responsible or implicated in most of the anti-U.S. terrorism during the 1990s, as well as the September 11, 2001, attack, was the al-Qaeda network, founded by Osama bin Laden. His father, Mohammed bin Laden, a native of Yemen, established a construction company in Saudi Arabia and became a billionaire through close connections to the royal family. Osama bin Laden, one of about 50 children fathered by Mohammed with several wives, used his several hundred million dollar inheritance to fund al-Qaeda (an Arabic word meaning "the base"). Bin Laden moved to Afghanistan during the mid-1980s to support the fight against the Soviet army and the country's Soviet-installed government. Calling the anti-Soviet fight a holy war, or *jihad*, bin Laden recruited militant Muslims from Arab countries to join the cause. (262) Bin Laden issued a declaration of war against the United States in 1996, because of U.S. support for Saudi Arabia and Israel.

Al-Qaeda is not a single unified organization, and the number involved is unknown; it also encompasses local franchises concerned with country-specific issues, as well as imitators and emulators ideologically aligned with al-Qaeda but not financially tied to it.

Jemaah Islamiyah is an example of an al-Qaeda franchise with local concerns, specifically to establish fundamentalist Islamic governments in Southeast Asia, whose terrorist activities have been concentrated in the world's most populous Muslim country, Indonesia. (263) Other terrorist groups have been loosely associated with al-Qaeda. Al-Qaeda's use of religion to justify attacks has posed challenges to both Muslims and non-Muslims alike. For many Muslims, the challenge was to express disagreement with the policies of the U.S. and Europe, yet disavow the use of terrorism. For many Americans and Europeans, the challenge was to distinguish between the peaceful but unfamiliar principles and practices of the world's 1.3 billion Muslims, and the misuse and abuse of Islam by a handful of terrorists.

(264)
State Support for Terrorism
Several states in the Middle East have provided support for terrorism in recent years, at three increasing levels of involvement:
- providing sanctuary for terrorists wanted by other countries;
- supplying weapons, money, and intelligence to terrorists;
- planning attacks using terrorists.

Libya
The government of Libya was accused of sponsoring a 1986 bombing of a nightclub in Berlin, Germany, popular with U.S. military personnel then stationed there, killing three (including one

U.S. soldier). U.S. relations with Libya had been poor since 1981, when U.S. aircraft shot down attacking Libyan warplanes while conducting exercises over waters the United States considered international but Libya considered inside its territory. In response to the Berlin bombing, U.S. bombers attacked the Libyan cities of Tripoli and Benghazi in a failed attempt to kill Colonel Muammar el-Qaddafi.

Libyan agents were found to have planted bombs that killed people on a flight over Lockerbie, Scotland in 1988, as well as a UTA flight over Niger in 1989. Following eight years of U.N. economic sanctions, Qaddafi turned over the suspects for a trial that was held in the Netherlands, under Scottish law. One of the two was acquitted while the other was sentenced to life imprisonment, but he was released in 2009 after he was diagnosed with terminal cancer. Libya renounced terrorism
in 2003 and has provided compensation for victims of Flight 103. Libya is no longer considered a state sponsor of terrorism.

Afghanistan

U.S. accusations of state-sponsored terrorism escalated after 9/11. The governments of first Afghanistan, then Iraq, and then Iran were accused of providing at least one of the three levels of state support for terrorists. As part of its war against terrorism, the U.S. government in cooperation with other countries, attacked Afghanistan in 2001 and Iraq in 2003 to depose those countries' government leaders considered supporters of terrorism.

The United States attacked Afghanistan in 2001 when its leaders, known as Taliban, sheltered Osama bin Laden and other al-Qaeda terrorists. The Taliban (Pashto for "students") had gained power in Afghanistan in 1995, imposing strict Islamic fundamentalist law on the population.

A civil war began when the King was overthrown in a bloodless coup in 1973 by a leader who was murdered five years later in a bloody coup by military officers sympathetic to the Soviet Union. The Soviet Union sent 115,000 troops to Afghanistan beginning in 1979 after fundamentalist Muslims, known as *mujahedeen*, or "holy warriors," started a rebellion against the pro-Soviet government.

Unable to subdue the mujahedeen, the Soviet Union withdrew its troops in 1989, and the Soviet-installed government in Afghanistan collapsed in 1992. After several years of infighting among the factions that had defeated the Soviet Union, the Taliban gained control over most of the country.

Six years of Taliban rule came to an end in 2001 following the U.S. invasion. Destroying the Taliban was necessary for the United States to go after al-Qaeda leaders, including Osama bin Laden, who were living in Afghanistan as guests of the Taliban. Removal of Taliban unleashed a new struggle for control of Afghanistan among the country's many ethnic groups. When U.S. attention shifted to Iraq and Iran, the Taliban were able to regroup and resume an insurgency against the U.S.-backed Afghanistan government.

Iraq

U.S. claims of state-sponsored terrorism proved more controversial in Iraq than in Afghanistan. The United States attacked Iraq in 2003 to depose Saddam Hussein. U.S. officials' justification for removing Hussein was that he had created biological and chemical weapons of mass destruction. The U.S. confrontation with Iraq predated the war on terrorism. From the time he became president of Iraq in 1979, Hussein's behavior had raised concern around the world. Iraq's 1990 invasion of neighboring Kuwait, which Hussein claimed was part of Iraq, was opposed by the international community. The 1991 U.S.-led Gulf War, known as Operation Desert Storm, drove Iraq out of Kuwait, although it failed to remove Hussein from power.

Desert Storm was supported by nearly every country in the United Nations. In contrast, few countries supported the U.S.-led attack in 2003 because they did not agree with the U.S. assessment that Iraq still possessed weapons of mass destruction. Inspectors sent by the United Nations had found evidence of weapons of mass destruction in Iraq during the 1980s. However, UN experts concluded that Iraq had destroyed those weapons in 1991 after its Desert Storm defeat. U.S. officials believed instead that Iraq still had the weapons hidden, though they were never able to find them, and their judgment may have been based on faulty intelligence.

The U.S. assertion that Hussein had close links with al-Qaeda was also challenged by most other countries, as well as by U.S. intelligence agencies. Hussein's Ba'ath Party, which ruled Iraq between 1968 and 2003, espoused different principles than the al-Qaeda terrorists. Lacking evidence of weapons of mass destruction and ties to al-Qaeda, the United States argued instead that Iraq needed a "regime change." The U.S. position drew little international support because sovereign states are reluctant to invade another sovereign state just because they dislike its leader, no matter how odious.

(266)
Having invaded Iraq and removed Hussein from power, the United States expected an enthusiastic welcome from the Iraqi people. Instead, the United States became embroiled in a complex and violent struggle among religious sects and tribes.

Iran
Hostility between the United States and Iran dates from 1979, when a revolution forced abdication of Iran's pro-U.S. Shah Mohammad Reza Pahlavi. Iran and Iraq fought a war between 1980 and 1988 over control of the Shatt al-Arab waterway, formed by the confluence of the Tigris and Euphrates rivers flowing into the Persian Gulf.

(268)
An estimated 1.5 million died in the war, until it ended when the two countries accepted a UN peace plan. When the United States launched its war on terrorism, Iran was a less immediate target than Afghanistan and Iraq. However, the United States accused Iran of harboring al-Qaeda members and of trying to gain influence in Iraq where the majority of people are Shiites. More troubling to the international community was evidence that Iran was developing a nuclear weapons program. Prolonged negotiations were undertaken to dismantle Iran's nuclear capabilities without resorting to yet another war in the Middle East.

Pakistan
The war on terror has spilled over from Pakistan's western neighbors, Afghanistan and Iran. Pakistan is a multiethnic state. Western Pakistan, along the border with Afghanistan, is a rugged, mountainous region inhabited by ethnic minorities where the Taliban have largely been in control.

Key Terms

Balance of power (p.257)	Gerrymandering (p.255)
Boundary (p.247)	Imperialism (p.245)
City-state (p.243)	Landlocked state (p.249)
Colonialism (p.244)	Microstate (p.242)
Colony (p.243)	Perforated state (p.248)
Compact state (p.247)	Prorupted state (p.247)
Elongated state (p.247)	Sovereignty (p.241)
Federal state (p.254)	State (p.241)
Fragmented state (p.248)	Unitary state (p.254)
Frontier (p.253)	

Test Prep Questions

1) Which of the following is NOT a political region that has a questionable status regarding statehood?
A) Korea
B) Japan
C) Taiwan
D) Western Sahara

2) The earliest dates developed in what region?
A) Mesopotamia
B) The Nile Valley
C) Europe
D) none of these

3) Which of the following was NOT a motivation for European Colonialism?
A) glory
B) God
C) goodness
D) gold

4) South Africa is a good example of what kind of a state, in terms of the five basic shapes?
A) prorupt
B) perforated
C) elongated
D) compact

5) Which of the following is NOT a form of gerrymandering?
A) excess vote
B) stacked vote
C) wasted vote
D) under vote

6) Which of the following countries is NOT a permanent member of the United Nations Security Council?
A) Germany
B) China
C) The United States
D) Russia

7) What does NATO stand for?
A) North American Trade Organization
B) North African Territory Organization
C) North Atlantic Treaty Organization
D) none of these

8) The Cold War era trade organization made up of Warsaw Pact members that disbanded in the 1990s was:
A) COMECON
B) UNEMART
C) COMEMART
D) UNECOM

9) What is the English translation of "al-Qaeda?"
A) "Holy War"
B) "The Base"
C) "Divine Wind"
D) "The Struggle"

10) Which of the following countries is NOT thought to be a state that has supported terrorism in recent years?
A) Libya
B) Afghanistan
C) Kuwait
D) Iran

Short Essay

1) Trace the development of the state concept from its beginnings, through the colonial era.
_____
_____
_____
_____
_____
_____

2) What are the five basic shapes of states? Cite examples of each.
_____
_____
_____
_____
_____
_____

3) Explain two ways that local government boundaries are drawn within countries, citing examples.
_____
_____
_____
_____
_____
_____
_____

Chapter 9
Development

Key Issues
1. Why does development vary among countries?
2. Where are more and less developed countries distributed?
3. Where does level of development vary by gender?
4. Why do less developed countries face obstacles to development?

(274)

The second half of the book concentrates on economic rather than cultural elements of human geography. This chapter examines the most fundamental global economic pattern — the division of the world into relatively wealthy regions and relatively poor ones. Earth's nearly 200 countries can be classified according to their level of **development**, which is the process of improving the material conditions of people through diffusion of knowledge and technology. Every *place* lies at some point along a continuum of development. A **more developed country (MDC)**, also known as a **relatively developed country** or simply as a **developed country,** has progressed further along the development continuum. A country in an earlier stage is a **less developed country (LDC)**, although many analysts prefer the term *developing country*. More developed countries cluster in some *spaces*, and less developed countries cluster in others. A number of economic, social, and demographic indicators distinguish more and less developed regions. The *scale* of the severe economic downturn that began in 2008 has illustrated the *globalization* of the economy in the twenty-first century. Individual countries have seen their economies severely buffeted by close *connections* to the global economy. A return to economic growth has necessitated taking advantage of *local diversity* in skills and resources.

Key Issue 1. Why Does Development Vary Among Countries?
- **Economic indicators of development**
- **Social indicators of development**
- **Demographic indicators of development**

The **Human Development Index (HDI)**, created by the United Nations, recognizes that a country's level of development is a function of *economic, social, and demographic* factors.

(275)

Economic Indicators of Development
To create the HDI, the UN selects one economic factor, two social factors, and one demographic factor that are thought to best reveal the level of development: the economic factor is gross domestic product per capita, the social factors are literacy rate and amount of education, and the demographic factor is life expectancy. The highest HDI possible is 1.0, or 100 percent. The highest-ranking countries are typically in Europe and include Canada. The highest HDI in recent years has been Norway, at 0.971 in 2009. The lowest ranked country in 2009 was Niger, with an HDI of 0.340. Thirty of the 32 lowest-ranking countries were located in sub-Saharan Africa.

Per capita income is a difficult figure to obtain. Geographers substitute per capita gross domestic product, a more readily available indicator. The **gross domestic product** (GDP) is the value of the total output of goods and services produced in a country, normally during a year.

In 2008, per capita GDP exceeded $30,000 in all MDCs, compared with less than $3,000 in LDCs. The gap has widened: Since 1980 per capita GDP increased from around $15,000 to $30,000 in MDCs, and from around $1,000 to $4,000 in LDCs.

Per capita GDP — or, for that matter, any other single indicator — cannot measure perfectly the level of a country's development. Few people are starving in less developed countries with per capita GDPs of a few thousand dollars. And not everyone is wealthy in a developed country such as the United States. Per capita GDP measures average (mean) wealth, not its distribution.

Types of Jobs
In addition to GDP per capita, three other economic indicators are especially useful in distinguishing between MDCs and LDCs: types of jobs, worker productivity, and availability of consumer goods. Average per capita income is higher in MDCs because people typically earn their living by different means than in LDCs. Jobs fall into three categories: primary (including agriculture), secondary (including manufacturing), and tertiary (including services). (276) Workers in the **primary sector** directly extract materials from Earth. The **secondary sector** includes manufacturers. The **tertiary** sector involves the provision of goods and services, retailing, banking, law, education, and government.

The contribution to GDP among primary, secondary, and tertiary sectors varies between MDCs and LDCs. The shares of GDP accounted for by the primary and secondary sectors are higher in LDCs than in MDCs, but that of the tertiary sector is higher in MDCs.

Productivity
Productivity is the value of a particular product compared to the amount of labor needed to make it. Productivity can be measured by the **value added** per worker, the gross value of the product minus the costs of raw materials and energy. Workers in more developed countries produce more with less effort because they have access to more machines, tools, and equipment to perform much of the work.

Consumer Goods
Part of the wealth generated in more developed countries is used to purchase goods and services. Especially important are goods and services related to transportation and communications, including motor vehicles, telephones, and computers. Products that promote better transportation and communications are accessible to virtually all residents in MDCs and are vital to the economy's functioning and growth. In contrast, in less developed countries, these products do not play a central role in daily life.

Most people in LDCs are familiar with these consumer goods, even though they cannot afford them. In many LDCs the "haves" are concentrated in urban areas; the "have-nots" live in the countryside. The minority who have these goods may include government officials, business owners, and other elites, whereas their lack among the majority who are denied access to these goods may provoke political unrest.

Technological change may help to reduce the gap in access to communications between MDCs and LDCs. Cell phone ownership is expanding rapidly in LDCs because these phones do not require costly investment of connecting wires to each individual building.

Social Indicators of Development
MDCs use part of their greater wealth to provide schools, hospitals, and welfare services. In turn, this well-educated, healthy, and secure population can be more economically productive.

Education and Literacy
In general, the higher the level of development, the greater are both the quantity and the quality of a country's educational services. Two measures of education are student/teacher ratio and literacy rate. In elementary or primary school, the number of students per teacher exceeds 30 in most LDCs, whereas it is

less than 20 in most MDCs. (278) The **literacy rate** is the percentage of a country's people who can read and write. It exceeds 98 percent in developed countries, compared to less than 60 percent in many LDCs.

Health and Welfare

The health of a population is influenced by diet. On average, people in MDCs receive more calories and proteins daily than they need, but in LDCs, most people receive less than the daily minimum allowance recommended by the United Nations. When people get sick, MDCs possess the resources to care for them. In most MDCs, health care is a public service that is available at little or no cost. In LDCs, private individuals must pay more than half of the cost of health care. The United States more closely resembles the pattern in LDCs. The MDCs use part of their wealth to protect people who, for various reasons, are unable to work. Economic growth has slowed, while the percentage of people needing public assistance has increased. Governments have faced a choice between reducing benefits or increasing taxes to pay for them.

Demographic Indicators of Development

The UN HDI utilizes life expectancy as a measure of development. Other demographic characteristics that distinguish more and less developed countries include infant mortality, natural increase, and crude birth rates.

(280)
Life Expectancy

Babies born today can expect to live into their sixties in LDCs compared to their seventies in MDCs. The gap in life expectancy is greater for females than for males. With longer life expectancies, MDCs have a higher percentage of elderly people who have retired and receive public support. The number of young people is six times higher than the number of older people in LDCs, whereas the two are nearly the same in MDCs.

(281)
Infant Mortality Rate

About 94 percent of infants survive in LDCs compared to more than 99.5 percent in MDCs. The infant mortality rate is greater in the LDCs for several reasons: malnutrition, lack of medicine, or poor medical practices.

Natural Increase Rate

The natural increase rate averages 1.5 percent annually in LDCs compared to only 0.2 percent in MDCs. Greater natural increase strains a country's ability to provide services that can make its people healthier and more productive.

Crude Birth Rate

LDCs have higher natural increase rates because they have higher crude birth rates. The annual crude birth rate is 23 per 1,000 in LDCs, compared to less than 12 per 1,000 in MDCs.

The crude death rate (CDR) does not indicate a society's level of development. The CDR is lower in LDCs than in MDCs, 8 per 1,000 compared to 10 per 1,000, for two reasons: diffusion of medical technology from MDCs, and second, the fact that MDCs have higher percentages of older people.

Key Issue 2. Where Are More and Less Developed Countries Distributed?
 - **More developed regions**
 - **Less developed regions**

The countries of the world can be categorized into nine major regions and three other distinctive regions according to their level of development. These regions have distinctive demographic and cultural

Study Guide for The Cultural Landscape: An Introduction to Human Geography, 10e

characteristics that have been discussed in earlier chapters. Subsequent chapters will show that the nine major regions also differ in economic characteristics. In a global economy, geographers are increasingly concerned with both the similarities and the differences in the economic patterns of the various regions.

(282)
More Developed Regions
Two of the nine major cultural regions — North America and Europe — are considered more developed. The distribution of more and less developed countries reflects a clear global pattern. If we draw a circle around the world at about 30° north latitude, nearly all of the LDCs lie south of the circle. The *north-south split* between MDCs and LDCs shows up clearly in world maps of measures of development, such as the HDI.

North America: HDI 0.95
The United States ranked only 13th in HDI in 2009. It ranked high in GDP per capita and literacy rate but lower than some other countries in education and life expectancy due to high dropout rates and inadequate healthcare coverage.

North America was once the world's major manufacturer of steel, automobiles and other goods, but in the past three decades, Japan, and Europe as well as LDCs, led by China, have eroded the region's dominance. Americans remain the leading consumers. The region has adapted to the loss of manufacturing jobs by holding the world's highest percentage of tertiary-sector employment, especially health care, leisure, and financial services. North America's financial institutions played a leading role in precipitating the recent deep recession. North America is the world's most important food exporter.

Europe: HDI 0.93
During the Cold War era, Europe was regarded as two regions — a democratic West closely linked economically and militarily with the United States and a Communist East linked to the Soviet Union. With the fall of communism, Europe is treated as a single world region. The elimination of most economic barriers within the European Union makes Western Europe the world's largest and richest market. Within Europe, development is the world's highest in a core area, however development lags in southern and eastern Europe, resulting in an overall HDI lower than North America. Europe is especially dependent on international trade, both among countries within Europe and with other regions. Europe provides high value goods and services, such as insurance, banking, and luxury motor vehicles. Government officials representing the region's wealthiest core area have been accused of protecting jobs in their countries rather than in the European Union as a whole. Most European governments have limited government spending because they fear high inflation once the economy recovers.

Most governments have been willing to sacrifice some economic growth in exchange for protection of existing jobs and social services.

(283)
Russia: HDI 0.73
Under communism, the Soviet Union had a centrally planned economy. Five-year plans prescribed production goals for the entire country, from quantities of minerals, manufactured goods and agricultural commodities to be produced to railways, roads, canals and houses to be built in each part of the country. After the Soviet Union dissolved in 1991, Russia rapidly and painfully converted to a market economy. Unemployment soared, and while a handful of Russians became very rich, most Russians saw their standard of living decline sharply. In the first years of the twenty-first century, Russia experienced economic growth, fueled in large measure by escalating production of oil. The severe worldwide recession caused a drop in demand, and with it the possibility of renewed decline in the HDI.

Japan: HDI 0.96

North America and Europe share many cultural characteristics. North America was colonized by European immigrants, so the regions share language, religion, and other political, economic, and cultural traditions. Japan, the third major center of development, has a different cultural tradition.

Japan's development is especially remarkable because it has an extremely unfavorable ratio of population to resources. Japan gained a foothold in the global economy by selling low-cost products and by taking advantage of an abundant supply of people willing to work hard for low wages. Japan then began to specialize in high-quality, high-value products. Japan's dominance was achieved in part by concentrating resources in rigorous educational systems and training programs to create a skilled labor force.

Oceania: HDI 0.90

Oceania is relatively marginal in the global economy because of its small number of inhabitants and peripheral location. Although the HDIs of Australia and New Zealand are comparable to those of other MDCs, the area's remaining people are scattered among sparsely inhabited islands that generally are less developed. Australia and New Zealand share many cultural characteristics with the United Kingdom. Australia and New Zealand are net exporters of food and other resources, especially to the United Kingdom. Increasingly, their economies are tied to Japan and other Asian countries.

Less Developed Regions

Six regions are classified as less developed. The level of development varies widely among the six regions. Latin America has the highest HDI, whereas South Asia and Sub-Saharan Africa lag behind the others.

(285)

Latin America

Latin American's population is highly concentrated along the Atlantic Coast. Overall, Latin Americans are more likely to live in urban areas than people in other LDCs. The level of development varies sharply within Latin America. Neighborhoods within the large cities enjoy a high level of development, and the coastal area as a whole has a relatively high GDP. Outside the coastal area, development is lower in Central America, several Caribbean Islands, and the interior of South America. Large areas of interior rain forest are being destroyed to sell the timber or to clear the land for settled agriculture.

The level of development is relatively high along the South Atlantic Coast between Curitiba, Brazil, and Buenos Aires, Argentina. Overall development in Latin America is hindered by inequitable income distribution. Latin American governments encourage redistribution of land to peasants but do not wish to alienate the large property owners, who generate much of the national wealth. Latin America's economy is closely linked to that of the United States, and the severe global recession has hit Latin America especially hard.

East Asia: HDI 0.77

The economy of East Asia — and the entire world, for that matter — is being driven in the twenty-first century increasingly by China. Now the world's second largest economy, behind the United States, China was the world's wealthiest country from ancient times until passed by Europe in the sixteenth century. As recently as the early nineteenth century, China still accounted for one-third of world GDP, but after a century of civil wars and foreign invasions, China had fallen far behind Europe and North America. China's watershed year was 1949, when the Communist party won a civil war and created the People's Republic of China.

(286)

The Communist government took control of most agricultural land. The system assured the production and distribution of enough food to support China's one-billion-plus population. In recent years, farmers have been permitted to hold long-term leases on land and control their own production.

In the twenty-first century, manufacturing has been increasing dramatically in China. With rising wealth, the world's largest population has been transformed into the world's largest market for consumer products. In partnership with Wal-Mart, China's manufacturing might is pushing down prices for consumer goods throughout the world. At the same time, the low wages being paid to China's factory workers are driving down factory pay around the world. Weaknesses remain in China's economic performance. Middle management is weak, quality control is minimal, banking is primitive, and legal protection is inadequate. Rapid development is straining resources. China is also responsible for an increasing share of the world's pollution.

Southwest Asia and North Africa: HDI 0.74
Much of Southwest Asia and North Africa is desert that can sustain only sparse concentrations of plant and animal life. This region — once more commonly called the Middle East — must import most products. However, it possesses one major economic asset: a large percentage of the world's petroleum reserves.

Governments in oil-rich states have used the billions of dollars generated from petroleum sales to finance economic development. However, not every country in the region has abundant petroleum reserves. Development possibilities are limited in countries that lack significant petroleum. The large gap in per capita income between the petroleum-rich countries and those that lack resources causes great tension in the region. The challenge for many Middle Eastern states is to promote development without abandoning the traditional cultural values of Islam.

(287)
The region also suffers from serious internal cultural disputes, as discussed in Chapters 6 through 8. Lack of resolution of the long-standing conflict between Israel and its neighbors has diverted resources from development to military conflict. Southwest Asia has also struggled with terrorism. Very few people endorse acts of violence. On the other hand, few supported the U.S.-led invasion of Iraq, and alternatives are sought to U.S.-influenced culture and development.

Southeast Asia: HDI 0.73
Southeast Asia's most populous country, Indonesia, includes 13,667 islands. Southeast Asia's other most populous countries are Vietnam, Thailand, and the Philippines.

The region's tropical climate limits intensive cultivation of most grains. Economic development is also limited in Southeast Asia by several mountain ranges, active volcanoes, frequent typhoons, and occasional tsunamis. This inhospitable environment traditionally kept population growth low. But Western medicine and technology has resulted in a rapid rate of increase.

Because of distinctive vegetation and climate, farmers in Southeast Asia concentrate on harvesting products that are used in manufacturing, such as palm oil and rubber. Southeast Asia also contains a large percentage of the world's tin as well as some petroleum reserves. Rice, the region's most important food, is now exported in large quantities from India, Malaysia, and Thailand. The region has suffered from a half century of nearly continuous warfare. Japan, the Netherlands, France, and the United Kingdom were all forced to withdraw from colonies.

Development has been rapid in Thailand, Singapore, Malaysia, and the Philippines. The region is a major manufacturer of textiles. Thailand is the region's center for automobiles and consumer goods. Economic growth in the region has slowed — funds for development were sometimes invested unwisely or stolen by corrupt officials. To restore economic confidence among international investors, Southeast Asian countries have been forced to undertake painful reforms that reduce the people's standard of living.

Central Asia: HDI 0.70
Most of the countries in Central Asia were once part of the Soviet Union. Within Central Asia, development is relatively high in Kazakhstan and Iran, as they are producers of petroleum. The level of

development is lower in the other "stan" republics, which rely upon mineral and agricultural products as their principal economic resources. Afghanistan probably has one of the world's lowest HDIs, but it hasn't been calculated for many years because of the extended war.

South Asia: HDI 0.61
South Asia includes India, Pakistan, Bangladesh, Sri Lanka, and the small Himalayan states of Nepal and Bhutan. The region has the world's second-highest population and second-lowest per capita income. The overall ratio of population to resources is unfavorable.

South Asia was a principal beneficiary of the Green Revolution: miracle rice and wheat seeds were widely dispersed, but agricultural productivity in South Asia also depends on climate. Agricultural output declines sharply if the monsoon rains fail to arrive.

(288)
India has become the world's fourth largest economy, behind the U.S., China, and Japan, and the rate of growth of its economy is second only to China's. India is the world's leading producer of jute, peanuts, sugarcane, and tea. It has multiple mineral reserves and is a leading producer of rice and wheat. The country has become a major manufacturer, although not as rapidly as China. India has become a major service provider as well; when you phone an airline, help desk, or a credit card company, chances are your call will be answered by someone located in India.

Sub-Saharan Africa: HDI 0.51
Africa has been divided into two regions. Countries north of the Sahara Desert share economic and cultural characteristics with Southwest Asia. South of the desert is sub-Saharan Africa. Sub-Saharan Africa has a number of assets. Despite these assets, sub-Saharan Africa has the least favorable prospect for development. And economic conditions in sub-Saharan Africa have deteriorated in recent years. Some of the region's economic problems are a legacy of the colonial era. Mining companies and other businesses were established to supply European industries with needed raw materials rather than to promote overall economic development.

Political problems have also plagued sub-Saharan Africa. European colonies were converted to states without regard for the distribution of ethnicities. The fundamental problem in many countries of sub-Saharan Africa is a dramatic imbalance between the number of inhabitants and the capacity of the land to feed the population.

Key Issue 3. Where Does Level of Development Vary by Gender?
- **Gender-related Development Index**
- **Gender Empowerment**

A country's overall level of development masks inequalities in the status of men and women.
(289) The United Nations has not found a single country in the world where its women are treated as well as its men. To measure the extent of each country's gender inequality, the United Nations has created two indexes. The **Gender-related Development Index (GDI)** compares the level of development of women with that of both sexes. The **Gender Empowerment Measure (GEM)** compares the ability of women and men to participate in economic and political decision making.

(290)
Gender-related Development Index
The GDI is constructed in a manner similar to the HDI. The GDI combines the same indicators of development used in the HDI, adjusted to reflect the differences in the accomplishments and conditions of men and women.

- **Economic Indicator of Gender Differences:** Per capita female income as a percentage of per capita male income.
- **Social Indicators of Gender Differences:** Number of females enrolled in school compared to number of males and percent of literate females compared to percent of literate males.
- **Demographic Indicator of Gender Differences:** Life expectancy of females compared to males.

Gender Empowerment

The GEM measures the ability of women to participate in the process of achieving improvements in their status, that is, to achieve political power. In every country of the world, both MDCs and LDCs, fewer women than men hold positions of economic and political power, according to the United Nations' GEM scoring system. The GEM is calculated by combining two indicators of economic power and two indicators of political power.

Economic Indicators of Empowerment: Per capita female income as a percentage of per capita male income and percentage of professional and technical jobs held by women.

Political Indicators of Empowerment: Percentage of administrative jobs held by women and percentage of members of the national parliament who are women.

A country with complete equality of power between men and women would have a GEM score of 1.0. As with GDI, countries with the highest GEMs are MDCs, especially in North America, Northern Europe, and Oceania. The lowest scores are in Africa and Asia, though lack of data prevents calculating scores in many LDCs. Every country has a lower GEM than GDI. A higher GDI compared to GEM means that women possess a greater share of a country's resources than power over allocation of those resources.

(294)
Key Issue 4. Why Do Less Developed Countries Face Obstacles to Development?
- **Development through self-sufficiency**
- **Development through international trade**
- **Financing development**
- **Fair trade**

To reduce disparities between rich and poor countries, LDCs must develop more rapidly. LDCs face two fundamental obstacles in trying to encourage more rapid development:
- Adopting policies that successfully promote development
- Finding funds to pay for development

To promote development, LDCs choose one of two models to promote development. One approach emphasizes international trade; the other advocates self-sufficiency. Each has important advantages and serious problems.

Development Through Self-Sufficiency. For most of the twentieth century, self-sufficiency, or balanced growth, was the more popular of the development alternatives. The world's two most populous countries, China and India, once adopted this strategy, as did most African and Eastern European countries.

Elements of Self-Sufficiency Approach. According to the self-sufficiency approach, a country should spread investment as equally as possible across all sectors of its economy, and in all regions. Reducing poverty takes precedence over encouraging a few people to become wealthy consumers. The approach nurses fledgling businesses by isolating them from competition of large international corporations. Countries promote self-sufficiency by setting barriers that limit the import of goods from other places. The approach also restricts local businesses from exporting to other countries. For many years India made effective use of many barriers to trade. Businesses were supposed to produce goods for consumption inside

India. If private companies were unable to make a profit selling goods only inside India, the government provided subsidies, such as cheap electricity, or wiped out debts. The government owned not just communications, transportation, and power companies, a common feature around the world, but also businesses such as insurance companies and automakers, left to the private sector in most countries.

(295)
Problems with the Self-Sufficiency Alternative. The experience of India and other LDCs revealed two major problems:

1. **Protection of inefficient businesses.** Businesses had little incentive to improve quality, lower production costs, reduce prices, or increase production. Companies protected from international competition do not feel pressure to keep abreast of rapid technological changes.

2. **Need for a large bureaucracy.** A complex administrative system encouraged abuse and corruption. Struggling to produce goods and services was less rewarding financially for many entrepreneurs than advising others on how to get around the complex government regulations. Other potential entrepreneurs earned more money by illegally importing goods and selling them on the black market.

(296)
Development Through International Trade
The international trade model of development calls for a country to identify its distinctive or unique economic assets. According to the international trade approach, a country can develop economically by concentrating scarce resources on expansion of its distinctive local industries.

Rostow's Development Model. A pioneering advocate of this approach was W. W. Rostow, who in the 1950s proposed a five-stage model of development. Several countries adopted this approach during the 1960s, although most continued to follow the self-sufficiency approach. The five stages were as follows:

1. **The traditional society**
2. **The preconditions for takeoff**
3. **The takeoff**
4. **The drive to maturity**
5. **The age of mass consumption**

According to the international trade model, each country is in one of these five stages of development. The model assumes that less developed countries will achieve development by moving along from an earlier to a later stage. A country that concentrates on international trade benefits from exposure to consumers in other countries. Concern for international competitiveness in the exporting takeoff industries will filter through less advanced economic sectors. Rostow's optimistic development model was based on two factors. First, the developed countries of Western Europe and North America had been joined by others in Southern and Eastern Europe and Japan.

Second, many LDCs contain an abundant supply of raw materials. In the past, European colonial powers extracted many of these resources without paying compensation to the colonies. In a global economy, the sale of these raw materials could generate funds for LDCs to promote development.

Examples of International Trade Approach
When most LDCs were following the self-sufficiency approach, two groups of countries chose the international trade approach during the mid-twentieth century.

The Four Asian Dragons. Among the first countries to adopt the international trade alternative were South Korea, Singapore, Taiwan, and the then-British colony of Hong Kong. Singapore and Hong Kong, British colonies until 1965 and 1997, respectively, have virtually no natural resources. Both comprise large cities surrounded by very small amounts of rural land. South Korea and Taiwan have traditionally taken their lead from Japan, and their adoption of the international trade approach was strongly influenced by Japan's success. Lacking natural resources, the four dragons promoted development by concentrating on producing a handful of manufactured goods. Low labor costs enabled these countries to sell products inexpensively in MDCs.

Petroleum-Rich Arabian Peninsula States. The Arabian Peninsula, once among the world's least developed regions, includes countries that were transformed overnight into some of the wealthiest, thanks to escalating petroleum prices during the 1970s.

(297)
Arabian Peninsula countries have used petroleum revenues to finance large-scale projects. The landscape has been further changed by the diffusion of consumer goods.

Problems with the International Trade Alternative
Three problems have hindered countries outside the four Asian dragons and the Arabian Peninsula from developing through the international trade approach:

1. Uneven resource distribution
2. Increased dependence on MDCs
3. Market decline

International Trade Approach Triumphs
In the late twentieth century, most countries embraced the international trade approach as the preferred alternative for stimulating development. Trade has increased more rapidly than wealth, a measure of the growing importance of the international trade approach. India, for example, dismantled its formidable collection of barriers to international trade during the 1990s.

Countries converted from self-sufficiency to international trade during the 1990s for one simple reason: overwhelming evidence that international trade better promoted development. The World Bank found that between 1990 and 2005 per capita GDP increased more than 4 percent annually in countries strongly oriented toward international trade, compared with less than 1 percent for countries strongly oriented toward self-sufficiency.

(298)
World Trade Organization. To promote the international trade development model, countries representing 97 percent of world trade established the World Trade Organization (WTO) in 1995. The WTO works to reduce barriers to international trade in two principal ways. First, through the WTO, countries negotiate reduction or elimination of international trade restrictions on manufactured goods and restrictions on the international movement of money by banks, corporations, and wealthy individuals. The WTO also promotes international trade by enforcing agreements.

The WTO has been sharply attacked by critics. Protesters routinely gather in the streets outside high-level meetings of the WTO. Progressive critics charge that the WTO is antidemocratic, because decisions made behind closed doors promote the interest of large corporations rather than the poor. Conservatives charge that the WTO compromises the power and sovereignty of individual countries because it can order changes in taxes and laws that it considers unfair trading practices.

Foreign Direct Investment
International trade requires corporations based in a particular country to invest in other countries. Investment made by a foreign company in the economy of another country is known as **foreign direct investment (FDI)**. FDI grew rapidly during the 1990s, from $130 billion in 1990 to $1.5 trillion in 2000.

The level declined to $647 billion in 2003, in the wake of the 9/11 al-Qaeda attacks on the United States, before returning to $1.5 trillion later in the decade.

(299)
Only one-fourth of FDI in 2007 went from an MDC to an LDC, and FDI is not evenly distributed among LDCs. Nearly one-third of all FDI went to China in 2007, while one-tenth went to African countries. The major sources of FDI are transnational corporations (TNCs). A **transnational corporation** invests and operates in countries other than the one in which its headquarters are located.

Financing Development
LDCs lack the money needed to finance development, so they obtain financial support from MDCs from two primary sources: loans from banks and international organizations, and direct investment by transnational corporations.

Loans. The two major lenders are the World Bank and the International Monetary Fund (IMF).

- The World Bank: includes the International Bank for Reconstruction and Development (IBRD) and the International Development Association (IDA). The IBRD loans to countries to reform institutions and implement transportation and social service projects. The IDA supports countries considered too risky for IBRD loans.

- The IMF: provides loans to countries experiencing balance-of-payments problems that threaten expansion of international trade; assistance is designed to help rebuild international reserves, intended to stabilize currency exchange rates, and pay for imports without having to impose harsh trade restrictions that would hamper the growth of world trade. Unlike the development banks, the IMF does not lend for specific projects.

The IMF and World Bank became specialized agencies of the United Nations when it was established in 1945. The theory behind borrowing money to build infrastructure is that new or expanded businesses attracted to an area will contribute additional taxes that the LDC uses in part to repay the loans and in part to improve its citizens' living conditions. The problem is that many of the new infrastructure projects are expensive failures. Also, billions in aid have been squandered, or spent on armaments by recipient nations.

(300)
Many LDCs have been unable to repay the interest on their loans, let alone the principal. Debt actually exceeds annual income in 18 countries. Financial institutions in more developed countries refuse to make further loans, so construction of needed infrastructure stops. The inability of many LDCs to repay loans also damages the financial stability of banks in the more developed countries.

Structural Adjustment Programs
The IMF, World Bank, and MDCs fear that canceling debts without strings attached will perpetuate bad habits in LDCs, therefore to obtain debt relief an LDC is required to prepare an outline for a **structural adjustment program**, identifying economic goals and strategies, including economic and government reforms. LDCs must direct benefits to the poor, not just the elite. Critics charge that poverty worsens under structural adjustment programs. Placing priority on reducing government spending and inflation may reduce education, health, and social services that benefit the poor.

(301)
In response to criticisms, the IMF and World Bank encourage innovative programs to reduce poverty and corruption, and consult more with average citizens.

Fair Trade

Fair Trade has been proposed as a variation of the international trade model of development. **Fair Trade** means that products are made and traded according to standards that protect workers and small businesses in LDCs. Standards for fair trade are set internationally by Fairtrade Labeling Organizations International. In North America, fair trade products have been primarily craft products. In Europe, most fair trade sales are in food. Two sets of standards distinguish fair trade: One set applies to workers on farms and in factories and the other set to producers.

Fair Trade Producer Standards

Fair trade advocates work with small businesses, especially worker-owned and democratically run cooperatives. Cooperatives benefit the local farmers and artisans who are members, rather than the absentee corporate owners interested only in maximizing profits. Because fair trade organizations bypass exploitative middlemen and work directly with producers, they are able to cut costs and return a greater percentage of the retail price to the producers. In some cases, the quality is higher because fair traders factor in the environmental cost of production.

Fair Trade Worker Standards

Critics of international trade charge that only a tiny percentage of the price a consumer pays for a good reaches the individual in the LDC responsible for making or growing it. Protection of workers' rights is not a high priority in the international trade model, according to its critics. In contrast, fair trade requires employers to pay workers fair wages, permit union organizing, and comply with minimum environmental and safety standards. Cooperatives are encouraged to reinvest profits back into the community, such as by providing health clinics, child care, and training.

Key Terms

Development (p. 274)
Fair trade (p. 301)
Foreign direct investment (p. 298)
Gender Empowerment Measure (GEM) (p. 289)
Gender-Related Development Index (GDI) (p. 289)
Gross domestic product (GDP) (p. 275)
Human Development Index (HDI) (p. 274)
Less developed country (LDC) (p. 274)
Literacy rate (p. 278)

More developed country (MDC) (p. 274)
Primary sector (p. 276)
Productivity (p. 276)
Secondary sector (p. 276)
Structural adjustment program (p. 300)
Tertiary sector (p. 276)
Transnational corporation (p. 299)
Value added (p. 276)

Test Prep Questions

1) Which of the following is NOT a factor used to calculate the HDI of a country?
A) literacy rate
B) GDP per capita
C) crude death rate
D) average life expectancy

2) What kind of factors are NOT generally considered when calculating the level of development of a country?
A) historical
B) economic
C) demographic
D) social

3) Which of the following jobs would be considered part of the <u>secondary</u> sector?
A) coal miner
B) bank teller
C) farmer
D) factory worker

4) Why do workers in LDCs show less productivity than workers in MDCs?
A) they use less-efficient technology
B) they don't work as hard
C) they aren't as smart
D) they aren't as educated

5) What demographic measurement does not strongly indicate a society's level of development?
A) natural increase rate
B) infant mortality rate
C) crude death rate
D) life expectancy

6) What more developed region is notable for having a core area with the world's highest level of development, but also an area that lags in development?
A) North America
B) Europe
C) Russia
D) Japan

7) Which of the following is NOT considered when calculating the Gender Empowerment Measure?
A) female literacy rate
B) per capita female income relative to men
C) percentage of members of the national parliament who are women
D) percentage of professional and technical jobs held by women

8) Which of the following is NOT one of Rostow's stages of development in the international trade approach?
A) the age of mass consumption
B) the point of diminishing returns
C) the preconditions for takeoff
D) the traditional society

9) Which of the following is NOT a problem with the international trade approach to development?
A) market decline
B) increased dependence on MDCs
C) uneven resource distribution
D) need for a large bureaucracy

10) Which of the following is NOT one of the four Asian Dragons?
A) Thailand
B) Taiwan
C) South Korea
D) Hong Kong

Short Essay

1) Identify the three different types of indicators used to measure development, and give specific examples of each explaining how they differ between LDCs and MDCs.

_____

_____

_____

_____

_____

2) Identify two <u>regions</u> that are characterized as being more developed, and two that are characterized as being less developed. Explain the factors that have either contributed to their development (in the case of the more developed regions), or hindered it (in the case of the less developed regions).

_____

_____

_____

_____

_____

_____

3) Explain the relationship between gender and development and the two methods we use to measure it.

_____

_____

_____

_____

_____

_____

_____

_____

Chapter 10
Agriculture

Key Issues
1. Where did agriculture originate?
2. Where are agricultural regions in LDCs?
3. Where are agricultural regions in MDCs?
4. Why do farmers face economic difficulties?

(308)

The previous chapter divided economic activities into primary, secondary, and tertiary sectors. This chapter is concerned with the principal form of primary-sector economic activity — agriculture. The next two chapters look at the secondary and tertiary sectors. In less developed *regions*, the farm products are most often consumed on or near the farm, whereas in MDCs farmers sell what they produce. The reason *why* farming varies around the world relates to the distribution across *space* of cultural and environmental factors. Despite increased knowledge of alternatives, farmers practice distinctive agriculture in different regions and on neighboring farms. Broad climate patterns influence the crops planted in a region, and local soil conditions influence the crops planted on an individual farm. Farmers choose from a variety of agricultural practices, based on their perception of the value of each alternative. These values are partly economic and partly cultural. How farmers deal with their physical environment varies according to dietary preferences, availability of technology, and other cultural traditions. Although individual farmers may make specific decisions on a very local *scale*, agriculture is as caught up in the *globalization* of the economy as other industries. After examining the origins and diffusion of agriculture, we will consider the agricultural practices used in LDCs and MDCs.

Key Issue 1. Where Did Agriculture Originate?
- **Origins of agriculture**
- **Subsistence and commercial agriculture**

The origins of agriculture cannot be documented with certainty, because it began before recorded history. Scholars try to reconstruct a logical sequence of events based on fragments. Improvements in cultivating plants and domesticating animals evolved over thousands of years.

(309)
Origins of Agriculture
Agriculture is deliberate modification of Earth's surface through cultivation of plants and rearing of animals to obtain sustenance or economic gain. Agriculture originated when humans domesticated plants and animals for their use. A **crop** is any plant cultivated by people.

Hunters and Gatherers
Before the invention of agriculture, all humans probably obtained the food they needed for survival through hunting for animals, fishing, or gathering plants. Hunters and gatherers lived in small groups. The men hunted game or fished, and the women collected berries, nuts, and roots. This division of labor sounds like a stereotype but is based on evidence from archaeology and anthropology. The group traveled frequently, establishing new home bases or camps. The direction and frequency of migration depended on the movement of game and the seasonal growth of plants at various locations. Today perhaps a quarter-million people, or less than 0.005 percent of the world's population, still survive by hunting and gathering. Contemporary hunting and gathering societies are isolated groups living on the periphery of world settlement, but they provide insight into human customs that prevailed in prehistoric times, before the invention of agriculture.

Invention of Agriculture

Why did nomadic groups convert from hunting, gathering, and fishing to agriculture? Geographers and other scientists agree that agriculture originated in multiple hearths around the world but do not agree on when and why. Southwest Asia was an early center of crop domestication; barley and wheat are thought to have been domesticated around 10,000 years ago, lentils and olives were also early domesticates from Southwest Asia. Rice is thought to have been domesticated in East Asia more than 10,000 years ago, and millet was domesticated at an early date as well. Sorghum was domesticated in central Africa around 8,000 years ago, and yams may have been domesticated even earlier. Millet and rice may have been domesticated in sub-Saharan Africa independently of the hearth in East Asia. In Latin America, two important hearths are thought to have emerged in Peru and Mexico around 4,000 to 5,000 years ago. Mexico is considered a hearth for beans and cotton, and Peru for the potato. Squashes may have been domesticated in the southeastern U.S. as well as Mexico. The most important contribution of the Americas, maize (corn) may have emerged in the two hearths around the same time.

Animals were also domesticated in multiple hearths at various dates. Southwest Asia is thought to have been the hearth for cattle, goats, pigs and sheep between 8,000 and 9,000 years ago. Domestication of the dog is thought to date from around 12,000 years ago, also in southwest Asia. The horse is considered to have been domesticated in Central Asia, and its diffusion is thought to be associated with that of the Indo-European language. Scientists do not agree on whether agriculture originated primarily because of environmental factors or cultural factors; probably a combination of both factors contributed. Those favoring environmental reasons point to the coinciding of domestication with the end of the last ice age, which resulted in a massive redistribution of humans, other animals, and plants.

(310)

Alternatively, human behavior may be primarily responsible for the origin of agriculture. A preference for living in a fixed place may have led hunters and gatherers to build permanent settlements. Over thousands of years, plant cultivation evolved from a combination of accident and deliberate experiment. That agriculture had multiple origins means that, from earliest times, people have produced food in distinctive ways in different regions.

Subsistence and Commercial Agriculture

The most fundamental differences in agricultural practices are between those in LDCs and those in MDCs. Farmers in LDCs practice subsistence agriculture, whereas farmers in MDCs practice commercial agriculture. **Subsistence agriculture** is the production of food primarily for consumption by the farmer's family. **Commercial agriculture** is the production of food primarily for sale off the farm.

(311)

Similarities between agriculture and climate maps are striking. Because of the problems involved with the concept of environmental determinism, geographers are wary of placing too much emphasis on the role of climate. Cultural preferences also explain agricultural differences in areas of similar climate, such as the lack of hog or wine production in areas where the climate is favorable for them. Five principal features distinguish commercial from subsistence agriculture: 1. purpose of farming; 2. percentage of farmers in the labor force; 3. use of machinery; 4. farm size; and 5. relationship of farming to other businesses.

Purpose of Farming. In LDCs, most people produce food for their own consumption. Some surplus may be sold but may not even exist some years. In commercial farming, farmers grow crops and raise animals primarily for sale. Agricultural products are sold to food-processing companies.

Percentage of Farmers in the Labor Force. In MDCs, around 5 percent of the workers are engaged directly in farming, compared to around 50 percent in LDCs. The percentage of farmers is even lower in the United States and Canada, at only around 2 percent. The number of farmers has declined dramatically in MDCs during the twentieth century. Both push and pull migration factors have been responsible.

Use of Machinery. In MDCs, a small number of farmers in more developed societies can feed many people because they rely on machinery to perform work. Traditionally, the farmer or local craftspeople made equipment from wood, but beginning in the late eighteenth century, factories produced farm machinery. The first all-iron plow was made in the 1770s. Factory-made farm machines have replaced or supplemented manual labor.

Transportation improvements also aid commercial farmers. Railroads in the nineteenth century, and highways and trucks in the twentieth century, have enabled farmers to transport crops and livestock farther and faster. Commercial farmers use scientific advances to increase productivity.

Some farmers conduct their own on-farm research. Electronics also aid commercial farmers. Global positioning systems (GPS) units determine precise coordinates for spreading different types and amounts of fertilizers. Both satellite imagery and yield monitors attached to combines monitor production outputs.

(313)
Farm Size. The average farm size is relatively large in commercial agriculture, especially in the United States and Canada. Commercial agriculture is increasingly dominated by a handful of large farms. In the United States, the largest 5 percent of farms produced 75 percent of the country's total agriculture. Large size is partly a consequence of mechanization. As a result of the large size and the high level of mechanization, commercial agriculture is an expensive business. This money is frequently borrowed from a bank and repaid after the output is sold. Although the United States currently has fewer farms and farmers than in 1900, the amount of land devoted to agriculture has increased. However, the amount of U.S. farmland has declined from its all-time peak in 1960. A serious problem in the United States has been the loss of the most productive farmland, known as **prime agricultural land**, as urban areas sprawl into the surrounding countryside.

Relationship of Farming to Other Businesses. Commercial farming is closely tied to other businesses. Commercial farming in MDCs has been called **agribusiness**, because the farm is integrated into a large food-production industry.

(314)
Although farmers are less than 2 percent of the U.S. labor force, more than 20 percent of U.S. labor works in food production related to agribusiness: food processing, packaging, storing, distributing, and retailing.

Key Issue 2. Where Are Agricultural Regions in Less Developed Countries?
- **Shifting cultivation**
- **Pastoral nomadism**
- **Intensive subsistence agriculture**
- **Plantation farming**

This section considers four agricultural types characteristic of LDCs: shifting cultivation, pastoral nomadism, intensive subsistence, and plantation farming. Intensive subsistence agriculture is divided into two regions, depending on the choice of crop.

Shifting Cultivation

Shifting cultivation is practiced in much of the world's Humid Low-Latitude, or A, climate regions, which have relatively high temperatures and abundant rainfall. It is practiced by roughly 250 million people across 36 million square kilometers (14 million square miles), especially in the tropical rainforests of South America, Central and West Africa, and Southeast Asia.

Characteristics of Shifting Cultivation

There are two distinctive features of **shifting cultivation**:
- Farmers clear land for planting by slashing vegetation and burning the debris (shifting cultivation is sometimes called **slash-and-burn agriculture**).
- Farmers grow crops on a cleared field for only a few years.

People who practice shifting cultivation generally live in small villages and grow food on the surrounding land, which the village controls.

The Process of Shifting Cultivation. Each year villagers designate an area for planting. They must remove the dense vegetation that typically covers tropical land. The debris is burned under carefully controlled conditions. Rains wash the fresh ashes into the soil, providing needed nutrients. Before planting, the cleared area, known by a variety of names in different regions, including **swidden**, *ladang*, *milpa*, *chena*, and *kaingin*, is prepared by hand. The cleared land can support crops only briefly, usually three years or fewer. Villagers leave the old site uncropped for many years. The villagers will return to the site, perhaps as few as 6 years or as many as 20 years later, to begin the process of clearing the land again. In the meantime, they may still care for fruit-bearing trees on the site.

Crops of Shifting Cultivation. The crops grown by each village vary by local custom and taste. The predominant crops include upland rice in Southeast Asia, maize (corn) and manioc (cassava) in South America, and millet and sorghum in Africa. Yams, sugarcane, plantain, and vegetables also are grown in some regions. The Kayapo people of Brazil's Amazon tropical rain forest plant in concentric rings. Plants that require more nutrients are located in the outer ring. (316) It is here that the leafy crowns of cut trees fall when the field is cleared. Most families grow only for their own needs, so one swidden may contain a large variety of intermingled crops. Families may specialize in a few crops and trade with villagers who have a surplus of others.

Ownership and Use of Land in Shifting Cultivation. Traditionally, land is owned by the village as a whole rather than separately by each resident. Today, private individuals now own the land in some communities, especially in Latin America. (317) Shifting cultivation occupies approximately one fourth of the world's land area, a higher percentage than any other type of agriculture. However, only 5 percent of the world's population engages in shifting cultivation.

Future of Shifting Cultivation

Land devoted to shifting cultivation is declining in the tropics at the rate of about 75,000 square kilometers (30,000 square miles), or 0.2 percent per year. The amount of Earth's surface allocated to tropical rain forests has already been reduced to less than half of its original area. Shifting cultivation is being replaced by logging, cattle ranching, and cultivation of cash crops.

To its critics, shifting cultivation is at best a preliminary step in economic development, and should be replaced by more sophisticated agriculture that yields more per land area.

Defenders of shifting cultivation consider it the most environmentally sound approach for the tropics. Practices used in other forms of agriculture may damage the soil, cause severe erosion, and upset balanced ecosystems. Large-scale destruction of the rain forests also may contribute to global warming. When large numbers of trees are cut, their burning and decay release large volumes of carbon dioxide. Elimination of shifting cultivation could also upset the traditional local diversity of cultures in the tropics. The activities of shifting cultivation are intertwined with other social, religious, political, and various folk customs.

(318)
As the importance of tropical rain forests to the global environment has become recognized, LDCs have been pressured to restrict further destruction of them. Bolivia agreed to set aside 1.5 million hectares (3.7 million acres) in a forest reserve in exchange for cancellation of 650 million dollars of its debt. In Brazil's Amazon rain forest, however, deforestation has increased 2.7 million hectares (7 million acres) per year during the 1990s to 3.1 million hectares (8 million acres) since 2000.

Pastoral Nomadism
Pastoral nomadism is a form of subsistence agriculture based on the herding of domesticated animals. The word *pastoral* refers to sheep herding. It is adapted to dry climates, where planting crops is impossible. Only about 15 million people are pastoral nomads, but they sparsely occupy about 20 percent of Earth's land area.

Characteristics of Pastoral Nomadism
Pastoral nomads depend primarily on animals rather than crops for survival. The animals provide milk, and their skins and hair are used for clothing and tents. Like other subsistence farmers, though, pastoral nomads consume mostly grain rather than meat. Some pastoral nomads obtain grain from sedentary subsistence farmers in exchange for animal products. More often, part of a nomadic group — perhaps the women and children — may plant crops at a fixed location while the rest of the group wanders with the herd. Other nomads might sow grain in recently flooded areas and return later in the year to harvest the crop.

Choice of Animals. Nomads select the type and number of animals for the herd according to local cultural and physical characteristics. The choice depends on the relative prestige of animals and the ability of species to adapt to a particular climate and vegetation.

Movements of Pastoral Nomads. Pastoral nomads do not wander randomly across the landscape but have a strong sense of territoriality. Every group controls a piece of territory and will invade another group's territory only in an emergency or if war is declared. (319) The precise migration patterns evolve from intimate knowledge of the area's physical and cultural characteristics. The selection of routes varies in unusually wet or dry years and is influenced by the condition of their animals and the area's political stability. Some pastoral nomads practice **transhumance**, which is seasonal migration of livestock between mountains and lowland **pasture** areas.

The Future of Pastoral Nomadism
Agricultural experts once regarded pastoral nomadism as a stage in the evolution of agriculture. Pastoral nomadism is now generally recognized as an offshoot of sedentary agriculture, not as a primitive precursor of it. Today pastoral nomadism is a declining form of agriculture, partly a victim of modern technology. Nomads used to be the most powerful inhabitants of the dry lands, but now, with modern weapons, national governments can control the nomadic population more effectively. Government efforts to resettle nomads have been particularly vigorous in China, Kazakhstan, and several Southwest Asia countries, including Egypt, Israel, Saudi Arabia, and Syria. Governments force groups to give up pastoral nomadism because they want the land for other uses. In the future, pastoral nomadism will be increasingly confined to areas that cannot be irrigated or that lack valuable raw materials.

Intensive Subsistence Agriculture
Shifting cultivation and pastoral nomadism are found in regions of low (population) density. But three-fourths of the world's people live in LDCs, and another form of subsistence agriculture is needed to feed most of them: **intensive subsistence agriculture**. In densely populated East, South, and Southeast Asia, most farmers practice intensive subsistence agriculture. The typical farm is much smaller than elsewhere in the world. Because the agricultural density is so high in parts of

East and South Asia, families must produce enough food for their survival from a very small area of land. They do this through careful agricultural practices, refined over thousands of years in response to local environmental and cultural patterns. Intensive subsistence farmers waste virtually no land. Paths and roads are kept as narrow as possible to minimize the loss of arable land. Little grain is grown to feed the animals.

Intensive Subsistence with Wet Rice Dominant
Wet rice occupies a relatively small percentage of Asia's agricultural land but is the region's most important source of food. Intensive wet-rice farming is the dominant type of agriculture in Southeast China, East India, and much of Southeast Asia.

Successful production of large yields of rice is an elaborate, time-consuming process that is done mostly by hand. Growing rice involves several steps: First, a farmer prepares the field for planting, using a plow drawn by water buffalo or oxen. The use of a plow and animal power is one characteristic that distinguishes subsistence agriculture from shifting cultivation. (320) Then the plowed land is flooded with water from rainfall, river overflow, or irrigation. The flooded field is called a **sawah** in the Austronesian language widely spoken in Indonesia, including Java. Europeans and North Americans frequently, but incorrectly, call it a **paddy**, the Malay word for wet rice. The customary way to grow rice is to grow seedlings on dry land in a nursery and then transplant the seedlings into the flooded field.

Wet rice is most easily grown on flat land, because the plants are submerged in water much of the time. One method of developing additional land suitable for growing rice is to terrace the hillsides of river valleys. Land is used even more intensively in parts of Asia by obtaining two harvests per year from one field, a process known as **double cropping**. Double cropping is common in places having warm winters but is relatively rare in India, where most areas have dry winters. Normally, double cropping involves alternating between wet rice and wheat, barley, or another dry crop, grown in the drier winter season.

Intensive Subsistence with Wet Rice Not Dominant
Climate prevents growing wet rice in portions of Asia, especially where summer precipitation levels are too low and winters are too harsh. Wheat is the most important crop, followed by barley. Other grains and legumes are grown for household consumption and some crops sold for cash, such as cotton, flax, hemp, and tobacco.

In milder parts of the region, more than one harvest can be obtained some years through skilled use of **crop rotation**.

Since the Chinese Communist Revolution in 1949, the government organized agricultural producer communes. By combining several small fields into a single large unit, the government hoped to promote agricultural efficiency, but people worked less efficiently for the commune than when working for themselves, and China has dismantled them. The communes still hold legal title to agricultural land as private individuals. Reorganization has been difficult because infrastructure was developed to serve large communal farms rather than small, individually managed ones, but production has increased greatly.

Plantation Farming
The plantation is a form of commercial agriculture found in the tropics and subtropics, especially in Latin America, Africa, and Asia. Plantations are often owned or operated by Europeans or North Americans and grow crops for sale primarily in MDCs. (322) A **plantation** is a large farm that specializes in one or two crops. Among the most important crops are cotton, sugarcane, coffee, rubber, tobacco, cocoa, jute, bananas, tea, coconuts, and palm oil. Crops such as tobacco, cotton,

and sugarcane, which can be planted only once a year, are less likely to be grown on large plantations today than in the past.

Because plantations are usually situated in sparsely settled locations, they must import workers. Managers try to spread the work throughout the year to make full use of the large labor force. Until the Civil War, plantations were important in the U.S. South, where the principal crop was cotton, followed by tobacco and sugarcane. Slaves brought from Africa performed most of the labor until the defeat of the South in the Civil War. Thereafter, plantations were subdivided and either sold to individual farmers or worked by tenant farmers.

Key Issue 3. Where Are Agricultural Regions in More Developed Countries?
- **Mixed crop and livestock farming**
- **Dairy farming**
- **Grain farming**
- **Livestock ranching**
- **Mediterranean agriculture**
- **Commercial gardening and fruit farming**
- **Importance of access to markets**

Commercial agriculture in MDCs can be divided into six main types. Each type is predominant in distinctive regions within MDCs, depending largely on climate.

Mixed Crop and Livestock Farming
Mixed crop and livestock farming is the most common form of commercial agriculture in the United States west of the Appalachians and east of 98° west longitude and in much of Europe from France to Russia.

Characteristics of Mixed Crop and Livestock Farming
The most distinctive characteristic of mixed crop and livestock farming is its integration of crops and livestock. Most of the crops are fed to animals rather than consumed directly by humans. Mixing crop and livestock farming permits farmers to distribute the workload more evenly through the year and reduces seasonal variations in income. In the U.S., corn is the crop most frequently planted in the mixed crop and livestock region because it generates a higher yield than other crops. Some is consumed by people as oil, margarine and other products, but most is fed to pigs and cattle. Soybeans have become the second most important crop in the region.

Crop Rotation
Mixed crop and livestock farming typically involves crop rotation. Crop rotation contrasts with shifting cultivation, in which nutrients depleted from a field are restored only by leaving the field fallow (uncropped) for many years. (323) A two-field crop-rotation system was developed in Northern Europe as early as the fifth century. Beginning in the eighth century, a three-field system was introduced. Each field yielded four harvests every six years, compared to three every six years under the two-field system. A four-field system was introduced in Europe during the eighteenth century. Each field thus passed through a cycle of four crops: root, cereal, rest crop, and another cereal. **Cereal grain**, such as oats, wheat, rye or barley, were sold for flour and beer production, and straw was retained for animal bedding. Root crops were fed to the animals during the winter. Clover and other "rest" crops were used for cattle grazing and restoration of nitrogen to the soil.

Dairy Farming
Dairy farming is the most important type of commercial agriculture practiced on farms near the large urban areas of the Northeast United States, Southeast Canada, and Northwest Europe. Dairying has also become important in South and East Asia.

(324)

Traditionally, fresh milk was rarely consumed except directly on the farm or in nearby villages. During the nineteenth century, demand for the sale of milk to urban residents increased. Rising incomes permitted urban residents to buy milk products, which were once considered luxuries.

Regional Distribution of Dairying

Dairying has become the most important type of commercial agriculture in the first ring outside large cities because of transportation factors. The ring surrounding a city from which milk can be supplied without spoiling is known as the **milkshed**. Improvements in transportation have permitted dairying to be undertaken farther from the market. As a result, nearly every farm in the U.S. Northeast and Northwest Europe is within the milkshed of at least one urban area.

(325)

Dairy farmers, like other commercial farmers, usually do not sell their products directly to consumers. The choice of product varies within the U.S. dairy region, depending on whether the farms are within the milkshed of a large urban area. Farms located farther from consumers are more likely to sell their output to processors. In the East, virtually all milk is sold to consumers living in large urban areas. Farther west, most milk is processed into cheese and butter. Countries likewise tend to specialize in certain products. New Zealand, the world's largest producer of dairy products, devotes about 5 percent to liquid milk, compared to over 50 percent in the United Kingdom.

Challenges for Dairy Farmers

Like other commercial farmers, dairy farmers face economic problems because of declining revenues and rising costs. Distinctive features of dairy farming have exacerbated the economic difficulties:
- **Labor-intensive.** Dairy farming requires constant attention throughout the year.
- **Winter Feed.** Dairy farmers also face the expense of feeding the cows in the winter, when they may be unable to graze on grass.

Grain Farming

Commercial **grain** agriculture is distinguished from mixed crop and livestock farming because crops on a grain farm are grown primarily for consumption by humans rather than by livestock. Wheat generally can be sold for a higher price than other grains such as rye, oats, and barley, and it has more uses as human food. Because wheat has a relatively high value per unit weight, it can be shipped profitably from remote farms to markets. Wheat is grown to a considerable extent for international trade and is the world's leading export crop. The ability to provide food for many people elsewhere in the world is a major source of economic and political strength for the United States and Canada.

The United States is by far the largest commercial producer of grain. Large-scale commercial grain production is found in only a few other countries, including Canada, Argentina, Australia, France, and the United Kingdom. Commercial grain farms are generally located in regions that are too dry for mixed crop and livestock agriculture.

Within North America, large-scale grain production is concentrated in three areas:
- The **winter wheat** belt extends through Kansas, Colorado, and Oklahoma.
- The **spring wheat** belt of the Dakotas, Montana, and southern Saskatchewan in Canada.
- The Palouse region of Washington State.

(326)

Large-scale grain production, like other commercial farming ventures in more developed countries, is heavily mechanized, conducted on large farms, and oriented to consumer preferences. The

McCormick **reaper** (a machine that cuts grain standing in the field) invented in the 1830s, first permitted large-scale wheat production. Today, the **combine** machine performs in one operation the three tasks of reaping, threshing, and cleaning. Unlike work on a mixed crop and livestock farm, the effort required to grow wheat is not uniform throughout the year. Some individuals or firms may therefore have two sets of fields — one in the spring-wheat belt and one in the winter-wheat belt.

Livestock Ranching

Ranching is the commercial grazing of livestock over an extensive area, practiced in more developed countries, where the vegetation is too sparse and the soil too poor to support crops.

The importance of ranching in the United States extends beyond the number of people who choose this form of commercial farming because of its prominence in popular culture. Cattle ranching in Texas, though, as glamorized in popular culture, actually dominated commercial agriculture for a short period — from 1867 to 1885.

Cattle ranching in the United States expanded because of demand for beef in the East Coast cities during the 1860s. Ranchers who could get their cattle to Chicago were paid $30 to $40 per head, compared to only $3 or $4 per head in Texas.

(327)

To reach Chicago, cattle were driven on hoof by cowboys over trails from Texas to the nearest railhead. The western terminus of the rail line reached Abilene, Kansas in 1867. The most famous route from Texas northward to the rail line was the Chisholm Trail.

Cattle ranching declined in importance during the 1880s after it came in conflict with sedentary agriculture. The early cattle ranchers in the West owned little land, only cattle.

The U.S. government, which owned most of the land used for open grazing, began to sell it to farmers to grow crops. For a few years, the ranchers tried to drive out the farmers. The farmers' most potent weapon proved to be barbed wire, first commercially produced in 1873. Ranchers were compelled to buy or lease land to accommodate their cattle. Sixty percent of cattle grazing today takes place on land leased from the U.S. government.

With the spread of irrigation techniques and hardier crops, land in the United States has been converted from ranching to crop growing. Cattle are still raised on ranches but are frequently sent for fattening to farms or to local feed lots.

Commercial ranching is conducted in several other MDCs. In Australia sheep are more common than cattle.

Ranching is rare in Europe, except in Spain and Portugal. In South America, a large portion of the pampas of Argentina, Southern Brazil, and Uruguay are devoted to grazing cattle and sheep.

Ranching has followed similar stages around the world: first, herding over open ranges, then ranching transformed into fixed farming by dividing the open land. Many of the farms converted to growing crops, and ranching was confined to the drier lands. Ranching has become part of the meat-processing industry rather than an economic activity carried out on isolated farms.

(328)

Mediterranean Agriculture

Mediterranean agriculture exists primarily in the lands that border the Mediterranean Sea. Farmers in California, central Chile, the southwestern part of South Africa, and southwestern Australia practice Mediterranean agriculture as well. Every Mediterranean area borders a sea. Prevailing sea winds provide moisture and moderate the winter temperatures. Summers are hot and dry. The land is very hilly. Farmers derive a smaller percentage of income from animal products in the Mediterranean region than in the mixed crop and livestock region. Some farmers living along the Mediterranean Sea traditionally used transhumance to raise animals, although the practice is now less common.

Most crops in Mediterranean lands are grown for human consumption rather than for animal feed. **Horticulture** — which is the growing of fruits, vegetables, and flowers — and tree crops form the commercial base of the Mediterranean farming. A combination of local physical and cultural characteristics determines which crops are grown in each area. In the lands bordering the Mediterranean Sea, the two most important cash crops are olives and grapes, although approximately half of the land is devoted to growing cereals, especially wheat for pasta and bread.

Cereals occupy a much lower percentage of the cultivated land in California than in other Mediterranean climates. Instead, much of California farmland is devoted to fruit and vegetable horticulture. The rapid growth of urban areas in California, especially Los Angeles, has converted high-quality agricultural land into housing developments. The loss of farmland has been offset by expansion of agriculture into arid lands. However, farming in dry lands requires massive irrigation to provide water.

Commercial Gardening and Fruit Farming
Commercial gardening and fruit farming is the predominant type of agriculture in the U.S. Southeast, frequently called **truck farming**, because "truck" was a Middle English word meaning bartering or the exchange of commodities. Truck farms grow fruits and vegetables. Some of these fruits and vegetables are sold fresh to consumers, but most are sold to large processors. (329) Truck farms are highly efficient large-scale operations that take full advantage of machines at every stage of the growing process. Labor costs are kept down by hiring migrant farm workers, some of whom are undocumented immigrants from Mexico. A handful of farms may dominate national output of some fruits and vegetables. A form of truck farming called *specialty farming* has spread to New England, growing crops that have limited but increasing demand among affluent consumers.

Key Issue 4. Why Do Farmers Face Economic Difficulties?
- **Issues for commercial farmers**
- **Issues for subsistence farmers**
- **Strategies to increase food supply**

Commercial and subsistence farmers both have difficulty generating enough income to continue farming. The underlying reasons are, however, different. Commercial farmers are producing a surplus of food, whereas many subsistence farmers are barely able to produce enough food to survive.

Challenges for Commercial Farmers
Commercial farmers produce large quantities of food and therefore face low prices for their output. Government subsidies help prop up farm income. Many believe that the future health of commercial farming rests with more sustainable practices.

Importance of Access to Markets
Because the purpose of commercial farming is to sell produce off the farm, the distance from the farm to the market influences the farmer's choice of crop to plant. Geographers use the von Thünen model to help explain the importance of proximity to market in the choice of crops on commercial farms. The model was first proposed in 1826 by Johann Heinrich von Thünen, a farmer in northern Germany. According to the model, in choosing an enterprise, a commercial farmer compares two costs: the cost of the land versus the cost of transporting products to market.

Von Thünen based his general model of the spatial arrangement of different crops on his experiences as owner of a large estate in northern Germany during the early nineteenth century. He found that specific crops were grown in different rings around the cities in the area.

(330)

The model assumed that all land in a study area had similar site characteristics and was of uniform quality, although von Thünen recognized that the model could vary according to topography and other distinctive physical conditions. The model also failed to understand that social customs and government policies influence the attractiveness of plants and animals for a commercial farmer. Although von Thünen developed the model for a small region with a single market center, it is also applicable on a national or global scale.

Overproduction in Commercial Farming

Commercial farmers suffer from low incomes because they produce too much food rather than too little. A surplus of food has been produced in part because of widespread adoption of efficient agricultural practices. Commercial farmers obtain greatly increased yields per area of land. Dairy farming also demonstrates the growth in productivity. Yield per cow nearly doubled in the period from 1980 to 2008.

Although the food supply has increased in MDCs, demand has remained constant, because the market for most products is already saturated. Demand is also stagnant for most agricultural products in more developed countries because of low population growth.

The U.S. government has three policies to attack the problem of excess productive capacity:

1. **Farmers are encouraged to avoid producing crops that are in excess supply.** The government encourages planting fallow crops.
2. **The government pays farmers when certain commodity prices are low.** The government sets a target price for the commodity and pays the farmers the difference between that price and what they receive in the market.
3. **The government buys surplus production and sells it or donates it to foreign governments.** In addition, low-income Americans receive food stamps in part to stimulate their purchase of additional food.

(331)

The United States has averaged about $16 billion a year on farm subsidies. Annual spending varies considerably from one year to the next. Farming in Europe is subsidized even more than in the United States. Supporters point to the preservation of rural village life in parts of Europe, while critics charge that Europeans pay needlessly high prices for food as a result of the subsidies.

Government policies in MDCs point out a fundamental irony in worldwide agricultural patterns. In an MDC such as the United States, farmers are encouraged to grow less food, whereas LDCs struggle to increase food production to match the rate of the growth in population.

Sustainable Agriculture

Some commercial farmers are converting their operations to sustainable agriculture, an agricultural practice that preserves and enhances environmental quality. Farmers practicing sustainable agriculture typically generate lower revenues than do conventional farmers, but they also have lower costs.

An increasingly popular form of sustainable agriculture is organic farming. However, some organic farms, especially the larger ones, may rely in part on nonsustainable practices. Worldwide, 0.24 percent of farmland was classified as organic in 2007. Australia was the leader, with 37 percent of the worldwide total.

Three principal practices distinguish sustainable agriculture (and at its best, organic farming) from conventional agriculture:
  • Sensitive land management
  • Limited use of chemicals
  • Better integration of crops and livestock

Sensitive Land Management. Sustainable agriculture protects soil in part through ridge tillage and limited use of chemicals. **Ridge tillage** is a system of planting crops on 4-to 8-inch ridges that are formed during cultivation or after harvest. Ridge tillage is attractive for two main reasons: lower production costs and greater soil conservation. Production costs are lower with ridge tillage in part because it requires less investment in tractors and other machinery than conventional planting. Ridge tillage features a minimum of soil disturbance from harvest to the next planting. Over several years the soil will tend to have increased organic matter, greater water holding capacity and more earthworms. The channels left by earthworms and decaying roots enhance drainage. Under sustainable agriculture, farmers control weeds with cultivation and minimal use of herbicides. Ridge tillage compares favorably with conventional farming for yields while lowering the cost of production.

Limited Use of Chemicals. In conventional agriculture, seeds are often genetically modified to survive when herbicides and insecticides are sprayed on the fields. (332) Widespread use of herbicides is artificially selecting for weeds resistant to the herbicide. Sustainable agriculture controls weeds with cultivation and minimal use of herbicides. (333) Researchers have found that combining mechanical weed control with some chemicals yields higher returns per acre than relying solely on one of the two methods. Ridge tillage also promotes decreased use of chemicals, which can be applied only to the ridges.

Integrated Crop and Livestock. Sustainable agriculture attempts to integrate the growing of crops and the raising of livestock as much as possible at the level of the individual farm. Animals consume crops grown on the farm and are not confined to small pens. Mixed crop and livestock is a common form of farming in many MDCs, including the Corn Belt in the United States. In conventional farming, many farmers choose to grow only crops or raise more animals than their crops can feed. Integration of crops and livestock is a return to the historical practice of mixed crop and livestock.

Sustainable agriculture is sensitive to the following complexities of biological and economic interdependencies between crops and livestock:

  1. Number of livestock
  2. Animal confinement
  3. Management of extreme weather conditions
  4. Flexible feeding and marketing

Challenges for Subsistence Farmers
Two economic issues discussed in earlier chapters influence the choice of crops planted by subsistence farmers:
  • Subsistence farmers must feed an increasing number of people because of rapid population growth.
  • Subsistence farmers must grow food for export instead of for direct consumption due to the adoption of the international trade approach to development.

Subsistence Farming and Population Growth

According to Ester Boserup, population growth compels subsistence farmers to consider new farming. For hundreds if not thousands of years, subsistence farming yielded enough food. Suddenly in the late twentieth century, the LDCs needed to provide enough food for a rapidly increasing population.

According to the Boserup thesis, subsistence farmers increase the supply of food through intensification of production, achieved in two ways:

1. **Adoption of new farming methods.** The additional labor needed to perform these operations comes from the population growth.

(334)
2. **Land is left fallow for shorter periods.** Boserup identified five basic stages in the intensification of farmland: Forest Fallow, Bush Fallow, Short Fallow, Annual Cropping, and Multicropping.

First, land is left fallow for shorter periods.

Subsistence Farming and International Trade

To expand production, subsistence farmers need higher-yield seeds, fertilizer, pesticides, and machinery. For many African and Asian countries, the main source of agricultural supplies is importing. To generate the funds they need to buy agricultural supplies, less developed countries must produce something they can sell in MDCs. In an LDC such as Kenya, families may divide by gender between traditional subsistence agriculture and contributing to international trade. The more land that is devoted to growing export crops, the less that is available to grow crops for domestic consumption. Rather than helping to increase productivity, the funds generated through the sale of export crops may be needed to feed the people who switched from subsistence farming to growing export crops.

Drug Crops. The export crops chosen in some LDCs, especially in Latin America and Asia, are those that can be converted to drugs. The United Nations estimated that in 1998 the incomes of 4 million people, primarily in Asia and Latin America, were dependent on cultivation of the opium poppy or coca leaf.

(335)
Afghanistan is the source of 80 percent of the world's opium; most of the remainder comes from Myanmar (Burma). One half of the world's coca leaf is grown in Columbia, and most of the remainder in neighboring Peru and Bolivia. The overwhelming majority of the marijuana that reaches the United States is grown in Mexico.

Strategies to Increase Food Supply

Four strategies increase the world's food supply:
- Expand the land area used for agriculture
- Increase the productivity of land now used for agriculture
- Identify new food sources
- Increase exports from other countries

Increase Food Supply by Expanding Agricultural Land. Historically, world food production increased primarily by expanding the amount of land devoted to agriculture. Today few scientists believe that further expansion of agricultural land can feed the growing world population. Cultivated land has been expanding in Africa at a rate of 1 percent per year, but population is increasing more than 2 percent per year. Worldwide, despite the recent decline in the natural increase, agricultural land is expanding more slowly than population.

Especially in semiarid regions, human actions are causing land to deteriorate to a desert-like

137

condition, a process called **desertification** (more precisely, semiarid land degradation). The United Nations estimates that desertification removes 27 million hectares (70 million acres) of land from agricultural production each year, an area roughly equivalent to Colorado.

Excessive water threatens other agricultural areas, especially drier lands that receive water from human-built irrigation systems. The United Nations estimates that 10 percent of all irrigated land is waterlogged, mostly in Asia and South America.

As urban areas grow in population and land area, farms on the periphery are replaced by homes, roads, shops, and other urban land uses.

Increasing Productivity. New agricultural practices have permitted farmers worldwide to achieve much greater yields from the same amount of land. (336) The invention and rapid diffusion of more productive agricultural techniques during the 1970s and 1980s is called the **green revolution**. The green revolution involves two main practices: the introduction of new higher-yield seeds and the expanded use of fertilizers. The new high-yield wheat, rice, and maize seeds were diffused rapidly around the world. India's wheat production, for example, more than doubled in five years. Other Asian and Latin American countries recorded similar productivity increases. The green revolution was largely responsible for preventing a food crisis in these regions during the 1970s and 1980s, but will these scientific breakthroughs continue in the twenty-first century?

To take full advantage of the new miracle seeds, farmers must use more fertilizer and machinery. The problem is that the cheapest way to produce nitrogen-based fertilizers is to obtain hydrogen from natural gas or petroleum. As fossil fuel prices increase, so do the prices for nitrogen-based fertilizers, which then become too expensive for many farmers in LDCs. Farmers need tractors, irrigation pumps, and other machinery to make the most effective use of the new miracle seeds. In LDCs, farmers cannot afford such equipment, nor, in view of high energy costs, can they buy fuel to operate the equipment.

Identifying New Food Sources. The third alternative for increasing the world's food supply is to develop new food sources. Three strategies being considered are to cultivate the oceans, to develop higher-protein cereals, and to improve palatability of rarely consumed foods.

Cultivating Oceans. Hope grew during the mid-twentieth century that increased fish consumption could meet the needs of a rapidly growing global population. However the population of some fish species declined because they were harvested faster than they could reproduce. The United Nations estimates that one-quarter of fish stocks have been overfished and one-half fully exploited, leaving only one-fourth underfished.

Developing Higher-protein Cereals. Scientists are experimenting with hybrids of the world's major cereals that have higher protein content. People can also obtain needed nutrition by consuming foods that are fortified during processing with vitamins, minerals, and protein-carrying amino acids. However, fortification has limited application in LDCs, where most people grow their own food rather than buy processed food.

Improving Palatability of Rarely Consumed Foods. A prominent example of an underused food resource in North America is the soybean. Although one of the region's leading crops, most is processed into animal feed, in part because many North Americans avoid consuming tofu, sprouts, and other recognizable products.

(338)
Other products that are made from soybeans but do not look like them are more widely accepted in North America. Krill (small crustaceans) could be an important source of food from the oceans, but unfortunately krill does not taste very good.

Increasing Trade. The fourth alternative for increasing the world's food supply is to export more food from countries that produce surpluses. The three top export grains are wheat, maize (corn), and rice. Few countries are major exporters of food, but increased production in the net-exporting countries could cover the gap elsewhere. The United States remains by far the largest grain exporter, accounting for one-half of global corn exports and one-fourth of wheat. Elsewhere in the world the picture has changed in the twenty-first century. From net importers of grain, South Asia and Southeast Asia have now become net exporters.

Japan is by far the world's leading grain importer, followed by China. On a regional scale, Southwest Asia (with Northern Africa) has become the leading net importer of all three major grains, and Saudi Arabia was the world's leading importer of rice in 2007. Sub-Saharan Africa also ranks among the leaders in net imports of all three grains.

Key Terms

Agribusiness (p.313)
Agriculture (p.309)
Cereal grain (p.323)
Chaff (p.320)
Combine (p.326)
Commercial agriculture (p.311)
Crop (p.309)
Crop rotation (p.321)
Desertification (p.335)
Double cropping (p.321)
Grain (p.325)
Green revolution (p.336)
Horticulture (p.328)
Hull (p.320)
Intensive subsistence agriculture (p.319)
Milkshed (p.324)
Paddy (p.320)
Pastoral nomadism (p.318)
Pasture (p.319)

Plantation (p.322)
Prime agricultural land (p.313)
Ranching (p.326)
Reaper (p.326)
Ridge tillage (p.331)
Sawah (p.320)
Shifting cultivation (p.314)
Slash-and-burn agriculture (p.314)
Spring wheat (p.325)
Subsistence agriculture (p.310)
Sustainable agriculture (p.331)
Swidden (p.315)
Thresh (p.320)
Transhumance (p.319)
Truck farming (p.328)
Wet rice (p.319)
Winnow (p.320)
Winter wheat (p.325)

Test Prep Questions

1) Which of the following was domesticated in the Americas?
A) rice
B) millet
C) corn
D) wheat

2) What region is thought to have been the hearth of the domestication of the largest number of animals useful for agriculture?
A) East Asia
B) Southwest Asia
C) sub-Saharan Africa
D) South America

3) Which of the following was NOT domesticated in the Americas?
A) barley
B) squash
C) beans
D) potatoes

4) Which of the following is NOT one of the principal features that distinguishes commercial agriculture from subsistence agriculture?
A) use of machinery
B) purpose of farming
C) choice of crop
D) farm size

5) What is another term for "shifting cultivation"?
A) sustainable agriculture
B) pastoral nomadism
C) subsistence agriculture
D) slash-and-burn agriculture

6) Which of the following statements about pastoral nomadism/pastoral nomads is FALSE?
A) Today, it is a declining form of agriculture.
B) They consume mostly grain rather than meat.
C) They depend upon animals rather than crops for survival.
D) They raise animals mostly to kill for food.

7) Which of the following is NOT an important plantation crop?
A) wheat
B) rubber
C) sugarcane
D) coffee

8) What type of agriculture typically involves crop rotation?
A) grain farming
B) Mediterranean agriculture
C) mixed crop and livestock farming
D) dairy farming

9) What are the two most important crops in Mediterranean agriculture?
A) citrus and nuts
B) olives and grapes
C) soybeans and corn
D) rice and beans

10) Which of the following is NOT a principal practice that distinguishes sustainable agriculture from conventional agriculture?
A) keeping prices low by reducing costs regardless of environmental impact
B) sensitive land management
C) limited use of chemicals
D) better integration of crops and livestock

Short Essay

1) What features distinguish commercial agriculture from subsistence agriculture?

_____

_____

_____

_____

_____

_____

_____

_____

_____

2) Compare and contrast pastoral nomadism with livestock ranching.

_____

_____

_____

_____

_____

_____

_____

_____

_____

3) Identify the three principal practices that distinguish sustainable agriculture from conventional agriculture and explain how they are sustainable.

_____

_____

_____

_____

_____

_____

Chapter 11
Industry

Key Issues
1. Where is industry distributed?
2. Why are situation factors important?
3. Where are site factors important?
4. Why are location factors changing?

(344)

The title of this chapter, "Industry," refers to the manufacturing of goods in a factory. The word is appropriate, because it also means persistence or diligence in creating value. Industry is much more highly clustered in *space* than is agriculture. Two connections are critical in determining the best location for a factory: *where* the markets for the product are located, and where the resources needed to make the product are located. A generation ago, industry was highly clustered in a handful of MDCs, but industry has diffused to LDCs. Geographers identify the *local diversity* in assets that enable some communities to compete successfully for industries, as well as handicaps that must be overcome to retain older companies.

Key Issue 1. Where Is Industry Distributed?
- **Origin of industry**
- **Industrial regions**

(345)
Origin of Industry
The **Industrial Revolution** was a series of improvements in industrial technology that transformed the process of manufacturing goods. Prior to the Industrial Revolution, industry was geographically dispersed across the landscape, as people made tools and agricultural equipment in their homes or obtained them in the local village. Home-based manufacturing was known as the **cottage industry** system. The term *Industrial Revolution* is somewhat misleading, because it was far more than industrial, and it didn't happen overnight. The Industrial Revolution resulted in new social, economic, and political inventions, not just industrial ones. The root of the Industrial Revolution was technology, involving several inventions that transformed the way in which goods were manufactured and created an unprecedented expansion in productivity, resulting in substantially higher standards of living. The invention most important to the development of factories was the steam engine, patented in 1769 by James Watt. Watt's steam engine could power factories far more efficiently than the watermills, then common in use. Industries impacted by the Industrial Revolution include:

- **Iron:** The first industry to benefit from Watt's steam engine, as it provided a practical way to keep the ovens constantly heated.
- **Coal:** The source of energy to operate the ovens and the steam engine.
- **Transportation:** Critical for diffusing the Industrial Revolution.
- **Textiles:** Transformed from a dispersed cottage industry to a concentrated factory system during the late eighteenth century.

(346)
- **Chemicals:** An industry created to bleach and dye cloth.
- **Food Processing:** Essential to feed the factory workers no longer living on farms.

143

Industrial Regions
Industry is concentrated in three of the nine world regions discussed in chapter 9: Europe, North America, and East Asia. Each of the three accounts for roughly one-fourth of the world's total industrial output. Outside these three regions, the leading industrial producers are Brazil and India.

Europe's Industrial Areas
Numerous industrial areas emerged in Europe, including several clustered in Western Europe centered on western Germany and extending north to the United Kingdom and south to Italy and Spain, and several in Eastern Europe, primarily in the former Soviet Union.

(347)
United Kingdom: Dominated world production of steel and textiles during the nineteenth century. Britain was saddled with what became outmoded and deteriorating factories and support services. The United Kingdom expanded industrial production in the late twentieth century by attracting new high-tech industries that serve the European market. Japanese companies have built more factories in the United Kingdom than in any other European country.

Rhine–Ruhr Valley: Western Europe's most important and most centrally located industrial area. Within the region, industry is dispersed rather than concentrated in one or two cities. This location at the mouth of Europe's most important river has made Rotterdam the world's largest port. Iron and steel manufacturing has concentrated in the Rhine–Ruhr Valley because of proximity to large coalfields. Access to iron and steel production stimulated other heavy-metal industries, such as railroad, machinery, and armaments to locate in the area. The city of Rotterdam, the world's largest port, lies at the mouth of several branches of the Rhine River as it flows into the North Sea.

Mid-Rhine: Western Europe's second most important industrial area. The German portion of the Mid-Rhine region lacks abundant raw materials, but it lies at the center of Europe's most important consumer market. The French portion of the Mid-Rhine region — Alsace and Lorraine — contains Europe's largest iron- ore field and is the production center for two-thirds of France's steel. Tiny Luxembourg is also one of the world's leading steel producers, because the Lorraine iron-ore field extends into the southern part of the country.

Po Basin: Southern Europe's oldest and most important industrial area. The Po Valley contains about two-thirds of Italy's manufacturing in one-fifth of its land area. Modern industrial development in the Po Basin began with establishment of textile manufacturing during the nineteenth century because of two key assets: inexpensive hydroelectricity, and a large labor supply willing to work for relatively low wages.

(348)
Northeastern Spain: Western Europe's fastest growing industrial area in the late twentieth century. Spain's leading industrial area, Catalonia, is centered on the city of Barcelona. The area is the center of Spain's textile industry and the location of its largest motor vehicle plant. Spain's motor-vehicle industry, while foreign-owned, is second largest in Europe, behind Germany's.

Moscow: Russia's oldest industrial area, centered around the country's capital and largest market. Moscow specializes in fabrics and products that require skilled labor.

St. Petersburg: Eastern Europe's second largest city, specializing in shipbuilding and other industries serving Russia's navy and ports in the Baltic Sea.

Volga: Russia's largest petroleum and natural gas fields. Also concentrated in this region are the motor vehicle, oil refining, chemical, and leather and fur industries.

Urals: Contains more than 1,000 types of minerals, the most varied collection found in any mining region in the world. Proximity to these inputs encouraged the Communists to locate iron and steel, chemicals, machinery, and metal fabricating in this area.

Kuznetsk: Russia's most important manufacturing district east of the Ural Mountains. Soviet planners took advantage of the area's coal and iron ore to invest in iron and steel factories there.

Donetsk: In Eastern Ukraine, an area of coal, iron ore, manganese, and natural gas. These assets make this region Eastern Europe's largest producer of iron and steel.

Silesia: Eastern Europe's leading industrial area outside the former Soviet Union. Silesia, which includes southern Poland and the northern Czech Republic, is an important steel production center, near coalfields.

North America's Industrial Areas

Industry arrived a bit later in the United States than in Europe, but it grew much faster. The first U.S. textile mill was opened in Pawtucket, Rhode Island, in 1791. The textile industry grew rapidly after 1808, when the U.S. government imposed an embargo on European trade to avoid entanglement in the Napoleonic Wars. The United States had become a major industrial nation by 1860, second only to the United Kingdom. Manufacturing in North America concentrated in the northeastern quadrant of the United States and in southeastern Canada. This manufacturing belt has achieved its dominance through a combination of historical and environmental factors. Early settlement gave eastern cities an advantage to become the country's dominant industrial center. The Northeast also had essential raw materials and good transportation. The Great Lakes and major rivers were supplemented in the 1800s by canals, railways, and highways. Within the North American manufacturing belt, several heavily industrialized areas developed:

New England: The oldest industrial area in the northeastern United States. It developed a textile industry in the early nineteenth century, importing cotton from southern states and shipping finished products to Europe.

Middle Atlantic: The largest U.S. market, it attracts industries that need proximity to a large number of consumers and that depend on foreign trade through one of this region's large ports.

Mohawk Valley: A linear industrial belt developed in upper New York State along the Hudson River and Erie Canal. Inexpensive, abundant electricity generated at nearby Niagara Falls has attracted aluminum, paper, and electrochemical industries to the region.

Pittsburgh–Lake Erie: The leading steel-producing area in the nineteenth century because of proximity to Appalachian coal and iron ore. Proximity to steelmakers attracted other manufacturers that made heavy use of steel in their own products.

Western Great Lakes: Centered on Chicago, the hub of the nation's transportation network, now the center of steel production. Automobile manufacturers and other industries locate in the western Great Lakes region to take advantage of this convergence of transportation routes.

Southern California: The leading industrial area outside of the Northeast. Los Angeles has become the country's largest area of clothing and textile production, the second-largest furniture producer, and a major food processing center. Immigrants from Latin America and Asia provide a large pool of low-wage workers.

Southeastern Ontario: Canada's most important industrial area, central to the Canadian and U.S. markets and near the Great Lakes and Niagara Falls. Inexpensive electricity has attracted aluminum manufacturing, paper making, flour mills, textile manufacturing, and sugar refining.

East Asia's Industrial Areas

Faced with isolation from world markets and a shortage of nearly all essential resources, East Asia has taken advantage of its most abundant resource: people. The region's two leading industrial countries — Japan and China — rank second and third in manufacturing value behind the United States.

Japan: Became an industrial power in the 1950s and 1960s, initially by producing goods in large quantity at cut-rate prices to consumers in other countries. Prices were kept low, despite high shipping costs, because workers received much lower wages than in Japan than in North America or Europe. Japan started training workers for highly skilled jobs, and "Made in Japan" now stands for high-quality motor vehicles, electronics, and precision instruments. Japan's manufacturing is concentrated in the central region between Tokyo and Nagasaki.

China: The world's largest supply of low-cost labor and the largest market for many consumer products. Policy changes in the 1990s opened China's market and labor force to transnational corporations. Rapid economic expansion put money in the pockets of enough of China's 1.3 billion people to encourage more manufacturing for domestic consumption. China's manufacturers have clustered in three areas along the east coast. Large and increasing gaps in wealth within China have been produced.

(350)

Key Issue 2. Why Are Situation Factors Important?
- **Proximity to inputs**
- **Proximity to markets**
- **Ship, rail, truck, or air?**

Having looked at the "where" question for industrial location, we can next consider the "why" question: Why are industries located where they are? Geographers try to explain why one location may prove more profitable for a factory than other locations.

Industry seeks to maximize profits by minimizing production costs. A company ordinarily faces two geographical costs: situation and site. **Situation factors** involve transporting materials to and from a factory. A firm seeks a location that minimizes the cost of transporting inputs to the factory and finished goods to the consumers.

Proximity to Inputs
The farther something is transported, the higher the cost, so a manufacturer tries to locate its factory as close as possible to both buyers and sellers.

- The optimal plant location is as close as possible to inputs if the cost of transporting raw materials to the factory exceeds the cost of transporting the product to consumers.
- The optimal plant location is as close as possible to the customer if the cost of transporting the product exceeds the cost of transporting inputs.

Every industry uses inputs — resources from the environment or parts made by other companies. An industry in which the inputs weigh more than the final product is a **bulk-reducing industry**. To minimize transport costs, these industries need to locate near the sources of inputs.

Copper: A Bulk-Reducing Industry
Copper production involves several steps. The first three steps provide good examples of bulk-reducing activities. The fourth step is not bulk reducing, so does not need to be near inputs.

1. Mining. The heavy, bulky ore extracted from the mines is mostly waste. Copper ore mined in North America is especially low-grade, less than .07 copper.
2. Concentration. Concentration mills crush the ore into fine particles, mix them with water and chemicals, and filter and dry them to produce copper concentrate, which is 25 percent copper.
3. Smelting. Smelters remove more impurities to make the copper 60-99 percent pure and are built near the concentration mills.
4. Refining. Purified copper produced by smelters is treated at refineries to produce 99.99 percent pure copper. Little further weight loss occurs, so proximity to mines, mills, and smelters is a less critical factor in determining location.

In general, metal processors such as the copper industry also try to locate near economical electrical sources and to negotiate favorable rates from power companies. Two-thirds of U.S. copper is mined in Arizona, so the state has most of the concentration mills and smelters. Most foundries are located near markets on the east and west coasts.

Steel: Changing Importance of Inputs
Steel is an alloy of iron that is manufactured by removing impurities in iron, such as silicon, phosphorus, sulfur, and oxygen, and adding desirable elements, such as manganese and chromium.

(351)
The two principal inputs in steel production are iron ore and coal. Steelmaking is a bulk-reducing industry that has located to minimize the transporting of these inputs. Steelmaking demonstrates that when the source of inputs or the relative importance of inputs changes, the optimal location for the industry changes. In the U.S., the distribution of steel production has changed several times because of changing inputs.

- **Mid-nineteenth century:** The U.S. steel industry concentrated around Pittsburgh in southwestern Pennsylvania, where iron ore and coal were both mined.
- **Late-nineteenth century:** Steel mills were built around Lake Erie. The location shift was largely influenced by the discovery of rich iron ore in the Mesabi Range, in northern Minnesota. Ore was transported via the Great Lakes and coal was shipped from Appalachia by train.
- **Early-twentieth century:** Most new steel mills were located near the southern end of Lake Michigan — Gary, Indiana, Chicago, and other communities. Changes in steelmaking required more iron in proportion to coal, so mills were built closer to the Mesabi Range.

• **Mid-twentieth century:** Most new U.S. steel mills were located near the East and West coasts. Iron ore increasingly came from other countries. Further, scrap iron and steel — widely available in the large metropolitan areas of the East and West coasts — became an important input in the steel-production process.

• **Late-twentieth century:** Most steel mills in the U.S. closed. Most of the survivors were around southern Lake Michigan and along the East Coast.

(352)
Proximity to Markets
The cost of transporting goods to consumers is a critical location factor for three types of industries: bulk-gaining, single-market, and perishable.

Bulk-Gaining Industries
A **bulk-gaining industry** makes something that gains volume or weight during production. To minimize transport costs, a bulk-gaining industry needs to locate near where the product is sold.

Fabricated Metals. A prominent example of a bulk-gaining industry is the fabrication of parts and machinery from steel and other metals.

Common fabricated products include televisions, refrigerators, and air conditioners. Machinery is fabricated for use in farms, factories, offices, and homes. Fabricators shape individual pieces of metal. Separate parts are joined together through welding, bonding, and fastening with bolts and rivets.

Because fabricated products typically occupy a larger volume than the sum of their individual parts, the cost of shipping the final product to consumers is usually the most critical factor.

Motor vehicles are fabricated in the U.S. at about 40 assembly plants from parts made at several thousand other plants. The critical location factor is minimizing transportation to the market.

Beverage Production. Beverage bottling is another good example of an industry that adds bulk. The principle input placed in a beverage container is water, which is relatively bulky, heavy, and expensive to transport. Because water is available where people live, bottlers can minimize costs by producing soft drinks near their consumers instead of shipping water (their heaviest input) long distances.

(354)
Single-Market Manufacturers
Single-market manufacturers are specialized manufacturers with only one or two customers. The optimal location for these factories is often proximity to the customer. An example of a single-market manufacturer is a producer of parts for motor vehicles. Parts makers now ship most of their products directly to assembly plants clustered in "auto alley." Proximity to the assembly plant is increasingly important because of the adoption of "just-in-time" delivery, where parts are delivered just in time to be used, often within minutes, rather than weeks or months in advance. The seat, for example, is an especially large and bulky object, and carmakers do not want to waste valuable space in their assembly plants by piling up an inventory of them. On the other hand, many parts do not need to be manufactured close to the customer, and for them changing site factors are more important.

Perishable Products
To deliver their products to consumers as rapidly as possible, perishable product industries must be

located near their markets. Processors of fresh food into frozen, canned, and preserved products can locate far from their customers. The daily newspaper is an example of a product other than food that is highly perishable because it contains dated information. Newspaper publishers must locate near markets to minimize transportation cost.

(355)
Difficulty with timely delivery is one of the main factors in the decline of newspapers. Electronic devices can deliver news more quickly than a newspaper.

Ship, Rail, Truck, or Air?
Firms seek the lowest-cost mode of transport, but the cheapest of the four alternatives changes with the distance that goods are being sent. The farther something is transported, the lower is the cost per kilometer (or mile). The cost per kilometer decreases at different rates for each of the four modes, because the loading and unloading expenses differ for each mode.

• **Trucks.** Most often used for short-distance delivery.
• **Trains.** Often used to ship to destinations that take longer than a day to reach, such as between the east and west coasts of the United States.
• **Ships.** Attractive for very long distances because the cost per kilometer is very low.
• **Air.** Most expensive for all distances, so is usually reserved for speedy delivery of small-bulk, high-value packages.

Modes of delivery are often mixed. Containerization has facilitated transfer of all packages between modes. Regardless of transportation mode, cost rises each time that inputs or products are transferred from one mode to another. Many companies that use multiple transport modes locate at a **break-of-bulk point,** a location where transfer among transportation modes is possible. Important break-of-bulk points include seaports and airports.

(356)
Key Issue 3. Why are Site Factors Important?
  • **Labor**
  • **Land**
  • **Capital**

Labor
Worldwide, around one-half billion people are engaged in industry. China has around one-fourth of all the world's manufacturing workers, India around one-fifth, and all MDCs combines around one-fifth.

Labor-Intensive Industries
A **labor-intensive industry** is one in which wages and other compensation paid to an employee constitute a high percentage of expenses. The reverse case, an industry with a much lower than average percentage of expenditures on labor, is considered capital intensive. The average wage paid to manufacturing workers exceeds $20 per hour in North America, Western Europe, and other MDCs and other benefits add substantially to the compensation. In LDCs, average wages are less than $5 per hour and include limited additional benefits. A labor-intensive industry is not the same as a high-wage industry. "Labor-intensive" is measured as a percentage, whereas "high-wage" is measured in currencies.

Textiles: Labor-Intensive
Production of apparel and **textiles**, which are woven fabrics, is a prominent example of an industry that generally requires less-skilled, low-cost workers. Spinning, weaving, and cutting and sewing are all labor intensive compared to other industries, but the importance of labor varies somewhat among them. Their global distributions are not identical because the three steps are not equally labor-intensive.

Textile and Apparel Spinning. The principal natural fiber is cotton, but synthetics account for three-fourths of the world thread production. (357) Because it is still a labor intensive industry, spinning is done primarily in low-wage countries. Synthetic fibers include regenerated synthetics, produced from natural raw materials, (rayon was the first commercially successful regenerated synthetic) and true synthetics, produced from materials like petrochemicals that do not naturally form fibers. Nylon was the first true synthetic fiber but polyester is now the leading true synthetic.

(358)
Textile and Apparel Weaving. For thousands of years, fabric has been woven or laced together by hand on a loom. As the process of weaving was physically hard work, weavers were traditionally men. For mechanized weaving, labor constitutes a high percentage of total production cost. Consequently, weaving is especially highly clustered in low-wage countries.

(359)
Textile and Apparel Assembly. Sewing is probably an even older human activity than spinning or weaving. The first functional sewing machine was invented by a French tailor, Barthelemy Thimonnier in 1830. Textiles are assembled into for main types of products — garments, carpets, home products, and industrial materials. MDCs play a larger role in assembly than in spinning and weaving because most consumers of assembled products are located in MDCs.

(360)
Land
Land suitable for constructing a factory can be found in many places, but if considered to encompass natural and human resources in addition to *terra firma,* "land" is a critical site factor.

Rural Sites
Early factories located inside cities due to a combination of situation and site factors. A city offered an attractive situation — proximity to a large local market and convenience in shipping to a national market by rail. A city also offered an attractive site — proximity to labor and sources of capital. To get the necessary space, early factories were multi-storied. Contemporary factories operate more efficiently as one-story buildings, and land is more likely to be available in suburban or rural locations. With trucks responsible for transporting inputs and products, proximity to major highways is more important for a factory.

Environmental Factors
Not every location has the same climate, topography, recreational opportunities, cultural facilities, and cost of living. Prior to the Industrial Revolution, many economic activities were located near rivers and close to forests, because running water and burning of wood were the two most important sources of energy. When coal became dominant in the late eighteenth century, industry began to concentrate in fewer locations. In the twentieth century, electricity became an important source of energy for industry. Although large industrial users usually pay a lower rate than do home consumers, industries with a

particularly high demand for energy may select a location with lower electrical rates. The aluminum industry, for example, requires a large amount of electricity. Aluminum plants have been built near dams to take advantage of the large amount of cheap hydroelectricity. (361)

A subsidiary of Alcoa even owns dams that generate power along the Cheoah, Little Tennessee, and Yadkin rivers in eastern Tennessee and western North Carolina.

Capital

The U.S. motor vehicle industry concentrated in Michigan early in the twentieth century largely because this region's financial institutions were more willing than eastern banks to lend money to the industry's pioneers. The most important factor in the clustering of high-tech industries in California's Silicon Valley — even more important than proximity to skilled labor—was the availability of capital. One-fourth of all capital in the United States is spent on new industries in the Silicon Valley. Financial institutions in many LDCs are short of funds, so new industries must seek loans from banks in MDCs. But enterprises may not get loans if they are located in a country that is perceived to have an unstable political system, a high debt level, or ill-advised economic policies.

Key Issue 4.   Why Are Location Factors Changing?
  • **Attraction of new industrial regions**
  • **Renewed attraction of traditional industrial regions**

Changing site factors have been especially important in stimulating industrial growth in new regions, internationally and within MDCs. At the same time, some industries remain in the traditional industrial regions, primarily because of changing situation factors.

Attraction of New Industrial Regions
Labor is the site factor that is changing especially dramatically in the twenty-first century.

Changing Industrial Distribution within MDCs
In the United States, industry has shifted from the Northeast toward the south and west. In Europe, government policies have encouraged relocation toward economically distressed peripheral areas.

(362)
Interregional Shift in the United States
The northeastern United States has lost 6 million jobs in manufacturing between 1950 and 2009. Meanwhile, 2 million manufacturing jobs were added in the South and West. Industrialization during the late nineteenth and early twentieth centuries largely bypassed the South, which had not recovered from losing the Civil War. As a result, the South was the poorest region of the United States. Industrial growth in the South since the 1930s has been stimulated in part by government policies to reduce historical disparities. The Tennessee Valley Authority brought electricity to much of the rural South.

Right-to-work Laws. The principal lure for many manufacturers was enactment by southern states of **right-to-work laws**. By enacting right-to-work laws, Southern states made it much more difficult for unions to organize factory workers, collect dues, and bargain with employers from a position of strength. Steel, textiles, tobacco products, and furniture industries have become dispersed through smaller communities in the South, many in search of a labor force willing to work for less money than in the North and willing to forgo joining a union.

Textile Production. The textile and apparel industry has been especially prominent in opening production in lower-wage locations while shutting production in higher-wage locations. The U.S. textile and apparel industry was heavily concentrated in the Northeast during the early twentieth century, then shifted to the South and West. Wage rates were much lower in the Southeast.

(363)
Southeastern mills were able to reach markets easily after the opening of the interstate highway system beginning in the in the 1950s.

Interregional Shifts in Europe. Manufacturing has diffused from traditional industrial centers in northwestern Europe toward southern and eastern Europe. European government policies have explicitly encouraged the industrial relocation. The European Union provides assistance to what it calls convergence regions and competitive and employment regions:

- **Convergence Regions:** Primarily Eastern and Southern Europe, where incomes lag behind Europe's average.
- **Competitive and Employment Regions:** Primarily Western Europe's traditional core industrial areas, which have experienced substantial manufacturing job losses in recent years.

The Western European country with the most rapid manufacturing growth rate since the late twentieth century has been Spain, especially since its admission to the European Union in 1986. Poland, Czech Republic, and Hungary have had the most industrial development East of Germany and West of Russia, though other countries in the region have shared in the growth. The region prefers to be called Central Europe, to signify its more central location in Europe's changing economy. Central Europe offers manufacturers labor and market proximity. Central European workers are less skilled but much cheaper than in Western Europe, more expensive but much more skilled than in Asia and Latin America. The region offers closer proximity to the wealthy markets of Western Europe.

International Shifts in Industry
Increasingly important industrial areas outside of North America and Europe include:

- **East Asia.** Rapid industrial growth in China means East Asia likely will account for an increasing share in World industrial production. South Korea is the world's leading producer of large container ships. (364) South Korea is a leading producer of steel and fabricated metal products, including motor vehicles.
- **South Asia.** Led by India, one of the fastest growing economies among large countries. Textiles are the dominant industry but motor vehicle production is growing rapidly.
- **Latin America.** The nearest low-wage region to the United States. *Maquiladora* plants have located in Mexico's far north to be as close as possible to the United States. Brazil is the leading industrial country in Latin America, although its industries serve primarily the domestic market, the region's largest.

Changing Distributions. The shift to new industrial regions can be seen clearly in steel and clothing. In 1980, 80 percent of world steel was produced in MDCs, but by 2008 its share of production declined to 40 percent.

(365)
China, now the world's largest steel producer, accounted for 38 percent of world steel output

in 2008, nearly as much as all MDCs combined. Labor-intensive industries have been especially attracted to LDCs. The number of apparel workers in the U.S. declined from 900,000 in 1990 to 150,000 in 2009. Mills in the Southeast have been unable to compete with manufacturers in countries paying less than $1 per hour. European countries have been even harder hit by international competition, as manufacturing wages exceed $30 per hour in much of Europe.

Outsourcing. Transnational corporations have been especially aggressive in using low-cost labor in LDCs. Despite greater transportation costs, transnational corporations can profitably transfer some work to LDCs, given the substantial difference in wages between LDCs and MDCs. Operations that require highly skilled workers remain in MDCs. This selective transfer of some jobs to LDCs is known as the **new international division of labor**. Transnational corporations allocate production to low-wage countries through **outsourcing**, which is turning over much of the responsibility for production to independent suppliers. Outsourcing contrasts with the approach typical of traditional mass production, called vertical integration, in which a company would control all phases of a highly complex production process.

(366)
Outsourcing has had a major impact on the distribution of manufacturing, because each step in the production process is now scrutinized closely in order to determine the optimal location.

Renewed Attraction of Traditional Industrial Regions
Two location factors influence industries to remain in traditional regions — availability of skilled labor and rapid delivery to market.

Proximity to Skilled Labor
Henry Ford boasted that he could take people off the street and put them to work with only a few minutes of training. That has changed for many industries, which now want skilled workers. The search for skilled labor has important geographic implications because it is an asset found principally in the traditional industrial regions. Computer manufacturing is an example of an industry that has concentrated in relatively high-wage, high-skilled regions of the United States, especially near universities in the Bay Area of California and Austin, Texas. Even the clothing industry has not completely abandoned the Northeast. Dresses, woolens, and other "high-end" clothing products require more skill in cutting and assembling the material.

Traditionally, factories assigned each worker one specific task to perform repeatedly. Some geographers call this approach **Fordist** or mass production, because the Ford Motor Company was one of the first to organize its production this way. (368) The term **post-Fordist** production is sometimes used to describe lean or flexible production. Three types of work rules distinguish post-Fordist lean production: 1. Teams; 2. Problem Solving; and 3. Leveling.

Just-in-Time Delivery
Proximity to market has become even more important in recent years because of the rise of just-in-time delivery. Just-in-time delivery reduces the money that a manufacturer must tie up in inventory. Leading computer manufacturers have eliminated inventory altogether. In some cases, though, just-in-time delivery merely shifts the burden of maintaining inventory to suppliers.

Wal-Mart, for example, holds low inventories but tells its suppliers to hold high inventories.

Just-in-time delivery means that producers have less inventory to cushion against disruptions in the arrival of needed parts.

Two kinds of disruptions can result from reliance on just-in-time delivery:
- **Labor unrest.** A strike at one supplier or in the logistics can shut down the entire production.
- **"Acts of God."** Most common are weather-related incidents, such as blizzards or floods.

Key Terms

Break-of-bulk point (p. 355)
Bulk-gaining industry (p. 352)
Bulk-reducing industry (p. 350)
Cottage industry (p. 345)
Fordist production (p. 368)
Industrial Revolution (p. 345)
Labor-intensive industry (p. 356)
Maquiladora (p. 344)
New international division of labor (p. 365)

Outsourcing (p. 365)
Post-Fordist (p. 368)
Right-to-work state (p. 362)
Site factors (p. 356)
Situation factors (p. 350)
Textile (p. 356)

Test Prep Questions

1) What invention was most important for the development of factories?
A) the loom
B) the watermill
C) the incandescent light bulb
D) the steam engine

2) Which of the following was NOT an industry impacted in the early part of the Industrial Revolution?
A) plastics
B) transportation
C) textiles
D) coal

3) Which of the following is NOT one of the world regions where industry is concentrated?
A) Europe
B) North America
C) Latin America
D) East Asia

4) Which of the following is NOT one of Europe's main industrial regions?
A) Rhine-Ruhr Valley
B) France's Loire Valley
C) Italy's Po Basin
D) Moscow

5) Which step in copper production is NOT bulk-reducing?
A) mining
B) concentration
C) refining
D) smelting

6) What is a good example of a bulk-gaining industry?
A) beverage bottling
B) meat packing
C) advertising
D) trucking

7) What mode of transportation has the lowest cost per kilometer or mile?
A) ship
B) train
C) air
D) truck

8) Which of the following is NOT a traditional site factor?
A) capital
B) land
C) labor
D) language

9) Which site factor is most responsible for the dramatic change in industrial locations that has taken place in the twenty-first century?
A) capital
B) land
C) labor
D) language

10) Which of the following is NOT a work rule of post-Fordist production?
A) rigidity
B) teamwork
C) problem solving
D) leveling

Short Essay

1) Describe the geographic distribution of industrial regions across the Earth.

_____

_____

_____

_____

_____

_____

_____

_____

_____

_____

2) Identify the three types of industries for which proximity to markets is a critical locational factor, and give examples of each.

_____

_____

_____

_____

_____

_____

_____

_____

3) Contrast interregional shifts in location of industry between the United States and Europe in the late twentieth and early twenty-first centuries.

_____

_____

_____

_____

_____

_____

_____

_____

_____

Chapter 12
Services

Key Issues
1. Where did services originate?
2. Why are contemporary services located?
3. Why are consumer services distributed in a regular pattern?
4. Why do business services cluster in large settlements?

(374)

A **service** is any activity that fulfills a human want or need and returns money to those who provide it. In sorting out where services are distributed in space, geographers see a close link between services and settlements, because services are located in settlements. A **settlement** is a permanent collection of buildings, where people reside, work, and obtain services. They occupy a very small percentage of Earth's surface, well under 1 percent, but settlements are home to nearly all humans, because few people live in isolation. The optimal location of industry, described in the last chapter, requires balancing a number of site and situation factors, but the optimal location for a service is simply near its customers. On the other hand, locating a service calls for far more precise geographic skills than locating a factory. The optimal location for a service may be a very specific place, such as a street corner. Within MDCs, larger cities offer a larger scale of services than do small towns, because more customers reside there. As they do for other economic and cultural features, geographers observe trends toward both globalization and local diversity in the distribution of services.

(375)
Key Issue 1. Where Did Services Originate?
- **Three types of services**
- **Services in early rural settlements**
- **Services in early urban settlements**

Services are provided in all societies, but in MDCs a majority of workers are engaged in the provision of services. In North America, three-fourths of workers are in services. The percentage varies widely in LDCs but is typically less than one-fourth.

Three Types of Services
The service sector of the economy is subdivided into three types: consumer services, business services, and public services. Each of these sectors is divided into several major subsections.

Consumer Services
Nearly one-half of all jobs in the United States are in **consumer services**. Four main types are retail, education, health, and leisure.

- **Retail and Wholesale Services**. About 15 percent of all U.S. jobs. Department stores, grocers, and motor vehicle sales and service account for nearly one half of these jobs; another one-fourth are wholesalers who provide merchandise to retailers.

- **Education Services.** About 10 percent of all jobs in the U.S. jobs. Two-thirds of educators are employed in public schools, one-third in private.

- **Health Services.** About 12 percent of all U.S. jobs in the U.S., primarily hospitals, doctors'

157

offices, and nursing homes.

- **Leisure and Hospitality Services.** About 10 percent of all U.S. jobs. Around 70 percent of these are in restaurants and bars; the other 30 percent is evenly divided between lodging and entertainment.

Business Services
Business services facilitate other businesses. Around 24 percent of all jobs in the U.S. are in the three types of business services: professional services, financial services, and transportation.

(376)

- **Financial Services.** About 6 percent of all U.S. jobs, often called "FIRE," an acronym for finance, insurance, and real estate.

- **Professional Services.** About 12 percent of all U.S. jobs. One-half is in technical services, and one-half in support services.

- **Transportation and Information Services.** About 6 percent of all U.S. jobs. One-half in transportation and one-half in information, as well as utilities such as water and electricity.

Public Services
The purpose of **public services** is to provide security and protection for citizens and businesses. About 17 percent of all U.S. jobs are in the public sector, 9 percent of public school employees are counted under education (consumer) services. One-fourth of public-sector employees work for the federal government, one-fourth for one of the state governments, and one-half for one of the local governments.

Changes in Number of Employees
Between 1972 and 2009, all of the growth in employment in the United States has been in services. Employment grew more rapidly in some services than in others. Business services expanded in professional services. Financial and transportation grew more slowly because of improved efficiency. In consumer services, health care had the most rapid increase. Recreation and entertainment also had large increases. Retailing did not increase. More stores opened with fewer employees.

Services in Early Rural Settlements
Before the establishment of permanent settlements as service centers, people lived as nomads, migrating in small groups across the landscape in search of food and water. No one knows the precise sequence of events through which settlements were established to provide services. Based on archaeological research, settlements probably originated to provide consumer and public services. Business services came later.

Early Consumer Services
The early permanent settlements may have been established to offer consumer services, specifically places to bury the dead. Having established a permanent resting place for the dead, the group might then install priests at the site to perform the service of saying prayers for the deceased. This would have encouraged the building of structures — places for ceremonies and dwellings.

(378)
Until the invention of skyscrapers in the late nineteenth century, religious buildings were often the tallest structures in a community. Settlements also may have been places to house families, permitting unburdened males to travel farther and faster in their search for food. Women kept "home

and hearth," making household objects, such as pots, tools, and clothing as well as educating the children. These household-based services evolved over thousands of years into institutions that create and store a group's values and heritage and transmit them from one generation to the next. People also needed tools, clothing, shelter, containers, fuel, and other material goods. Men gathered the materials. Women used these materials to manufacture household objects and maintain their dwellings. The variety of consumer services expanded as people began to specialize. Settlements took on a retail-service function.

Early Public Services

Public services probably followed the religious activities into early permanent settlements. The group's political leaders also chose to live permanently in the settlement. The settlement likely was a good base from which the group could defend nearby food sources against competitors. For defense, the group might surround the settlement with a wall. Thus, settlements became citadels.

Early Business Services

Everyone in settlements needed food, which was supplied by the group through hunting or gathering. People brought objects and materials they collected or produced into the settlement and exchanged them for items brought by others. The settlement served as neutral ground where several groups could safely come together to trade goods and services. To facilitate this trade, officials in the settlement provided producer services, such as regulating the terms of transactions.

Services in Early Urban Settlements

Urban settlements date from the beginning of documented history in the Middle East and Asia. A handful of urban settlements provided business and public services, as well as some consumer services with large market areas. Virtually all settlements were rural, because the economy was based on the agriculture of the surrounding fields.

Services in Ancient Cities

Urban settlements may have originated in Mesopotamia and diffused at an early date to Egypt, China, and South Asia's Indus Valley. Or they may have originated independently in each of the four hearths.

Earliest Urban Settlements. Among the oldest well-documented urban settlements is Ur in Mesopotamia (present-day Iraq). Archaeologists have unearthed ruins in Ur that date from approximately 3000 B.C. Ancient Ur was compact, perhaps covering 100 hectares (250 acres), and was surrounded by a wall. The most prominent structure was a temple, known as a ziggurat. Surrounding the ziggurat were residential areas containing a dense network of narrow, winding streets and courtyards. Titris Hoyuk, in present-day Turkey, occupied a 50-hectare (125-acre) site and apparently had a population of about 10,000. Recent evidence unearthed from about 2500 B.C. suggests that early urban settlements were well-planned communities. Houses varied in size but were of similar design. Houses were apparently occupied by an extended family, because they contained several cooking areas.

Ancient Athens. Settlements were first established in the eastern Mediterranean about 2500 B.C., trading centers for the thousands of islands dotting the Aegean Sea and the eastern Mediterranean.

(379)

The settlement provided the government, military protection, and other public services for the surrounding hinterland. They were organized into **city-states**. Athens, the largest city-state in ancient Greece, was probably the first city to attain a population of 100,000.

Ancient Rome. The rise of the Roman Empire encouraged urban settlement. Settlements were established as centers of administrative, military, and other public services, as well as retail and other consumer services. The city of Rome — the empire's center for administration, commerce, culture, and all other services — grew to at least 250,000 inhabitants, although some claim that the population may have reached a million. With the fall of the Roman Empire in the fifth century A.D., urban settlements declined and trade diminished. Large urban settlements shrank or were abandoned. For several hundred years, Europe's cultural heritage was preserved largely in monasteries and isolated rural areas.

Services in Medieval Cities

Urban life began to revive in Europe in the eleventh century as feudal lords established new urban settlements. They gave residents charters of rights to establish independent cities in exchange for their military service.

(381)

By the fourteenth century, Europe was covered by a dense network of small market towns serving the needs of particular lords. The largest medieval European urban settlements served as power centers for the lords and church leaders, as well as major market centers. European urban settlements were usually surrounded by walls in medieval times. Dense and compact within the walls, medieval urban settlements lacked space for construction, so ordinary shops and houses nestled into the side of the walls and large buildings. Most of the world's largest cities were in Asia, not Europe, however, from the collapse of the Roman Empire until the diffusion of the Industrial Revolution across Europe during the nineteenth century. Beijing (China) competed with Constantinople as the world's most populous city for several hundred years, until London claimed the distinction during the early 1800s.

Key Issue 2. Where Are Contemporary Services Located?
- **Services in rural settlements**
- **Services in urban settlements**

Services are clustered in settlements. Rural settlements are centers for agriculture and provide a small number of services; urban settlements are centers for consumer and business services. One half of the people in the world currently live in a rural settlement, and the other half in an urban settlement.

Services in Rural Settlements

A **clustered rural settlement** is a place where a number of families live in close proximity to each other, with fields surrounding the collection of houses and farm buildings. A **dispersed rural settlement**, typical of the North American rural landscape, is characterized by farmers living on individual farms.

Clustered Rural Settlements

A clustered rural settlement typically includes homes, barns, tool sheds, and other farm structures, plus personal services, such as religious structures and schools. In common language such a settlement is called a hamlet or village.

(382)

The fields must be accessible to the farmers and are thus generally limited to a radius of 1 or 2 kilometers (one-half to 1 mile) from the buildings. In some places, individual farmers own or rent the land; in other places, the land is owned collectively by the settlement or by a lord. Farmers typically have responsibility for scattered parcels in several fields. This pattern encouraged living in a clustered rural settlement to minimize travel time to the various fields. Traditionally, when the population of a settlement grew too large for the capacity of the surrounding fields, new settlements were established nearby. Clustered rural settlements are often arranged in one of two types of patterns: circular and linear.

Circular Rural Settlements. These comprise a central open space surrounded by structures. Examples include:
- Kraal villages in southern Africa, which have enclosures for livestock in the center, surrounded by a ring of houses.
- Gewandorf settlements, once found in rural Germany, consisted of a core of houses, barns, and churches, encircled by different types of agricultural activities.

(383)
Linear Rural Settlements. These comprise buildings clustered along a road, river, or dike to facilitate communications. The fields extend behind the buildings in long, narrow strips. Long lot farms can be seen today along the St. Lawrence River in Québec. In the French long-lot system, houses were erected along a river. Narrow lots from 5 to 1000 kilometers deep were established perpendicular to the river so that each original settler had river access.

Clustered Settlements in Colonial America
New England colonists built clustered settlements centered on an open area called a common. Clustered settlements were favored by New England colonists for several reasons:

- They typically traveled to the New World in a group. The settlement was usually built near the center of the land grant.
- The colonists wanted to live close together to reinforce common cultural and religious values.
- They clustered their settlements for defense against Indian attacks.

Each villager owned several discontinuous parcels on the periphery of the settlement, to provide the variety of land types needed for different crops. Beyond the fields the town held pastures and woodland for the common use of all residents. The contemporary New England landscape contains remnants of the old clustered rural settlement pattern; many towns still have a central common surrounded by the church, school, and various houses, but today's residents work in shops and offices rather than on farms.

(384)
Dispersed Rural Settlements
Outside of New England, dispersed rural settlements were more common in the American colonies. With the introduction of farm machinery, farms operated more efficiently at a larger scale.

Dispersed Rural Settlements in the United States. The Middle Atlantic colonies were settled by a more heterogeneous group of people than those in New England. Further, most Middle Atlantic colonists came individually rather than as a cohesive religious group. Dispersed settlement patterns dominated in the American Midwest in part because the early settlers came primarily from the Middle Atlantic colonies. In New England, a dispersed distribution began to replace the clustered settlements in the eighteenth century. Eventually people bought, sold, and exchanged land to create large, continuous holdings instead of several isolated pieces. A shortage of land eventually forced immigrants and children to strike out alone and claim farmland on the frontier. In addition, the cultural bonds that had created clustered rural settlements had weakened.

Dispersed Rural Settlements in Great Britain. To improve agricultural production, a number of European countries converted their rural landscapes from clustered settlements to dispersed patterns. A prominent example was the **enclosure movement** in Great Britain, between 1750 and 1850. Because the enclosure movement coincided with the Industrial Revolution, villagers who were displaced from farming moved to urban settlements and became workers in factories and services. The enclosure movement brought greater agricultural efficiency, but it destroyed the self-contained world of village life.

Services in Urban Settlements

The population of urban settlements exceeded that of rural settlements for the first time in human history in 2008. The percentage of people living in urban settlements had increased from 3 percent in 1800 to 30 percent in 1950, and 47 percent in 2000.

Differences Between Urban and Rural Settlements

Louis Wirth argued in the 1930s that an urban dweller follows a different way of life than does a rural dweller, and he defined a city as a permanent settlement that has three characteristics — large size, high population density, and socially heterogeneous people.

(385)

Large Size. If you live in a rural settlement, you know most of the other inhabitants and may even be related to many of them. In contrast, if you live in an urban settlement, you can know only a small percentage of the other residents. Most of these relationships are contractual; consequently, the large size produces different social relationships than those formed in rural settlements.

High Density. Each person in an urban settlement plays a special role or performs a specific task to allow the complex urban system to function smoothly. High density encourages people to compete for survival in limited space.

Social Heterogeneity. A person has greater freedom in an urban settlement to pursue an unusual profession, sexual orientation, or cultural interest. In a rural settlement, unusual actions might be noticed and scorned, but urban residents are more tolerant of diverse social behavior.

In MDCs, social distinctions between urban and rural residents have blurred. According to Wirth's definition, nearly everyone in an MDC is urban.

Increasing Percentage of People in Cities

The process by which the population of urban settlements grows, known as **urbanization**, has two dimensions — an increase in the number of people living in cities and an increase in the percentage of people living in cities. The distinction is important because they occur for different reasons and have different global distributions. A large percentage of people living in urban settlements reflects a country's level of development.

(386)

The percentage of urban dwellers is high in MDCs because over the past 200 years rural residents have migrated from the countryside to work in the factories and services concentrated in cities. Because the percentage living in urban areas simply cannot increase much more in MDCs, the process of urbanization has largely ended.

Increasing Number of People in Cities

MDCs have a higher percentage of urban residents but LDCs have more of the very large urban settlements.

(387)

Eight of the ten most populous cities are currently in LDCs. In LDCs, migration from the countryside is fueling half the increase in population in urban settlements, even though job opportunities may not be available.

Key Issue 3.   Why Are Consumer Services Distributed in a Regular Pattern?
- **Central place theory**
- **Market-area analysis**
- **Hierarchy of services and settlements**

Consumer services and business services do not have the same distributions.   Consumer services generally follow a regular pattern based on size of settlements.

(388)
Central Place Theory
Central place theory helps to explain how the most profitable location can be identified. A **central place** is a market center for the exchange of goods and services by people attracted from the surrounding area.   Central places compete against each other.   This competition creates a regular pattern of settlements, according to central place theory.

Market Area of a Service
The area surrounding a service from which customers are attracted is the **market area** or **hinterland**. To establish the market area, a circle is drawn around the node of service on a map.   The closer to the periphery of the circle, the greater is the percentage of consumers who will choose to obtain services from other nodes. To represent market areas in central place theory, geographers draw hexagons around settlements. Hexagons represent a compromise between circles and squares.

Size of Market Area
To determine the extent of a market area, geographers need two pieces of information about a service: its range and its threshold.

(389)
Range of a Service.   The **range** is the maximum distance people are willing to travel to use a service. The range is the radius of the circle (or hexagon) drawn to delineate a service's market area. If firms at other locations compete by providing the service, the range must be modified.   The range of a service is irregularly shaped to take in only the territory for which the proposed site is closer than competitors'.   Retailers typically define their range as the maximum distance that two-thirds to three-fourths of their customers will travel. The range must be modified further because most people think of distance in terms of time, rather than a linear measure like kilometers or miles. The irregularly shaped circle must be drawn to acknowledge that travel time varies with road conditions.

Threshold of a Service.   The second piece of geographic information needed to compute a market area is the **threshold**, which is the minimum number of people needed to support the service.   How potential consumers inside the range are counted depends on the product. Developers of shopping malls, department stores, and large supermarkets typically count only higher-income people.

Market-Area Analysis
Retailers and other service providers make use of market-area studies to determine whether locating in the market would be profitable and where the best location would be within the market area.

Profitability of a Location

The range and threshold together determine whether a good or service can be profitable in a particular location. (391) A store may need a larger threshold and range to attract some of the available customers if competitors are located nearby.

Optimal Location within a Market
According to geographers, the best location is the one that minimizes the distance to the service for the largest number of people.

Best Location in a Linear Settlement. In a linear community like an Atlantic Ocean resort, the service should be located where half of the customers are to the north and half to the south. What if a different number of customers live in each block of the city? To compute the optimal location in these cases, geographers have adapted the **gravity model** from physics. The gravity model predicts that the optimal location of a service is directly related to the number of people in the area and inversely related to the distance people must travel to access it.

Best Location in a Nonlinear Settlement. Most settlements are more complex than a single main street. Geographers still apply the gravity model to find the best location.

(392)
Hierarchy of Services and Settlements
Small settlements are limited to services that have small thresholds, short ranges, and small market areas. Larger settlements provide services having larger thresholds, ranges, and market areas. However, neighborhoods within large settlements also provide services having small thresholds and ranges.

(393)
Nesting of Services and Settlements
MDCs have numerous small settlements with small thresholds and ranges, and far fewer large settlements with large thresholds and ranges. The nesting pattern can be illustrated with overlapping hexagons of different sizes for different levels of market area. In his original study, Walter Christaller showed that the distances between settlements in southern Germany followed a regular pattern. He identified seven sizes of settlements (market hamlet, township center, county seat, district city, small state capital, provincial head capital, and regional capital city). Brian Berry has documented a similar hierarchy of settlements in parts of the U.S. Midwest. The principle of nesting market areas also works at the scale of services within cities.

Rank-Size Distribution of Settlements
In many MDCs, geographers observe that ranking settlements from largest to smallest (population) produces a regular pattern or hierarchy. This is the **rank-size rule**, in which the country's nth-largest settlement is 1/n the population of the largest settlement.

If the settlement hierarchy does not have a rank-size distribution of settlements, instead, it may follow the **primate city rule**, in which the largest settlement has more than twice as many people as the second-ranking settlement. In this distribution, the largest city is called a **primate city**. Copenhagen, Denmark, London, United Kingdom, and Bucharest, Romania are all primate cities.

The existence of a rank-size distribution of settlements is not merely a mathematical curiosity. (394) The absence of the rank-size distribution in an LDC indicates that there is not enough wealth in the society to pay for a full variety of services.

Periodic Markets

Services at the lower end of the central place hierarchy may be provided at a periodic market, which is a collection of individual vendors who come together to offer goods and services in a location on specified days. A periodic market provides goods to residents of LDCs and rural areas in MDCs. In urban areas, periodic markets offer residents fresh food brought in that morning from the countryside.

The frequency of periodic markets varies by culture.
• **Muslim countries:** Typically conform to the weekly calendar. Once a week, in each of six cities, and non market on Friday, the Muslim day of rest.
• **Rural China:** A three-city 10-day cycle, according to G. William Skinner. Three 10-day cycles fit into a lunar month.
• **Korea:** Two 15-day cycles fit in a lunar month.
• **Africa:** Varies from 3 to 7 days. Variations in the cycle stem from ethnic differences.

Key Issue 4.   Why Do Business Services Cluster in Large Settlements?
• **Hierarchy of business services**
• **Business services in LDCs**
• **Economic base of settlements**

Business services disproportionately cluster in a handful of settlements, and individual settlements specialize in particular business services.

Hierarchy of Business Services
Geographers distinguish four levels of urban settlements according to their importance in the provision of business services. At the top are a handful of urban settlements known as world cities that play an especially important role in global business services.

Services in World Cities

Business services, including law, banking, insurance, accounting, and advertising, concentrate in disproportionately large numbers in world cities. (395) New forms of transportation and communications were expected to reduce the need for clustering of economic activities in large cities. To some extent, economic activities have decentralized, especially manufacturing, but modern inventions reinforce rather than diminish the primacy of world cities in the global economy.

Business Services in World Cities.   The clustering of business services in the modern world city is a product of the Industrial Revolution. Modern industry is managed by large corporations formed to minimize the liability to any individual owner. A board of directors located far from the factory building makes key decisions. Support staff also far from the factory account for the flow of money and materials. This work is done in offices in world cities. World cities offer many financial services to these businesses. Lawyers, accountants, and other professionals cluster in world cities.

Consumer Services in World Cities.   Because of their large size, world cities have retail services with extensive market areas, but they may even have more retailers than large size alone would predict. (396) Luxury and highly specialized products are especially likely to be sold there. Leisure services of national significance are especially likely to cluster in world cities, in part because they require large thresholds and large ranges, and in part because of the presence of wealthy patrons.

Public Services in World Cities.   World cities may be centers of national or international political power. Most are national capitals. Also clustered in the world cities are offices for groups having business with the government. Unlike other world cities, New York is not a national capital. But as the home of the world's major international organization, the United Nations, it attracts thousands of UN diplomats and bureaucrats, as well as employees of organizations with business at the United Nations.   Brussels is a world city because it is the most important center for European Union activities.

Four Levels of Business Services
According to the hierarchy of business services in urban settlements, cities can be divided into four levels of importance:

• **World Cities.** Subdivided into three tiers:
  • Dominant World Cities. London, New York, and Tokyo.
  • Major World Cities. Chicago, Los Angeles, and Washington, D.C. in North America, and Brussels, Frankfurt, Paris, and Zurich in Western Europe. Only two of the nine second-tier world cities — São Paulo and Singapore — are in less developed regions.
  • Secondary World Cities. Four in North America (Houston, Miami, San Francisco, Toronto), seven in Asia, five in Western Europe, four in Latin America, and one each in Africa (Johannesburg) and the South Pacific (Sydney).

• **Command and Control Centers.** These contain the headquarters of many large corporations, concentrations of business services, educational, medical, and public institutions. Two levels of command and control centers can be identified: regional centers and subregional centers.

• **Specialized Producer-Service Centers**. These offer a narrower and more highly specialized variety of services. One group of these cities specializes in the management and R&D activities related to specific industries. A second group specializes as centers of government and education, notably state capitals that also have a major university.

• **Dependent Centers.** These provide relatively unskilled jobs and depend (for their economic health) on decisions made in the world cities, regional command and control centers, and specialized producer-service centers. Four subtypes of dependent centers can be identified in the United States: resort, retirement, and residential centers; manufacturing centers; industrial and military centers; mining and industrial centers.

Business Services in LDCs
In the global economy, LDCs specialize in two distinct types of business services:
  • Offshore financial services
  • Back-office functions

Offshore Financial Services
Small countries, usually islands and microstates, exploit niches in the circulation of global capital by offering offshore financial services that provide two important functions:
  • **Taxes**. Taxes on income, profits, and capital gains are typically low or nonexistent.
  • **Privacy**. Bank secrecy laws can help individuals and businesses evade disclosure in their home countries.

The privacy laws and low tax rates can also provide havens to tax dodges and other illegal schemes.

(397)
In the Cayman Islands, it is a crime to discuss confidential business — defined as matters learned on the job — in public. Other offshore centers include the British and U.S. Virgin Islands, Bahamas,

Andorra, Liechtenstein, and Monaco in Europe, Belize and Panama in Central America, Bahrain in the

Middle East, and Liberia in Africa.

Back Offices

The second type of business service found in peripheral regions is back-office functions, also known as business-process outsourcing (BPO). Typical back-office functions include processing insurance claims, payroll management, transcription work, and other routine clerical activities. Traditionally, companies housed their back-office staff in the same office building downtown as their management staff, or at least in nearby buildings. Proximity was considered important for supervision and rapid turnaround of information. For many business services, improved telecommunications have eliminated the need for spatial proximity. Selective LDCs have attracted back offices for two reasons related to labor:

- Low Wages. Most back-office workers earn a few thousand dollars per year — higher than wages paid in most sectors of the economy, but only one-tenth the wages paid to workers performing similar jobs in MDCs.
- Ability to Speak English. Only a handful of LDCs possess a large labor force fluent in English. India, Malaysia, and the Philippines have substantial numbers of workers with English-language skills, a legacy of British and American colonial rule.

Workers in back offices are often forced to work late at night, when it's daytime in the U.S., peak demand for inquiries.

Economic Base of Settlements

A settlement's distinctive economic structure derives from its **basic industries**, which export primarily to consumers outside the settlement. **Nonbasic industries** are enterprises whose customers live in the same community, essentially consumer services. A community's unique collection of basic industries defines its **economic base**. A settlement's economic base is important, because exporting by the basic industries brings money into the local economy, thus stimulating the provision of more nonbasic consumer services for the settlement. A community's basic industries can be identified by computing the percentage of the community's workers employed in different types of businesses. If the percentage is much higher in the local community, (compared to the country), then that type of business is a basic economic activity.

Specialization of Cities in Different Services

Each type of basic activity has a different spatial distribution. The concept of basic industries originally referred to manufacturing. Most communities that have an economic base of manufacturing durable goods are clustered between northern Ohio and southeastern Wisconsin, near the southern Great Lakes. Nondurable manufacturing industries, such as textiles, are clustered in the Southeast, especially in the Carolinas. But in a post-industrial society such as the United States, increasingly the basic economic activities are in business, consumer, or public services. Geographers Ó hUalláchain and Reid have documented examples of settlements that specialize in particular types of business services:

- **Examples of settlements specializing in business services:**
  - General business: Chicago, Los Angeles, New York, and San Francisco.
  - Computing and data processing: Boston and San Jose (399)
  - High-tech industries support services: Austin, Orlando, and Raleigh-Durham
  - Military activities support services: Albuquerque, Colorado Springs, Huntsville, Knoxville, Norfolk
  - Management consulting services: Washington D.C.

- **Examples of settlements specializing in consumer-services:**

• Entertainment and recreation: Atlantic City, Las Vegas, and Reno
• Medical services: Rochester, Minnesota.

• **Examples of settlements specializing in public services:**
  • State capitals
  • Large universities
  • Military bases

Distribution of Talent

Individuals possessing special talents are not distributed uniformly among cities. (400) The principal enticement for talented individuals to cluster in some cities more than others is cultural rather than economic, according to research conducted by Richard Florida. Florida found a significant positive relationship between the distribution of talent and the distribution of diversity in the largest U.S. cities. Attracting talented individuals is important for a city, because these individuals are responsible for promoting economic innovation.

Key Terms

Basic industries (p. 398)
Business services (p. 375)
Central place (p. 388)
Central place theory (p. 388)
City-state (p. 379)
Clustered rural settlement (p. 381)
Consumer services (p. 375)
Dispersed rural settlement (p. 381)
Economic base (p. 398)
Enclosure movement (p. 384)
Gravity model (p. 391)

Market area (or hinterland) (p. 388)
Nonbasic industries (p. 398)
Primate city (p. 393)
Primate city rule (p. 393)
Public services (p. 376)
Range (of a service) (p. 389)
Rank-size rule (p. 393)
Service (p. 374)
Settlement (p. 374)
Threshold (p. 489)
Urbanization (p.3 85)

Test Prep Questions

1) Which of the following is NOT considered a main type of business service?
A) financial
B) recreational
C) professional
D) information

2) Where were the earliest cities thought to have originated?
A) Mesopotamia
B) South Asia
C) ancient Greece
D) ancient Rome

3) What region of the United States was remarkable for its clustered rural settlements?
A) the South
B) New England
C) the Mid-Atlantic
D) the Midwest

4) Louis Wirth argued that urban settlements, compared to rural settlements, had all the following characteristics EXCEPT:

A) large size
B) high density
C) social heterogeneity
D) greater pressure to conform

5) A country with a high percentage of urban residents would most likely be:

A) an MDC
B) an LDC
C) in stage 1 of the demographic transition
D) in stage 2 of the demographic transition

6) A country with a relatively large number of large (by world standards) cities would most likely be:

A) an MDC
B) an LDC
C) in stage 3 of the demographic transition
D) in stage 4 of the demographic transition

7) The basic shape of market in central place theory is:

A) a square
B) a hexagon
C) a circle
D) a geometrically irregular shape.

8) Which of the following cities would be considered a primate city?

A) New York
B) London
C) Los Angeles
D) Chicago

9) Which of the following is NOT one of the three dominant world cities?

A) London
B) New York
C) Berlin
D) Tokyo

10) According to Richard Florida, what is the single most powerful enticement that attracts talented people to one city over another?

A) cultural diversity
B) high wages
C) low rents
D) economic considerations in general

Short Essay

1) Identify the three types of services in the tertiary sector of the economy, and give examples.

_____

_____

_____

_____

_____

_____

_____

_____

2) Compare and contrast the concepts of percentage vs. number of people in cities as they pertain to MDCs and LDCs.

_____

_____

_____

_____

_____

_____

_____

_____

_____

_____

3) Explain the concepts of range and threshold, and how they relate to market area.

_____

_____

_____

_____

_____

_____

_____

_____

Chapter 13
Urban Patterns

Key Issues
1. Why do services cluster downtown?
2. Where are people distributed within urban areas?
3. Why do inner cities face distinctive challenges?
4. Why do suburbs face distinctive challenges?

(406)
This chapter looks at where people and activities are distributed within urban spaces. We all experience the interplay between *globalization* and *local diversity* of urban settlements. Many downtowns have a collection of high-rise buildings, towers, and landmarks that are identifiable even to people who have never visited them. On the other hand, suburban houses, streets, schools, and shopping centers look very much alike from one American city to another. In *regions* of MDCs, people are increasingly likely to live in suburbs. People wish to spread across the landscape to avoid urban problems, but at the same time they want convenient *connections* to the city's jobs, shops, culture, and recreation. Although different internal structures characterize urban areas in the United States and elsewhere, the problems arising from current spatial trends are similar. Geographers describe where different types of people live and try to explain the reasons for the observed patterns.

Key Issue 1.   Why Do Services Cluster Downtown?
- **CBD land uses**
- **Competition for land in the CBD**
- **CBDs outside North America**

Downtown is the best-known and the most visually distinctive area of most cities. The downtowns of most North American cities have different features than those in the rest of the world.

CBD Land Uses
Downtown is known to geographers by the more precise term **central business district (CBD)**. The CBD is compact, but contains a large percentage of the shops, offices, and public institutions.

(407)
The center is the easiest part of the city to reach from the rest of the region and is the focal point of the region's transportation network.

Retail Services in the CBD
In the past, three types of retail services clustered in the CBD, because they require accessibility to everyone in the region — retailers with a high threshold, those with a long range, and those that serve people who work in the CBD.

Retail Services with a High Threshold. High-threshold shops, such as department stores, traditionally preferred a CBD location to be accessible to many people. Rents were highest there because this location had the highest accessibility for the most customers. In recent years, many high threshold shops such as large department stores have closed their downtown branches. The customers for downtown department stores now consist of downtown office workers, inner-city residents, and tourists.

Retail Services with a High Range. High-range retailers are often specialists, with customers who patronize them infrequently. Like those with high thresholds, high-range retailers have moved with department stores to suburban locations. These retailers survive in some CBDs if they combine retailing with recreational activities. New shopping areas that attract high-range retailers have been built in several North American CBDs. These downtown malls attract suburban shoppers as well as out-of-town tourists because in addition to shops, they offer unique recreation and entertainment experiences.

Retail Services Serving Downtown Workers. A third type of retail activity in the center serves the many people who work in the center and shop during lunch or working hours. (408) These businesses sell office supplies, computers, and clothing, or offer shoe repair, rapid photocopying, dry cleaning, and soon. In contrast to the other two types of retailers, shops that appeal to nearby office workers are expanding in the CBD, in part because the number of downtown office workers has increased and in part because downtown offices require more services.

Business Services in the CBD

Offices cluster in the center for accessibility. Despite the diffusion of modern telecommunications, many professionals still exchange information with colleagues primarily through face-to-face contact. Offices are centrally located to facilitate rapid communication of fast-breaking news through spatial proximity. A central location also helps businesses that employ workers from a variety of neighborhoods. Firms that need highly specialized employees are more likely to find them in the central area, perhaps currently working for another company downtown.

Competition for Land in the CBD

The center's accessibility produces extreme competition for the limited sites available. As a result, land values are very high in the CBD, and it is too expensive for some activities.

High Land Costs

Tokyo's CBD probably contains Earth's most expensive land. Tokyo's high prices result from a severe shortage of buildable land. Buildings in most areas are legally restricted to less than 10 meters in height (normally three stories) for fear of earthquakes. Two distinctive characteristics of the central city follow from the high land cost. First, land is used more intensively in the center. Second, some activities are excluded because of the high cost of space.

Intensive Land Use. The intensive demand for space has given the CBD a three-dimensional character, pushing it vertically. A vast underground network exists beneath most central cities. The typical "underground city" includes multistory parking garages, loading docks and utility lines. Subways run beneath the streets of larger central cities.

(409)
Cities such as Minneapolis, Montreal, and Toronto have built extensive pedestrian passages and shops beneath the center. These underground areas segregate pedestrians from motor vehicles and shield them from harsh winter weather.

Skyscrapers. Demand for space in the CBD has also made high-rise structures economically feasible. Suburban houses, shopping malls, and factories look much the same from one city to another, but each city has a unique downtown skyline resulting from its high-rise buildings. The first skyscrapers were built in Chicago in the 1880s, made possible by two inventions: the elevator and iron-frame building construction. The first high-rises caused great inconvenience to neighboring structures because they blocked light and air movement. Artificial lighting, ventilation, central heating, and air-conditioning have helped solve these problems. Skyscrapers are an interesting example of "vertical geography." The nature of an activity influences which floor it occupies in a typical high-rise.

Activities Excluded from the CBD

High rents and land shortage discourage two principal activities in the CBD: industrial and residential.

Lack of Industry in the CBD. Modern factories require a large parcel of land to spread operations among one-story buildings. Suitable land is generally available in suburbs. Port cities have transformed their waterfronts from industry to commercial and recreational activities. CBD waterfronts have become major tourist attractions in a number of North American cities, including Boston, Toronto, Baltimore, and San Francisco, as well as in European cities such as Barcelona and London.

Lack of Residents in CBDs. Many people used to live downtown. Poorer people jammed into tiny overcrowded apartments, and richer people built mansions downtown. In the twentieth century most residents abandoned downtown living because of a combination of pull and push factors. They were pulled to suburbs that offered larger homes with private yards and modern schools. (410) And they were pushed from CBDs by high rents that business and retail services were willing to pay and from the dirt, crime, congestion, and poverty that they experienced living downtown. In the twenty-first century the population of many U.S. CBDs has increased. Downtown living is especially attractive to people without school-age children.

CBDs Outside North America

CBDs outside North America are less dominated by commercial considerations. European cities display a legacy of low-rise structures and narrow streets, built as long ago as medieval times. Some European cities have tried to preserve their historic core by limiting high-rise buildings and the number of cars. More people live downtown in cities outside North America. Although constructing large new buildings is difficult, many shops and offices still wish to be in the center of European cities. The alternative to new construction is renovation of older buildings, which is more expensive, and as a result rents are much higher in the center of European cities than in U.S. cities of comparable size.

Key Issue 2. Where Are People Distributed within Urban Areas?
•**Models of urban structure**
•**Applying the models outside North America**

People are not distributed randomly within an urban area. Geographers describe where people with particular characteristics are likely to live within an urban area, and they offer explanations for why these patterns occur.

Models of Urban Structure

Sociologists, economists, and geographers have developed three models to help explain where different types of people tend to live in an urban area: the concentric zone, sector, and multiple nuclei models. The three models describing the internal social structure of cities were all developed in Chicago, a city on a prairie. Except for Lake Michigan to the east, few physical features have interrupted the region's growth.

Concentric Zone Model

The concentric zone model was the first to explain the distribution of different social groups within urban areas.   It was created in 1923 by sociologist E.W. Burgess.   According to the **concentric zone model**, a city grows outward from a central area in a series of concentric rings.

1. CBD: The innermost ring, where nonresidential activities are concentrated.
2. A zone in transition, which contains industry and poorer quality housing. Immigrants to the city first live in this zone.
3. A zone of working-class homes, which contains modest older houses occupied by stable, working-class families.
(411)
4. A zone of better residences, which contains newer and more spacious houses for middle-class families.
5. A commuters' zone, beyond the continuous built-up area of the city.

Sector Model
A second theory of urban structure, the **sector model**, was developed in 1939 by land economist Homer Hoyt.   According to Hoyt, the city develops in a series of sectors, not rings.   Certain areas of the city are more attractive for various activities, originally because of an environmental factor or even by mere chance.   As a city grows, activities expand outward in a wedge, or sector, from the center. The best housing is therefore found in a corridor extending from downtown to the outer edge of the city. Industrial and retailing activities develop in other sectors, usually along good transportation lines. To some extent, the sector model is a refinement of the concentric zone model rather than a radical restatement. (412)   Hoyt and Burgess both claimed that social patterns in Chicago supported their model.

Multiple Nuclei Model
Geographers C. D. Harris and E. L. Ullman developed the multiple nuclei model in 1945. According to the **multiple nuclei model**, a city is a complex structure that includes more than one center around which activities revolve.   Examples of these nodes include a port, neighborhood business center, university, airport, and park. The theory also states that some activities are attracted to particular nodes while others try to avoid them.   For example, a university node may attract well-educated residents, pizzerias, and bookstores, whereas an airport may attract hotels and warehouses.

Geographic Applications of the Models
The three models help us understand where people with different social characteristics tend to live within an urban area.   Effective use of the models depends on the availability of data at the scale of individual neighborhoods.   Urban areas in the United States are divided into **census tracts**, which contain approximately 5,000 residents and correspond where possible to neighborhood boundaries. Every decade, the U.S. Bureau of the Census publishes data summarizing the characteristics of the residents living in each tract.

Social Area Analysis.   The spatial distribution of any of these social characteristics can be plotted on a map of the community's census tracts. Social scientists can compare the distributions of characteristics and create an overall picture of where various types of people tend to live.   This kind of study is known as **social area analysis**.

Critics point out that the models are too simple and fail to consider the variety of reasons that lead people to select particular residential locations. Because the three models are all based on conditions that existed between the two world wars, critics also question their relevance to contemporary urban patterns. But if the models are combined rather than considered independently, they help geographers explain where different types of people live in a city.   The models say that most people prefer to live near others having similar characteristics.

(413)
Putting the three models together, we can identify, for example, the neighborhood in which a high-income, Asian-American owner-occupant is most likely to live.

Applying the Models Outside North America
American urban areas differ from those elsewhere in the world.   Social groups in other countries may not have the same reasons for selecting particular neighborhoods.

European Cities
In contrast to most U.S. cities, wealthy Europeans still live in the inner rings of the upper class sector, not just in the suburbs. A central location provides proximity to the region's best shops, restaurants, cafes, and cultural facilities. As in the United States, wealthier people in European cities cluster along a sector extending out from the CBD. In the past, low-income people also lived in the center of European cities. Social segregation was vertical: Wealthier people lived on the first or second floors, while poorer people occupied the dark, dank basements, or they climbed many flights of stairs to reach the attics.

(414) Today, low-income people are less likely to live in European inner-city neighborhoods. Poor-quality housing has been renovated for wealthy people, or demolished.   Building and zoning codes prohibit anyone from living in basements, and upper floors are attractive to wealthy individuals once elevators are installed.

People with lower incomes have been relegated to the outskirts of European cities. Many residents of these dreary suburbs are persons of color or recent immigrants from Africa or Asia who face discrimination and prejudice by "native" Europeans.   European officials encouraged the construction of high-density suburbs to help preserve the countryside from development and to avoid the inefficient sprawl that characterizes American suburbs.

Less Developed Countries
In LDCs, as in Europe, the poor are accommodated in the suburbs, whereas the rich live near the center of cities, as well as in a sector extending from the center.   The similarity between European and LDC cities is not a coincidence.   Most cities in less developed countries have passed through three stages of development — pre-European colonization, the European Colonial period, and postcolonial independence.

Precolonial Cities.   Few cities existed in Africa, Asia, and Latin America before the Europeans established colonies. Most people lived in rural settlements.

Cities were often laid out surrounding a religious core, such as a mosque in Muslim regions. Government buildings and the homes of wealthy families surrounded the mosque and bazaar. Families with less wealth and lower status located farther from the core, and recent migrants to the city lived on the edge. Commercial activities were arranged in a concentric and hierarchical pattern:

- Higher-status businesses directly related to religious practices were located closest to the mosque.
- In the next ring were secular businesses.
- Food products were sold in the next ring, and then came blacksmiths, basket makers, and potters.
- A quarter would be reserved for Jews, a second for Christians, and a third for foreigners

In Mexico, the Aztecs founded Mexico City — which they called Tenochtitlán — on a hill known as Chapultepec. Forced by other people to leave the hill, they migrated a few kilometers south.

Then in 1325 they moved to a marshy island in Lake Texcoco. (415)   Over the next two centuries, the Aztecs conquered the neighboring peoples and extended their control through much of present day Mexico.

Colonial Cities.   When Europeans gained control of Africa, Asia, and Latin America, they expanded existing cities to provide colonial services as well as housing for Europeans who settled in the colony. Colonial cities were either left to one side or demolished because they were totally at variance with European ideas.

Colonial cities followed standardized plans.   All Spanish cities in Latin America, for example, were built according to the Laws of the Indies, drafted in 1573. Cities were to be constructed on a gridiron street plan centered on a church and central plaza and neighborhoods centered around smaller plazas with parish churches or monasteries. (416)   After the Spanish conquered Tenochtitlán, they destroyed the city, and dispersed or killed most of the inhabitants.   The city, renamed Mexico City, was rebuilt around a main square, called the Zócalo, in the center of the island, on the site of the Aztecs' sacred precinct.   The Spanish reconstructed the streets in a grid pattern extending from the Zócalo. In other examples, Fès (Fez), Morocco, now consists of two separate and distinct towns — one that existed before the French gained control and one built by the French colonialists. On the other hand, the French Colonial city of Saigon, Vietnam (now Ho Chi Minh City), was built by completely demolishing the existing city without leaving a trace.

Cities Since Independence.   Following independence, cities have become the focal points of change in LDCs.   Millions of people have migrated to the cities in search of work. Geographers Ernest Griffin and Larry Ford show that in Latin American cities, wealthy people push out from the center in a well-defined elite residential sector on either side of a narrow spine that contains offices, shops, and amenities, and services like water and electricity.   In Mexico City, Emperor Maximilian (1864–1867) designed a 14-lane, tree-lined boulevard patterned after the Champs-Elysées in Paris. The boulevard (now known as the Paseo de la Reforma) extended 3 kilometers southwest from the center to Chapultepec. The Reforma between downtown and Chapultepec became the spine of an elite sector. Physical factors influenced the movement of wealthy people toward the west along the Reforma. Because elevation was higher than elsewhere in the city, sewage flowed eastward and northward away from Chapultepec. In 1903, most of Lake Texcoco was drained by a gigantic canal and tunnel project. However, the lake bed was a less desirable residential location than the west side, because prevailing winds from the northeast stirred up dust storms from the dried-up lake bed. As Mexico City's population grew rapidly during the twentieth century, the social patterns inherited from the nineteenth century were reinforced.

Squatter Settlements.   The LDCs are unable to house the rapidly growing number of poor people.   A large percentage of poor immigrants to urban areas in LDCs live in **squatter settlements**. The United Nations estimated that 175 million people worldwide lived in squatter settlements in 2003. Squatter settlements have few services, because neither the city nor the

residents can afford them. Electricity service may be stolen by running a wire from the nearest power line.

(418)
In the absence of bus service or available private cars, a resident may have to walk two hours to reach a place of employment. At first, squatters do little more than camp on the land or sleep in the street. Families then erect primitive shelters with scavenged materials.

Key Issue 3. Why Do Inner Cities Have Distinctive Challenges?
- **Inner-city physical issues**
- **Inner-city social issues**
- **Inner-city economic issues**

Most of the land in urban settlements is devoted to housing.

(419)
Inner cities in the United States contain concentrations of low-income people with a variety of physical, social, and economic problems very different from those faced by suburban residents.

Inner-City Physical Issues
The major physical problem faced by inner-city neighborhoods is the poor condition of the housing, most of which was built before 1940.

Process of Deterioration
As the number of low-income residents increase in the city, the territory they occupy expands. Middle-class families move out of a neighborhood to newer housing farther from the center and sell or rent their houses to lower-income families.

Filtering. Large houses built by wealthy families in the nineteenth century are subdivided by absentee landlords into smaller dwellings for low-income families. This process is known as **filtering**. Landlords stop maintaining houses when the rent they collect becomes less than the maintenance cost. The building soon deteriorates and grows unfit for occupancy. At this point in the filtering process, the owner may abandon the property because the rents that can be collected are less than the cost of taxes and upkeep. Governments that aggressively go after landlords to repair deteriorated properties may in fact hasten abandonment, because landlords will not spend money on repairs that they are unable to recoup in rents. Inner-city neighborhoods that housed perhaps 100,000 a century ago contain less than 10,000 inhabitants today. Schools and shops close because they are no longer needed with rapidly declining populations. Through the filtering process, many poor families have moved to less deteriorated houses farther from the center.

Redlining. Some banks engage in **redlining** — drawing lines on a map to identify areas in which they will refuse to loan money. Although redlining is illegal, enforcement of laws against it is frequently difficult. The Community Reinvestment Act requires banks to demonstrate that inner-city neighborhoods within its service area receive a fair share of its loans.

Urban Renewal
North American and European cities have demolished much of their substandard inner-city housing through **urban renewal** programs. The land is then turned over to private developers or to public agencies to construct new buildings or services. Urban renewal has been criticized for destroying the social cohesion of older neighborhoods and reducing the supply of low-cost housing.

Public Housing. In the United States, **public housing** is reserved for low-income households, who must pay 30 percent of their income for rent. In the U.S., public housing accounts for only 1 percent of all dwellings, compared to 14 percent in the United Kingdom. Elsewhere in Western Europe, governments typically subsidize construction cost and rent for a large percentage of the privately built housing.

Most of the high-rise public-housing projects built in the United States and Europe during the 1950s and early 1960s are now considered unsatisfactory environments for families with children. Some observers claim that the high-rise buildings caused the problem, because too many low-income families are concentrated into a high-density environment. Public-housing authorities have demolished high-rise public-housing projects in recent years in U.S. and European cities. The U.S. government has stopped funding new public housing. In Britain, the supply of public housing has also declined because the government has forced local authorities to sell some of the dwellings to the residents.

Renovated Housing.   In some cases, nonprofit organizations renovate housing and sell or rent them to low-income people.   But more often, the renovated housing attracts middle-class people. Most cities have at least one substantially renovated inner-city neighborhood where middle-class people live.   In a few cases, inner-city neighborhoods never deteriorated, because the community's social elite maintained them as enclaves of expensive property.   The process by which middle-class people move into deteriorated inner-city neighborhoods and renovate the housing is known as **gentrification**. Gentrified inner-city neighborhoods also attract middle-class individuals who work downtown.

(421)
In cities where gentrification is especially strong, ethnic patterns are being altered.

Cities encourage the process by providing low-cost loans and tax breaks.   Public expenditures for renovation have been criticized as subsidies for the middle class at the expense of poor people, who are forced to move because the rents are suddenly too high for them.   Cities try to reduce the hardship on poor families forced to move. U.S. law requires that they be reimbursed both for moving expenses and for rent increases over a four-year period.   Western European countries have similar laws.   Cities are also renovating old houses specifically for lower-income families.

Inner-City Social Issues
Beyond the pockets of gentrified neighborhoods, inner cities contain primarily low-income people who face a variety of social problems.   Inner-city residents constitute a permanent underclass who live in a culture of poverty.

Underclass
Inner-city residents frequently are referred to as a permanent **underclass** because they are trapped in an unending cycle of economic and social problems.

The future is especially bleak for the underclass because they are increasingly unable to compete for jobs.   The gap between skills demanded by employers and the training possessed by inner-city residents is widening.

Inner-city residents do not even have access to the remaining low-skilled jobs, such as custodians and fast-food servers, because they are increasingly in the distant suburbs.

Some members of the underclass are homeless.   Accurate counts are impossible to obtain, but an estimated one to two million Americans sleep in doorways, on heated street grates, and in bus and subway stations.

(422)
Single men constitute two-fifths of the homeless. Homelessness is also a serious problem in LDCs

Culture of Poverty
Inner-city residents are trapped as permanent underclass because they live in a culture of poverty. Unwed mothers give birth to three-fourths of the babies in U.S. inner-city neighborhoods, and

three-fourths of children in the inner city live with only one parent. Because of inadequate child-care services, single mothers may be forced to choose between working to generate income and staying at home to take care of the children. In principle, government officials would like to see more fathers living with their wives and children, but they provide little incentive for them to do so. If the husband moves back home, his wife may lose welfare benefits, leaving the couple financially worse off together than apart. Although drug use is a problem in both the suburbs and rural areas, rates of use in recent years have increased most rapidly in the inner cities. Violence erupts when two gangs fight over the boundaries between their drug distribution areas. Many neighborhoods in the United States are segregated by ethnicity. Even small cities display strong social distinctions among neighborhoods. A family seeking a new residence usually considers only a handful of districts, where the residents' social and financial characteristics match their own.

Inner-City Economic Issues

The concentration of low-income residents in inner-city neighborhoods of central cities has produced financial problems. The severe recession in recent years has aggravated those problems. Low-income inner-city residents require public services, but they can pay very little of the taxes to support those services. A city has two choices to close the gap between the cost of services and the funding available from taxes:

- **Reduce Services.** Aside from the hardship imposed on individuals laid off from work, cutbacks in public services also encourage middle-class residents and industries to move from the city.

(423)
- **Raise Tax Revenues.** Spending public money to increase the downtown tax base can take scarce funds away from projects in inner city neighborhoods, such as subsidized housing and playgrounds.

During the mid-twentieth century, inner-city fiscal problems were alleviated by increasing contributions from the federal government. Federal aid has declined by two-thirds since the 1980s. To offset a portion of these lost federal funds, some state governments increased financial assistance to cities.

Impact of the Recession

One of the principal causes of the severe recession that began in 2008 was a collapse in the housing market, primarily in the inner city. Despite having poor credit histories, first-time home buyers were approved for mortgages without background checks. These were known as subprime mortgages. In the first year of the recession, 10 percent of all Americans with mortgages were behind in their payments or already in foreclosure. In many cases, the amount of the mortgages exceeded the value of the house once prices had fallen.

Annexation

For many cities, economic problems are exacerbated by their inability to annex peripheral land. **Annexation** is the process of legally adding land area to a city.

Normally, land can be annexed into a city only if a majority of residents in the affected area vote in favor of doing so. Peripheral residents generally desired annexation in the nineteenth century, because the city offered better services. Today, however, cities are less likely to annex peripheral land because the residents prefer to organize their own services rather than pay city taxes for them. As a result, today's cities are surrounded by a collection of suburban jurisdictions. Some of these peripheral jurisdictions were small, isolated towns. Others are newly created communities whose residents wish to live close to the large city but not be legally part of it.

(424)
Key Issue 4. Why Do Suburbs Face Distinctive Challenges?
- **Urban expansion**
- **The peripheral model**
- **Suburban segregation**
- **Transportation and suburbanization**

In 1950, only 20 percent of Americans lived in suburbs compared to 40 percent in cities and 40 percent in small towns and rural areas. In 2000, after half a century of rapid suburban growth, 50 percent of Americans lived in suburbs, compared to only 30 percent in cities and 20 percent in small towns and rural areas.

Urban Expansion
Until recently in the U.S., as cities grew, they expanded by adding peripheral land. Now cities are surrounded by a collection of suburban jurisdictions whose residents prefer to remain legally independent of the large city.

Annexation
The process of legally adding land area to a city is **annexation**. Normally, land can be annexed into a city only if a majority of residents in the affected area vote in favor of doing so. Peripheral residents generally desired annexation in the nineteenth century, because the city offered better services. Today, however, cities are less likely to annex peripheral land because the residents prefer to organize their own services rather than pay city taxes for them. Some of these peripheral jurisdictions were small, isolated towns. Others are newly created communities whose residents wish to live close to the large city but not be legally part of it.

Defining Urban Settlements
Instead of annexing peripheral areas, cities now are surrounded by suburbs. As a result, several definitions have been created to characterize cities and their suburbs:
• City: a legal entity
• Urbanized area: a continuously built-up area
• Metropolitan area: a functional area

The City. The term *city* defines an urban settlement that has been legally incorporated into an independent, self-governing unit. In the United States, a city that is surrounded by suburbs is sometimes called a **central city**.

Urbanized Area. An **urbanized area** consists of a central city plus its contiguous built-up suburbs where population density exceeds 1,000 persons per square mile (400 persons per square kilometer).

(425)
Approximately 70 percent of the U.S. population lives in urban areas, including about 30 percent in central cities and 40 percent in surrounding jurisdictions. Working with urbanized areas is difficult because few statistics are available about them. Urbanized areas do not correspond to government boundaries.

Metropolitan Statistical Area. The concept of urbanized area also has limited applicability because it does not accurately reflect the full influence that an urban settlement has in contemporary society. The area of influence of a city extends beyond legal boundaries and adjacent built-up jurisdictions. Therefore, we need another definition of urban settlement to account for its more extensive zone of influence. The U.S. Bureau of the Census has created a method of measuring the functional area of a city, known as the **metropolitan statistical area (MSA)**. An MSA includes the following:

- A central city with a population of at least 50,000
- The county within which the city is located
- Adjacent counties with a high population density and a large percentage of residents working in the central city's county

The MSAs are widely used because many statistics are published for counties, the basic MSA building block. One problem is that some MSAs include extensive land area that is not urban. The MSAs comprise some 20 percent of total U.S. land area, compared to only 2 percent for urbanized areas. The urbanized area typically occupies only 10 percent of an MSA land area but contains over 90 percent of its population. The census has also designated smaller urban areas as **micropolitan statistical areas**. These include an urbanized area of between 10,000 and 50,000 inhabitants, the county in which it is found, and adjacent counties tied to the city. About 10 percent of Americans live in a micropolitan statistical area. Metropolitan and micropolitan statistical areas together are known as **core based statistical areas (CBSAs)**. Recognizing that some of the have close ties, the census has combined them into **combined statistical areas (CSAs)**. The 124 CSAs, plus the remaining 187 MSAs and 406 micropolitan statistical areas not combined into CSAs together are known as **primary census statistical areas (PCSAs)**.

(426)
Local Government Fragmentation
The fragmentation of local government in the United States makes it difficult to solve regional problems of traffic, solid-waste disposal, and construction of affordable housing. The large number of local government units has led to calls for a metropolitan government that could coordinate — if not replace — the numerous local governments in an urban area. Most U.S. metropolitan areas have a **council of government**, which is a cooperative agency consisting of representatives of the various local governments in the region. Strong metropolitan-wide governments have been established in a few places in North America. Two kinds exist:

- **Consolidations of City and County Governments.** Examples include Indianapolis and Miami. Government functions that were handled separately by city and county are combined into a joint operation in the same office building.
- **Federations.** Examples include Toronto and other large Canadian cities. Toronto's metropolitan government was created in 1953 through federation of 13 municipalities. A two-tier system of government existed until 1998, when the municipalities were amalgamated into a single government.

Overlapping Metropolitan Areas
Some adjacent MSAs overlap. A county between two central cities may send a large number of commuters to jobs in each. In the northeastern United States, large metropolitan areas form one continuous urban complex, extending from north of Boston to south of Washington, D.C.

(427)
Geographer Jean Gottmann named this region Megalopolis, a Greek word meaning "great city," others have called it the Boswash corridor. Other continuous urban complexes exist in the United States: the southern Great Lakes and southern California. Among important examples in other MDCs are the German Ruhr, Randstad in the Netherlands, and Japan's

Tokaido. Within Megalopolis, the downtown areas of individual cities retain distinctive identities. But at the periphery of the urban areas, the boundaries overlap. Once considered two separate areas, Washington and Baltimore were combined into a single metropolitan statistical area after the 1990 census. However, that combination did not do justice to the distinctive character of the two cities, so the census again divided them into two separate MSAs after the 2000 census, but grouped them into one combined statistical area.

(427)
The Peripheral Model

North American urban areas follow what Chauncey Harris (creator of the multiple nuclei model) calls the peripheral model. According to the **peripheral model**, an urban area consists of an inner city surrounded by large suburban residential and business areas tied together by a beltway or ring road.

The peripheral model points to problems of sprawl and segregation that characterize many suburbs. Around the beltway are nodes of consumer and business services, called **edge cities**. Edge cities originated as suburban residences then shopping malls were built. Now edge cities contain manufacturing centers. Specialized nodes emerge in the edge cities: a collection of hotels and warehouses around an airport, a large theme park, a distribution center near the junction of the beltway and a major long-distance interstate highway.

Density Gradient

As you travel outward from the center of a city, you can watch the decline in the density at which people live. This density change in an urban area is called the **density gradient**. According to the density gradient, the number of houses per unit of land diminishes as distance from the center city increases.

(428)
Two changes have affected the density gradient in recent years:

- **Fewer People Living in the Center.** The density gradient thus has a gap in the center, where few live.
- **Fewer Differences in Density Within Urban Areas.** The number of people living on a hectare of land has decreased in the central residential areas through population decline and abandonment of old housing. At the same time, density has increased on the periphery through construction projects and diffusion of suburbs across a larger area.

The result of the two changes is to flatten the density gradient and reduce the extremes of density between inner and outer areas traditionally found within cities.

Cost of Suburban Sprawl

U.S. suburbs are characterized by **sprawl**, which is the progressive spread of development over the landscape. Developers frequently reject land adjacent to built-up areas in favor of detached isolated sites, depending on the price and physical attributes of the alternatives. The periphery of U.S. cities therefore looks like Swiss cheese, with pockets of development and gaps of open space. Roads and utilities must be extended to connect isolated new developments to nearby built-up areas. Sprawl also wastes land. Some prime agricultural land may be lost through construction of isolated housing developments; in the interim, other sites lie fallow, while speculators await the most profitable time to build homes on them. The low-density suburb also wastes more energy, especially because the automobile is required for most trips. (429) The supply of land for construction of new housing is more severely restricted in European urban areas by designating areas of mandatory open space. London, Birmingham, and several other British cities are surrounded by **greenbelts**, or rings of open space. New housing is built either in older suburbs inside the greenbelts or in planned extensions to small towns and new towns beyond the greenbelts. Restriction of the supply of land has driven up house prices in Europe.

Several U.S. states have taken strong steps in the past few years to curb sprawl, reduce traffic congestion, and reverse inner-city decline. Legislation and regulations to limit suburban sprawl and preserve farmland has been called **smart growth**. Oregon and Tennessee have defined growth boundaries within which new development must occur. New Jersey, Rhode Island, and Washington were also early leaders in enacting strong state-level smart-growth initiatives. Maryland enacted especially strong smart growth legislation in 1998. State money must be spent to "fill in" already urbanized areas.

Suburban Segregation

Public opinion polls in the U.S. show people's strong desire for suburban living. It is no surprise then that the suburban population has grown much faster than the overall population in the United States. Suburbs offer varied attractions — a detached single family dwelling rather than a row house or apartment, private land surrounding the house, space to park cars, and a greater opportunity for home ownership. The modern residential suburb is segregated, and in two ways:

- **Segregated Social Classes.** Housing in a given suburban community is usually built for people of a single social class, with others excluded by virtue of the cost, size, or location of the housing.
- **Segregated Land Uses.** Residents are separated from commercial and manufacturing activities.

Residential Segregation

The homogeneous suburb is a twentieth-century phenomenon. In older cities, activities and classes were more likely to be separated vertically rather than horizontally. Poorer people lived on the higher levels or in the basement, the least attractive parts of the building. Once cities spread out over much larger areas, the old pattern of vertical separation was replaced by territorial segregation. Large sections of the city were developed, appealing to people with similar incomes and lifestyles.

Zoning ordinances, developed in Europe and North America in the early decades of the twentieth century, encouraged spatial separation. They prevented mixing of land uses within the same district. The strongest criticism of U.S. residential suburbs is that low-income and minority people are unable to live in them because of the high cost of the housing and the unfriendliness of established residents. Legal devices, such as requiring each house to sit on a large lot and the prohibition of apartments, prevent low-income families from living in many suburbs. (430) In some metropolitan areas, the inner-city social and economic problems described earlier are found in older suburbs immediately adjacent to the central city. Inner suburbs become home to lower-income people displaced from gentrifying urban neighborhoods. Meanwhile, middle class residents move from the inner suburbs to newer homes on the periphery, and the inner suburbs are unable to generate revenue to provide for the needs of a poorer population.

Suburbanization of Businesses

Businesses have moved to suburbs — manufacturers because land costs are lower, and service providers because most of their customers are there.

Suburbanization of Retailing

Since the end of World War II, downtown sales have not increased, whereas suburban sales have risen at an annual rate of 5 percent. The low density of residential construction discourages people from walking to stores, and restrictive zoning practices often exclude shops from residential areas. Retailing has been increasingly concentrated in planned suburban shopping malls of varying sizes. Corner shops have been replaced by supermarkets in small shopping centers. Malls have become centers for activities in suburban areas that lack other types of community facilities.

Suburbanization of Factories and Offices
Factories and warehouses have migrated to suburbia for more space, cheaper land, and better truck access. Modern factories and warehouses are spread over a single level. Industries increasingly receive inputs and distribute products by truck. Offices that do not require face-to-face contact increasingly are moving to suburbs where rents are much lower than in the CBD.

(431)
Transportation and Suburbanization
Urban sprawl makes people more dependent on transportation for access to work, shopping, and leisure activities.   More than half of all trips are work-related.   Shopping or other personal business and social journeys each account for approximately one-fourth of all trips.   Historically, the growth of suburbs was constrained by transportation problems.   People lived in crowded cities because they had to be within walking distance of shops and places of employment.   Cities then built street railways and underground railways.   Many so-called streetcar suburbs built in the nineteenth century still exist and retain unique visual identities.

Motor Vehicles
The suburban explosion in the twentieth century has relied on motor vehicles rather than railroads, especially in the United States.   Rail lines restricted nineteenth-century suburban development to narrow ribbons within walking distance of the stations.

Motor vehicle ownership is nearly universal among American households, with the exception of some very poor families, older individuals, and people living in the centers of large cities. Outside the big cities, public transportation service is extremely rare or nonexistent.   The U.S. government has encouraged the use of cars and trucks by paying 90 percent of the cost of limited-access high-speed interstate highways and by policies that keep the price of fuel below the level found in Europe.

The motor vehicle is an important user of land in the city.   An average city allocates about one-fourth of its land to roads and parking lots. (432)   European and Japanese cities have been especially disrupted by attempts to insert new roads and parking areas in or near to the medieval central areas.   Technological improvements may help congestion by increasing road capacity or by reducing the demand to drive on them.

(433)
Public Transit
Because few people in the United States live within walking distance of their place of employment, urban areas are characterized by extensive commuting. As much as 40 percent of all trips made into or out of a CBD occur during four hours of the day — two in the morning and two in the afternoon. **Rush hour**, or peak hour, is the four consecutive 15-minute periods that have the heaviest traffic.

Advantages of Public Transit. In larger cities, public transportation is better suited than motor vehicles to moving large numbers of people. Public transportation is cheaper, less polluting, and more energy-efficient than the automobile. Motor vehicles have costs beyond their purchase and operation: delays imposed on others, increased need for highway maintenance, construction of new highways, and pollution. In most cities around the world, extensive networks of bus, tram, and subway lines have been maintained, and funds for new construction have been provided in recent years. Smaller cities have shared the construction boom. In France alone, new subway lines have been built in Lyon and Marseille, and hundreds of kilometers of entirely new tracks have been laid between the country's major cities to operate a high speed train.

Public Transit in the United States. In the U.S., public transit is used primarily for rush-hour commuting by workers in and out of the CBD. But in some cities, public transit service is minimal or nonexistent. Early in the twentieth century, U.S. cities had 50,000 kilometers (50,000 miles) of street railways and trolleys that carried 15 billion passengers a year, but only a few hundred kilometers of track remain. The one exception to the downward trend in public transportation is rapid transit. Cities such as Boston and Chicago have attracted new passengers through construction of new subway lines and modernization of existing service. The federal government has permitted Boston, New York, and other cities to use funds originally allocated for interstate highways to modernize rapid transit service instead. Subway ridership in the United States increased from 2 billion in 1995 to 3 billion in 2006. The trolley, now known as fixed light-rail transit, is making a modest comeback in North America. California, the state that most symbolizes the automobile-oriented American culture, leads in construction of new fixed light-rail transit lines. Los Angeles — the city perhaps most associated with the motor vehicle — has planned the most extensive new light-rail system.

(434)
Low-income people tend to live in inner-city neighborhoods, but the job opportunities are in suburban areas not well served by public transportation. Despite modest recent successes, most public transportation systems are caught in a vicious circle, because fares do not cover operating costs. As patronage declines and expenses rise, the fares are increased, which drives away passengers and leads to service reduction and still higher fares. The United States does not fully recognize that public transportation is a vital utility deserving of subsidy to the degree long assumed by European governments.

Key Terms

Annexation (p. 424)
Census tract (p. 412)
Central business district (CBD) (p. 406)
City (p. 424)
Combined Statistical Area (CSA) (p. 425)
Concentric zone model (p. 410)
 Core based statistical area (CBSA) (p. 425)
 Council of government (p. 426)
 Density gradient (p. 427)
 Edge city (p. 427)
 Filtering (p. 419)
 Gentrification (p. 420)
 Greenbelt (p. 429)
Metropolitan statistical area (MSA) (p. 425)
Micropolitan statistical area (p. 425)

Multiple nuclei model (p. 412)
Peripheral model (p. 427)
Public housing (p. 420)
Redlining (p. 433)
Rush (or peak) hour (p. 433)
Sector model (p. 411)
Smart growth (p. 429)
Social area analysis (p. 412)
Sprawl (p. 428)
Squatter settlement (p. 417)
Underclass (p. 421)
Urban renewal (p. 420)
Urbanized area (p. 424)
Zoning ordinance (p. 429)

Test Prep Questions

1) What types of activities are generally NOT found in CBDs?
A) retailers with a high range
B) manufacturing industries
C) retailers with a high threshold
D) face-to-face business services

2) The concentric zone model sees the city structured as a series of what?
A) nodes
B) wedges
C) rings
D) regions

3) The three models of urban structure all agree on one thing:
A) There are five major zones in a city.
B) Most people tend to prefer to live near others who have the same characteristics.
C) Cities and suburbs make up a functional region.
D) The models apply to cities all over the world.

4) Where do the poor generally live in European cities?
A) in the basements and attics of inner city buildings
B) in housing projects in the inner city
C) in single family homes in the suburbs
D) in housing projects in the suburbs

5) What was a common feature for cities in LDCs during the colonial period?
A) standardized plans
B) squatter settlements
C) concentric patterns
D) religious hierarchies

6) Drawing lines on a map to identify areas in which banks refuse to loan money is known as:
A) gentrification
B) filtering
C) urban renewal
D) redlining

7) When a city faces an eroding tax base, it can:
A) increase services
B) raise tax revenues
C) use federal funds to offset the loss
D) none of these

8) What definition of an urban settlement is most useful for gathering statistical data about the functional region?

A) city
B) metropolitan statistical area
C) megalopolis
D) urbanized area

9) How are North American Suburbs segregated?

A) according to land use
B) by social class
C) through the use of zoning ordinances
D) all of these

10) What is the exception in the downward trend in public transportation?

A) rapid transit
B) busses
C) automobiles
D) high-speed rail

Short Essay

1) Explain what kinds of services are found in North American CBDs and why they are located there, and what kinds of activities are excluded from the CBD and why.

_____

_____

_____

_____

_____

_____

_____

_____

2) Identify the three basic issues that cause inner cities to face distinctive challenges and the particular problems associated with them.

_____

_____

_____

_____

_____

_____

———————————————————————————————

———————————————————————————————

———————————————————————————————

———————————————————————————————

3) Explain the three ways in which cities are defined, and discuss the usefulness of each definition.

———————————————————————————————

———————————————————————————————

———————————————————————————————

———————————————————————————————

———————————————————————————————

———————————————————————————————

———————————————————————————————

———————————————————————————————

———————————————————————————————

Chapter 14
Resource Issues

Key Issues
1. Why are resources being depleted?
2. Why are resources being polluted?
3. Why are resources being reused?
4. Why should resources be conserved?

(440)
Geographers study the troubled relationship between human actions and the physical environment in which we live. A **resource** is a substance in the environment that is useful to people, is economically and technologically feasible to access, and is socially acceptable to use. Resources include food, water, soil, plants, animals, and minerals. The problem is that most resources are limited, and Earth has a tremendous number of consumers. Geographers observe two major misuses of resources:
1. We deplete scarce resources — especially petroleum, natural gas, and coal.
2. We destroy resources through the pollution of air, water, and soil.

Nowhere is the globalization trend more pronounced than in the study of resources. Global uniformity in cultural preferences means that people in different places value similar natural resources, although not everyone has the same access to them. In a global environment, all places are connected, so the misuse of a resource in one place affects the well-being of people everywhere.

Key Issue 1. Why Are Resources Being Depleted?
- **Energy resources**
- **Mineral resources**

Two kinds of natural resources are especially valuable to humans: minerals and energy resources. (441) MDCs want to preserve current standards of living, and LDCs are struggling to attain a better standard. All this demands tremendous energy resources, so as we deplete our current sources of energy, we must develop alternative ones.

Energy Resources
Historically, people relied on power supplied by themselves or by animals, known as **animate power**. **Biomass fuel**, such as wood, plant material, and animal waste, remains the most important source of fuel in some LDCs, but during the Industrial Revolution, MDCs converted to **inanimate power**, generated from machines.

Energy Supply and Demand
Around one-half of the world's energy is consumed in MDCs and one-half in LDCs, but MDCs contain around one-third the population of LDCs, so per capita consumption of energy is around three times higher in MDCs.

Three of Earth's substances provide five-sixths of the world's energy:

- **Coal.** Supplanted wood as the leading energy source in North America and Europe in the late 1800s.
- **Petroleum.** First pumped in 1859, not an important resource until the diffusion of motor vehicles.

189

• **Natural Gas.** Originally burned off as waste from oil drilling, now used to heat homes.

In MDCs, other energy comes primarily from nuclear and hydroelectric power. Burning wood and hydroelectric power provides much of the remaining energy in LDCs. Energy is used in three principal places:

1. **Businesses.** The main energy resource is coal, followed by natural gas and oil.
2. **Homes.** Energy is used primarily for heating of living space and water. Natural gas is the most common source, followed by petroleum (heating oil and kerosene).
3. **Transportation.** Almost all transportation systems operate on petroleum products. Only subways, streetcars, and some trains run on coal-generated electricity.

Petroleum, natural gas, and coal are known as **fossil fuels**. A fossil fuel is the residue of plants and animals that became buried millions of years ago. Two characteristics of fossil fuels cause great concern for the future:

1. **The supply of fossil fuels is finite.** Once the present supply is consumed, we must look to other resources for energy.
2. **Fossil fuels are distributed unevenly around the globe.** Some regions enjoy a generous supply, others have little.

Finiteness of Fossil Fuels
To understand Earth's resources, we distinguish between those that are renewable and those that are not:

• **Renewable energy** is replaced continually or at least within a human lifespan;
• **Nonrenewable energy** forms so slowly that it cannot be renewed.

The world faces an energy problem in part because we are rapidly depleting the remaining supply of the three fossil fuels, especially petroleum. We can use other resources for heat, fuel, and manufacturing, but they are likely to be more expensive and less convenient to use than fossil fuels.

Proven Reserves. How much of the fossil-fuel supply remains? Despite the critical importance of this question for the future, no one can answer it precisely. The amount of energy remaining in deposits that have been discovered is called a **proven reserve**. Proven reserves can be measured with reasonable accuracy. Proven reserves can be measured with reasonable accuracy — about 1.3 trillion barrels of petroleum, about 175 trillion cubic meters of natural gas, and about 1 quadrillion metric tons of coal.

At the current world petroleum consumption rate of about 31 billion barrels a year, Earth's proven petroleum reserves of 1.3 trillion barrels will last 43 years.

(442)
At current rates, reserves of natural gas will last for about 49 years and coal would last 131 years.

Potential Reserves. The energy in undiscovered deposits that are thought to exist is a **potential reserve**. Potential reserves can be converted to proven reserves in several ways:
• **Undiscovered Fields.** The largest, most accessible deposits of fossil fuels already have been exploited. Newly discovered reserves generally are smaller and more remote.
• **Enhanced Recovery from Already Discovered Fields.** When it was first exploited,

190

petroleum "gushed" from wells and coal was quarried in open pits. But now extraction is harder.

- **Unconventional Sources.** They are called unconventional because we do not currently have economically feasible, environmentally sound technology to extract them. Canada has especially abundant oil sands in Alberta. Utah, Wyoming, and Colorado also contain abundant oil shale. The shale must be extracted through mining, and current technology makes refining the oil expensive. Adverse environmental impact of using these sources may be high.

(443)

Uneven Distribution of Fossil Fuels

Geographers observe two important inequalities in the global distribution of fossil fuels: Some regions have abundant reserves, whereas others have little; the heaviest consumers of fossil fuel are in different regions than most of the reserves. Unequal possession and consumption of fossil fuels have been major sources of global instability.

Location of Reserves. Why do some regions have abundant reserves of one or more fossil fuels, but other regions have little? This partly reflects how fossil fuels form. Coal forms in tropical locations. Thanks to the slow movement of Earth's drifting continents, the tropical swamps of 250 million years ago have relocated to the mid latitudes. China is responsible for extracting 39 percent of the world's coal, and the United States 16 percent.

Sources of petroleum and natural gas formed from sediment deposited on the seafloor. Some reserves still lie beneath seas, but other reserves are located beneath land that had been under water millions of years ago. Southwest Asia produces 40 percent of the world's petroleum, central Asia 15 percent, Russia, 11 percent, and the U.S. 10 percent. Russia and the U.S. each account for 18 percent of current natural gas production, although Russia possesses more than one-fourth of the world's reserves. Southwest and central Asia account for nearly two-thirds of the world's proven petroleum reserves. Canada is thought to have 13 percent of the world petroleum reserves, second behind Saudi Arabia.

(444)

Taken as a group, MDCs have historically possessed a disproportionately high percentage of the world's proven fossil fuel reserves, but this dominance is ending in the twenty-first century. The U.S. still has extensive coal reserves, but its petroleum and natural gas reserves are being depleted rapidly.

(445)

Consumption of Fossil Fuels. Because MDCs consume more energy than they produce, they must import fossil fuels, especially petroleum, from LDCs.

(446)

Because of more rapid economic development in LDCs, the MDCs face greater competition in obtaining the world's remaining supplies of fossil fuels. China is forecast to take over the top energy consumer ranking from the U.S. around 2015.

Control of World Petroleum

The sharpest conflicts over energy will be centered on the world's limited proven reserves of petroleum. The U.S. produced more petroleum than it consumed during the first half of the twentieth century. U.S. petroleum imports increased from 14 percent of total consumption in 1954 to 58 percent in 2009. European countries and Japan have always depended on foreign petroleum. China changed from a net exporter to an importer during the 1990s.

OPEC. At first, Western companies set oil prices and paid Asian countries only a small percentage of their oil profits. Several LDCs possessing substantial petroleum reserves created the Organization of Petroleum Exporting Countries (OPEC) in 1960. OPEC's Arab members were angry at North American and Western European countries for supporting Israel during that nation's 1973 war with the Arab states of Egypt, Jordan, and Syria. So during the winter of 1973–1974, they flexed their new economic muscle with a boycott — Arab OPEC states refused to sell petroleum to the nations that had supported Israel. Soon gasoline supplies dwindled in MDCs. Each U.S. gasoline station received a small ration of fuel. European countries took more drastic action — the Netherlands, for example, banned all but emergency motor vehicle travel on Sundays.

(447)
OPEC lifted the boycott in 1974 but raised petroleum prices from $3 per barrel to more than $35 by 1981. The rapid escalation in petroleum prices during the 1970s caused severe economic problems in MDCs, and manufacturers were forced out of business. The LDCs were hurt even more. They depended on low-cost petroleum imports to spur economic development, and their fertilizer costs shot up. North American and Western European states encouraged OPEC countries to invest in American and European real estate, banks, and other safe and profitable investments. Comparable investment opportunities were limited in less developed countries.

Changing Supply and Demand. The price of petroleum plummeted during the 1980s and settled during the 1990s at the lowest level in modern history, adjusting for inflation. Conservation measures dampened demand for petroleum in most developed countries. The average vehicle driven in the United States got 14 miles per gallon in 1975, compared to 22 miles per gallon in 2000. With petroleum prices remaining low, consumption increased; Americans bought more gas-guzzling trucks and sport-utility vehicles, and drove longer distances, and once again petroleum imports reached record levels. As in the 1970s, Americans were once again unprepared for the shock of steep oil price rises in the twenty-first century. Supplies were disrupted, yet global demand continues to increase, especially from LDCs led by China. At some point extracting the remaining petroleum reserves will prove so expensive and environmentally damaging that use of alternative energy sources will accelerate, and dependency on petroleum will diminish. The issues for the world are whether dwindling petroleum reserves are handled wisely and other energy sources are substituted peacefully. Given the massive growth in LDCs, MDCs may have little influence.

Mineral Resources
Earth has 92 natural elements, but about 99 percent of the crust is composed of 8 elements: oxygen, silicon, aluminum, iron, calcium, sodium, potassium, and magnesium. The eight most common elements combine with rare ones to form approximately 3,000 different minerals, all with their own properties of hardness, color, and density, as well as spatial distribution. Minerals are either metallic or nonmetallic. Each mineral potentially is a resource, if people find a use for it. When a new technological process or product is invented, demand can suddenly increase for a mineral that had little use in the past. Conversely, when a new process or product replaces an older one, demand may decline for a mineral important in the past. Mineral deposits are not uniformly distributed around the world. A handful of countries accounts for most of the world's supply of particular minerals. Further, the leading producers at this time are not always the countries with the most extensive reserves, an indication that the relative fortunes of states may change in the future.

(448)
Nonmetallic Minerals

Building stones, including large stones, coarse gravel, and fine sand, account for 90 percent of nonmetallic mineral extraction. Nonmetallic minerals are also used for fertilizer. All four are abundant elements in nature with wide distributions. However, mining is highly clustered where the minerals are most easily and cheaply extracted.

• **Phosphorus:** One-fourth of the world's supply is mined in the United States; another one-third in Morocco and China. Morocco possesses one-half the world's reserves.

• **Potassium:** Obtained primarily from the evaporation of seawater. Principal sources include former Soviet Union countries, Canada, the U.S., and the Dead Sea, shared by Israel and Jordan.

• **Calcium:** High levels concentrated in the of the Western U.S. and Canada, as well as Russia's steppes.

• **Sulfur:** The United States and Canada are responsible for one-fourth of the world's production, with another one-fifth coming from China and Russia.

(449)

Nitrogen, obtained from the atmosphere, is an even more important fertilizer. Capturing it from the atmosphere utilizes a lot of energy, so supply and demand is more associated with energy resources than other fertilizer elements. Another group of nonmetallic minerals — gemstones — are valued highly for their color and brilliance when cut and polished. Diamonds are especially useful in manufacturing. Two-thirds of the world's diamonds are currently mined in Australia, Botswana, and Russia.

Metallic Minerals: Ferrous

Metallic minerals have properties that are especially valuable for fashioning machinery, vehicles, and other essential components of an industrialized society. Many metals are also capable of combining with other metals to form alloys with yet other distinctive properties. Metals are known as ferrous or nonferrous. **Ferrous** metals include iron ore and other alloys used in the production of iron and steel. The term "ferrous" refers to the Latin word for iron.

Iron Ore. By far the world's most widely used ferrous metal is iron, which accounts for 5 percent of Earth's crust by weight and 95 percent of ferrous metal mineral extraction.

(450)

Iron is prized for its many assets: a good conductor of heat and electricity, able to be attracted by a magnet and to be magnetized, and malleable into useful shapes. The critical importance of iron to the past four thousand years of human history is reflected by the application of the term "Iron Age" to the period. Mining of iron ore, from which iron is extracted, is concentrated in a handful of countries. Iron deposits of indifferent quality but close to market are actively mined, whereas large known deposits in remote areas are ignored for now, although they may become more important in the future once more accessible deposits are exhausted.

Other Ferrous Metals. Several less common ferrous metals are important for alloying with iron to produce steel: chromium, manganese, molybdenum, nickel, tin, titanium, magnesium, and tungsten.

Metallic Minerals: Nonferrous

Nonferrous metals are utilized to make products other than iron and steel. The most abundant nonferrous metal is aluminum.

Aluminum (Bauxite). Rarely used commercially prior to the twentieth century, aluminum is now in greater demand than any metal except iron. World reserves of aluminum are so large — more than 1,000 years at current rates of use — that it is essentially regarded as inexhaustible at realistic projections of future demand.

Other Nonferrous Metals. Other especially important nonferrous metals include copper, lead, and zinc. World supplies for some nonferrous metals are extremely limited — less than 60 years for copper, 25 years for lead, and 45 years for zinc.

Precious Metals. Nonferrous metals also include precious metals — silver, gold, and the platinum group. In addition to jewelry, both silver and gold are used in a variety of industrial applications, such as electrical and electronic products, and silver is a component of photographic film, whereas gold is important in dentistry.

(451)
The principal use of the platinum group is in motor-vehicle catalytic converters to treat exhaust emissions, as well as fuel cells

Key Issue 2. Why Are Resources Being Polluted?
  •   **Air pollution**
  •   **Water pollution**
  •   **Land pollution**

In our consideration of resources, consumption is half of the equation — waste disposal is the other half. We rely on air, water, and land to remove and disperse our waste. Pollution occurs when more waste is added than a resource can accommodate.

Air Pollution
Air pollution is a concentration of trace substances at a greater level than occurs in average air. The most common air pollutants are carbon monoxide, sulfur dioxide, nitrogen oxides, hydrocarbons, and solid particulates. Three human activities generate most air pollution: motor vehicles, industry, and power plants. In all three cases, pollution results from the burning of fossil fuels.

Global Scale Air Pollution
Air pollution concerns geographers at three scales — global, regional, and local. Air pollution may contribute to global warming and damage the atmosphere's ozone layer. It may also be damaging the atmosphere's ozone layer.

Global Warming. Human actions, especially the burning of fossil fuels, may be causing Earth's temperature to rise. The average temperature of Earth's surface has increased by 1° Celsius (2° Fahrenheit) during the past century. Earth is warmed by sunlight that is converted to heat. When the heat tries to pass back through the atmosphere to space, some gets through and some is trapped. A concentration of trace gases in the atmosphere can block or delay the return of some of the heat leaving the surface heading for space. When fossil fuels are burned, one of the trace gasses, carbon dioxide, is discharged. Plants and oceans absorb much of the discharges, but increased fossil-fuel burning during the past 200 years has caused the level of carbon dioxide in the atmosphere to rise by more than one-fourth. Contributing to the warming has been the buildup of carbon dioxide emissions at an annual rate of more than 1 percent, although scientists disagree on whether it caused most or only a small percentage of the warming. The anticipated increase in Earth's temperature, caused by carbon dioxide trapping some of the radiation emitted by the surface, is called the **greenhouse effect**.

(452)
Global warming of only a few degrees could melt the polar ice caps and raise the level of the oceans many meters. Coastal cities would flood. Global patterns of precipitation could shift. The shifts in coastlines and precipitation patterns could require massive migration and be accompanied by political disputes.

Global-Scale Ozone Damage. The stratosphere contains a concentration of **ozone** gas. The ozone layer absorbs dangerous ultraviolet (UV) rays from the Sun. Earth's protective ozone layer is threatened by pollutants called **chlorofluorocarbons (CFCs)**. In 2007, virtually all countries agreed to cease using CFCs, by 2020 in MDCs by 2030 in LDCs.

Regional-Scale Air Pollution
At the regional scale, air pollution may damage a region's vegetation and water supply through acid deposition. Sulfur oxides and nitrogen oxides, emitted by burning fossil fuels, enter the atmosphere, where they combine with oxygen and water. Tiny droplets of sulfuric acid and nitric acid form and return to Earth's surface as acid deposition. When dissolved in water, the acids may fall as acid precipitation — rain, snow, or fog. Acid precipitation damages lakes, killing fish and plants. On land, concentrations of acid in the soil can injure plants by depriving them of nutrients and can harm soil worms and insects. Buildings and monuments made of marble and limestone have suffered corrosion from acid rain. Geographers are particularly interested in the effects of acid precipitation because the worst damage is not experienced at the same location as the emission of the pollutants. Acid rain falling in Ontario, Canada, for example, can be traced to emissions from coal-burning power plants in the U.S. Great Lakes region. Eastern Europe has suffered especially severely from acid precipitation, a legacy of Communist policies that encouraged the construction of factories and power plants without pollution control devices.

(453)
The destruction of trees has harmed Eastern Europe's seasonal water flow. In dense forests, snow used to melt slowly and trickle into rivers. Now, on the barren sites, it melts and drains quickly, causing flooding in the spring and water shortages in the summer. Perhaps the most severe impact is on human life. A 40-year-old man living in Poland's polluted southern industrial area has a life expectancy 10 years less than his father had at the same age. The United States has reduced sulfur dioxide emissions significantly since the 1970s, and many European countries have also made significant cuts. Despite this, acid precipitation continues to damage forests and lakes.

Local Scale Air Pollution
At the local scale, air pollution is especially severe in places where emission sources are concentrated, such as urban areas. Urban air pollution has three basic components:

- **Carbon monoxide:** Produced from incomplete burning in power plants and vehicles.
(454)
- **Hydrocarbons:** Also result from incomplete combustion, as well as evaporation of paint solvents. Hydrocarbons and nitrogen oxides in the presence of sunlight form **photochemical smog**.
- **Particulates:** Include dust and smoke particles.

The severity of air pollution depends on the weather.

(455)

According to the American Lung Association, the two worst U.S. metropolitan areas for concentrations of particulates are Los Angeles and Pittsburgh. Mexico City may have the world's most serious air pollution problem. Progress in controlling urban air pollution is mixed. In MDCs, air has improved where strict clean-air regulations are enforced. Limited emission controls in LDCs are contributing to severe urban air pollution.

Water Pollution

Water serves many human purposes. These uses depend on fresh, clean, unpolluted water, but clean water is not always available, because people also use water for purposes that pollute it. Pollution is widespread, because it is easy to dump waste into a river and let the water carry it downstream where it becomes someone else's problem. Water can decompose some waste, but the volume of discharge often exceeds the capacity of many rivers and lakes to accommodate it.

Water Pollution Sources

Three main sources generate most water pollution:

- **Water-Using Industries**: Steel, chemicals, paper products, and food processing are major industrial polluters of water.
- **Municipal Sewage**: In MDCs, sewers carry wastewater to a municipal treatment plant, where most — but not all — of the pollutants are removed. In LDCs, sewer systems are rare, and wastewater usually drains untreated into rivers and lakes.
- **Agriculture**: Fertilizers and pesticides spread on fields to increase agricultural productivity are carried into rivers and lakes by the irrigation system or natural runoff.

(456)

Point-source pollution enters a stream at a specific location, whereas nonpoint-source pollution comes from a large diffuse area:

- Manufacturers and municipal sewage systems tend to pollute through point sources, such as a pipe from a waste-water treatment plant.
- Farmers tend to pollute through nonpoint sources, such as by permitting fertilizer to wash from a field during a storm.

Point-source pollutants are usually smaller in quantity and much easier to control.

Impact on Aquatic Life

Aquatic plants and animals consume oxygen, but so do the decomposing organic waste that humans dump into the water. The oxygen consumed by the decomposing organic waste constitutes the **biochemical oxygen demand (BOD)**. If too much waste is discharged into the water, the water becomes oxygen-starved and fish die. When runoff carries fertilizer from farm fields into streams or lakes, the fertilizer nourishes excessive aquatic plant production that consumes too much oxygen. Either type of pollution unbalances the normal oxygen level, threatening aquatic plants and animals. Some of the residuals may become concentrated in the fish, making them unsafe for human consumption. Many factories and power plants use water for cooling and then discharge the warm water back into the river or lake. Fish adapted to cold water, such as salmon and trout, might not be able to survive in the warmer water.

Wastewater and Disease

Since passage of clean water laws, most treatment plants meet high water-quality standards.

Improved treatment procedures have resulted in cleaner rivers and lakes in MDCs. The Thames was once a major food source for Londoners, but during the Industrial Revolution it became the principal location for dumping waste. The fish died, and the water grew unsafe to drink. The British government began a massive cleanup during the 1960s to restore the Thames to health. A salmon was caught in the Thames just upstream from London in 1982, the first since 1833.

In LDCs, sewage often flows untreated directly into rivers. The drinking water, usually removed from the same rivers, may be inadequately treated as well. Waterborne diseases such as cholera, typhoid, and dysentery are major causes of death. Some LDCs regard water pollution as a small price to pay for participating in a global economy.

Land Pollution
When we consume a product, we also consume an unwanted byproduct, the container in which the product is packaged. About 2 kilograms (4 pounds) of solid waste per person is generated daily in the United States.

(458)
Paper products, such as corrugated cardboard and newspapers, account for the largest percentage of solid waste in the U.S., especially among residences and retailers.
Even consumers who carefully dispose of solid waste are contributing to a major pollution problem.

Solid Waste Disposal
The **sanitary landfill** is by far the most common strategy for disposal of solid waste in the United States. We *disperse* air and water pollutants into the atmosphere, rivers, and eventually the ocean, but we *concentrate* solid waste in thousands of landfills. Chemicals released by the decomposing solid waste can leak from the landfill into groundwater. This can contaminate water wells, soil, and nearby streams. The number of landfills in the U.S. has declined by three-fourths since 1990. Better compaction methods and expansion of large regional landfills have provided expanded capacity. Some communities now pay to use landfills elsewhere. Incineration and recycling have both increased rapidly. Burning the trash reduces its bulk by about three-fourths, demanding far less landfill space. Incineration also provides energy that generates electricity. Burning releases some toxins into the air, and some remain in the ash.

Hazardous Waste
Disposing of hazardous waste is especially difficult. Hazardous wastes include heavy metals (including mercury, cadmium, and zinc), PCB oils from electrical equipment, cyanides, strong solvents, acids, and caustics. If poisonous industrial residuals are not carefully placed in protective containers, the chemicals may leach into the soil and contaminate groundwater or escape into the atmosphere. Companies in the United States that release chemicals classified as toxic by the E.P.A. must report the amounts released. About 47 million tons of hazardous wastes were discharged in the United States in 2007.

(459)
Some European and North American firms have tried to transport their waste to West Africa, often unscrupulously.

Key Issue 3. Why Are Resources Being Reused?
  • **Renewing resources**

- **Recycling resources**

Depletion and destruction of resources can be reduced through reuse. Renewable resources can be substituted for nonrenewable ones. Recycling unwanted resources can replace the discharging of these products into the environment.

Renewing Resources
Energy poses an especially strong challenge in substituting renewable energy resources for nonrenewable ones. Although renewable resources can be harnessed for energy, continued reliance on petroleum, natural gas, and coal continues to be the cheaper alternative.

Nuclear Energy
The big advantage of nuclear power is the large amount of energy released from a small amount of material. Nuclear power supplies about one-sixth of the world's electricity. Europe and the U.S. are each responsible for generating one-third of the world's nuclear power, and about 30 countries make some use of nuclear power. The countries most highly dependent on nuclear power are clustered in Europe. Dependency on nuclear power varies widely among U.S. states. Twenty states and the District of Columbia have no nuclear power plants. Nuclear power presents serious problems.

Potential Accidents. A nuclear power plant produces electricity from energy released by splitting uranium atoms in a controlled environment, a process called **fission**. One product of all nuclear reactions is **radioactive waste**.

Nuclear power plants cannot explode, like a nuclear bomb, however, it is possible to have a runaway reaction, which overheats the reactor, causing a meltdown, possible steam explosions, and scattering of radioactive material into the atmosphere. This happened in 1986 at Chernobyl in the north of Ukraine, near the Belarus border. Half of the eventual victims may be residents of European countries other than Ukraine and Belarus.

Radioactive Waste. When nuclear fuel fissions, the waste is highly radioactive and lethal, and it remains so for many years. Plutonium can be harvested from it for making nuclear weapons. No one has yet devised permanent storage for radioactive waste. It must be isolated for several thousand years. The United States is Earth's third-largest country in land area, yet it has failed to find a suitable underground storage site because of worry about groundwater contamination.

(460)
Bomb Material. Nuclear power has been used in warfare twice, in August 1945, when the United States dropped an atomic bomb on first Hiroshima and then Nagasaki, Japan. No government has since dared to use them in a war, because leaders have recognized that a full-scale nuclear conflict could terminate human civilization. Russia and the U.S. each have several thousand nuclear weapons; China, France and the United Kingdom have several hundred; India and Pakistan have several dozen; and North Korea has a handful. Israel is suspected of having nuclear weapons, but has not admitted to it. Iran has been developing the capability. Diffusion of nuclear programs to countries sympathetic to terrorists has been particularly worrying to the rest of the world.

Limited Uranium Reserves. Like fossil fuels, uranium is a nonrenewable resource. Proven reserves are limited — about 124 years at current rates of use. One-fourth of the proven reserves are in Australia and one-sixth are in Kazakhstan. Uranium ore naturally contains only 0.7 percent U-235; a greater concentration is needed for power generation. A **breeder reactor** turns uranium into a renewable resource by generating plutonium, also a nuclear fuel. However, plutonium is more lethal than uranium. It is also easier to fashion into a bomb. Because of these risks, few breeder reactors have been built, and none are in the United States.

High Cost. Nuclear power plants cost several billion dollars to build, primarily because of elaborate safety measures. Uranium is mined in one place, refined in another, and used in still another. Generating electricity from nuclear plants is much more expensive than from coal burning plants. The future of nuclear power has been seriously hurt by the combination of high risk and cost. Some countries in North America and Western Europe have curtailed construction of new plants. On the other hand, countries without nuclear power are moving toward introducing it, including Poland, Turkey, Indonesia, and Vietnam.

(461)
Australia, with the most extensive reserves of uranium, is debating expansion. Advances in safety and reactor technology, combined with the high cost of other power sources, are driving the renewed interest.

Nuclear Fusion. Some nuclear power issues could be addressed through nuclear **fusion**, which is the fusing of hydrogen atoms to form helium. Fusion releases spectacular amounts of energy, but fusion can occur only at very high temperatures. Alternatives such as fusion do not offer immediate solutions to energy shortages in the twenty-first century but may become more practical if the price of current energy resources substantially rises.

Leading Renewable Energy Sources
The two leading renewable energy sources currently are biomass and hydroelectric. Geothermal, wind, and solar are also currently used but are less common.

Biomass. More than one-half of renewable energy comes from biomass, including wood and crops. When carefully harvested, wood is a renewable resource that can be used to generate electricity and heat. Crops such as sugarcane, corn, and soybeans, can be processed into motor vehicle fuels. The potential for increasing the use of biomass for fuel is limited, for several reasons:
- When wood is burned for fuel instead of being left in the forest, the fertility of the forest may be reduced.
- Burning biomass may be inefficient, because the energy used to produce the crops may be as much as the energy supplied by the crops.
- Biomass already serves other essential purposes other than energy, such as providing much of Earth's food, clothing, and shelter.

Hydroelectric Power. Water has been a source of mechanical power since before recorded history. It turned water wheels to operate machines. Over the last hundred years, the energy of moving water has been used to generate electricity, called **hydroelectric power**. Hydroelectric power is the world's second most popular source of electricity, after coal, supplying about a fourth of worldwide demand. Many LDCs depend on hydroelectric power for most of their power.

China is the world's leading producer of hydroelectric power. Unfortunately, its Three

Gorges dam, under construction across the Yangtze River, is widely regarded as an environmental disaster for the resulting decline in water quality in the river, endangerment of wildlife, and extinction of rare species of vegetation in a region known for biodiversity.

Wind Power. Wind has also long been a source of energy, the most obvious being sailboats and windmills. One-third of the U.S. is considered windy enough to make wind power economically feasible. Twenty percent of Denmark's electricity is wind generated. Construction of a windmill modifies the environment much less severely than a dam. Some oppose windmills because they can be noisy and lethal for birds and bats, and can constitute a visual blight when constructed on mountaintops or offshore in places of outstanding beauty.

Geothermal Energy. Natural nuclear reactions make the Earth's interior hot. In volcanic areas hot rocks can encounter groundwater producing steam that can be tapped by wells. Energy from this hot water or steam is called **geothermal energy**. Harnessing geothermal energy is most feasible at the rifts along Earth's surface where crustal plates meet.

Solar Energy

The ultimate renewable resource is solar energy supplied by the sun. Solar sources currently supply the U.S. with only 1 percent of electricity, but the potential for growth is limitless. The sun's energy is free and ubiquitous and cannot be exclusively owned, bought, or sold; it does not damage the environment or cause pollution.

Passive Solar Energy. Solar energy is harnessed through either passive or active means. **Passive solar energy systems** capture energy without special devices. Reliance on passive solar energy increased during the nineteenth century when construction innovations first permitted hanging of massive glass "curtains" on a thin steel frame. With electricity and petroleum cheap and abundant after World War II and through most of the twentieth century, passive solar energy rarely played a major role in construction of homes and commercial buildings. In recent years building construction and remodeling have made more use of passive solar energy through advances in glass technology.

Active Solar Energy. Active solar energy systems collect solar energy and convert it either to heat energy or to electricity. In direct electric conversion, solar radiation is captured with **photovoltaic cells** which convert light energy to electrical energy. (464) In indirect electric conversion, solar radiation is first converted to heat, then to electricity. In heat conversion, solar radiation is concentrated with large reflectors and lenses to heat water or rocks.

Generating Electricity Through Solar. Solar power can be produced at a central station and distributed by an electric company, as coal and nuclear-generated electricity is now supplied. With coal still relatively cheap, there is little interest in solar technology. In MDCs, solar electricity is used in spacecraft, calculators, and sites where conventional power is unavailable. In LDCs, the largest and fastest-growing market for photovoltaic cells includes the 2 billion people who lack electricity, especially residents of remote villages. But the cost of cells must drop and their efficiency must improve for solar power to expand rapidly.

Renewable Energy in Motor Vehicles

The most serious obstacle to decreasing reliance on nonrenewable energy is its importance as motor vehicle fuel. Several alternative sources of fuel are becoming available.

Batteries. Battery power was popular in early motor vehicles, especially in 1900 in large cities of the northeast where their relative quietness and cleanliness made them popular as taxicabs. Women preferred them because they were easy to start. The main shortcomings of the electric car in the early 1900s remain unchanged a century later. Electric-powered vehicles have a more limited range, cost more to operate, and recharging the batteries can take several hours. To address these issues, carmakers offer a variety of vehicles that combine electric and gasoline power.

Biofuels. Motor-vehicle fuel, known as ethanol, can be produced from biomass material, specifically the sugars found in many crops. Corn is the principal source of ethanol in the United States. However to grow and process the corn takes a lot of energy, supplied primarily by fossil fuels, so using ethanol may not actually reduce dependency on fossil fuels. Because of the limitations of using corn, engineers are looking at other sources of biofuels, such as sugarcane in Brazil.

(465)
Some vehicles with diesel engines can be run on biodiesel, a fuel made from vegetable oil and fats.

Hydrogen Fuel Cells. Hydrogen fuel cells convert hydrogen and oxygen into water, producing electricity and heat in the process. The oxygen for the fuel cell reaction comes from the air, so it is free and ubiquitous. For motor vehicles, getting tanks of liquid or gaseous hydrogen to motorists will require a new distribution system. Increasing and wildly fluctuating petroleum prices have stimulated interest in alternative-fuel vehicles.

Recycling Resources
Recycling increased in the United States from 7 percent of all solid waste in 1970 to 10 percent in 1980, 17 percent in 1990, and 33 percent in 2007. The amount of solid waste generated by Americans increased by 54 million tons between 1990 and 2007, and the amount recycled increased by 51 million tons, so about the same amount went into landfills or incinerators. The percentage of recovered materials varies widely by product.

Recycling Collection
Recycling involves two main series of activities. First, materials that would otherwise be "thrown away" are collected and sorted.

(466)
Then the materials are manufactured into new products for which a market exists.

Pickup and Processing. Recyclables are collected in four primary methods: curbside, drop-off centers, buyback centers, and deposit programs. Regardless of the collection method, recyclables are sent to a materials recovery facility to be sorted and prepared into marketable commodities for manufacturing.

Manufacturing. Once cleaned and separated, the recyclables are ready to be manufactured into a marketable product. Four major manufacturing sectors accounted for more than half of the recycling activity — paper mills, steel mills, plastic converters, and iron and steel foundries.

- **Paper:** Most types can be recycled; the key is collecting large quantities of clean, well-

sorted, uncontaminated and dry paper.
• **Plastic:** Different plastic types must not be mixed.
• **Glass:** Can be used repeatedly with no loss in quality and is 100 percent recyclable.
• **Aluminum:** Aluminum scrap is readily accepted for recycling, although other metals are rarely accepted.

Other Pollution by Reduction Strategies
In addition to recycling, two other basic strategies can reduce pollution:
   • Reducing the amount of waste discharged into the environment.
   • Expanding the capacity of the environment to accept discharges.

Reducing Discharges. Pollution can be prevented if the amount of waste being discharged into the environment is reduced to a level that the environment can assimilate.

(467)
The mix of various inputs can be adjusted to produce a higher ratio of product to waste. The amount of waste can also be reduced if the production system produces less of the product — or if production ceases altogether — because of lower consumer demand. Emissions-trading systems can reduce discharges, especially into the atmosphere. To reduce sulfur dioxide discharges, the United States introduced a market through an amendment to the 1990 Clean Air Act. Power companies can buy and sell allowances to emit sulfur dioxide.

Increasing Environmental Capacity. The second way to handle pollution is to increase environmental capacity to accept waste discharges. The capacity of air, water, and land to accept waste is not fixed, but varies among places and at different times. A deep, fast-flowing river has a greater capacity to absorb wastewater than a shallow, slow-moving one. Wastewater can be stored when the river level is low and released when the river is high. Similarly, exhaust released into stagnant air irritates, whereas exhaust released in windy conditions is quickly dispersed. Environmental capacity can also be increased by transforming the waste so that it is discharged into a resource that has the capacity to assimilate it. For example, a coal-burning power plant discharges gases into the atmosphere, causing air pollution. To reduce air pollution, wet scrubbers are installed to wash particulates from the gas before it is released to the atmosphere. Wet scrubbers capture the particulates in water, which then can be discharged into a stream. If the stream is polluted by the discharge, then the wastewater can be cleaned in a settling basin where the particulates drop out. This transforms the residue into a solid waste for disposal on land.

Comparing Pollution Reduction Strategies
Relying on an increase in the capacity of the environment to accept discharges is risky. Recent history is filled with examples of wastes discharged in the environment with the belief that they would be dispersed or isolated safely: CFCs in the stratosphere, garbage offshore, and toxic chemicals beneath Love Canal. Tall smokestacks built to reduce sulfur dioxide discharges around coal-burning industries were successful at dispersing sulfur over a larger area. But the result of the dispersal was that acid precipitation fell hundreds of kilometers away. Reducing discharges into the environment (by either changing the production process or recycling) is usually the preferred alternative.

Key Issue 4. Why Should Resources Be Conserved?
   • **Sustainable development**

- **Biodiversity**

Because it is one part natural science and one part social science, geography is especially sensitive to the importance of protecting the natural environment while meeting human needs. "Conservation" is a concept that reflects balance between nature and society.

Sustainable Development
Sustainable development is "development that meets the needs of the present without compromising the ability of future generations to meet their own needs," according to the United Nations.

Conservation, Preservation, and Sustainability
Conservation is the sustainable use and management of natural resources such as wildlife, water, air, and Earth deposits to meet human needs, including food, medicine, and recreation.

(468)
Conservation differs from **preservation**, which is maintenance of resources in their present condition, with as little human impact as possible. Preservation does not regard nature as a resource for human use. In contrast, conservation is compatible with development, but only if natural resources are utilized in a careful rather than a wasteful manner. An increasingly important approach to careful utilization of resources is sustainable development, based on promotion of biodiversity.

Sustainability and Economic Growth
The UN's "sustainable development" definition originated in the 1987 Brundtland Report. The report argued that sustainable development had to recognize the importance of economic growth while conserving natural resources. Environmental protection, economic growth, and social equity are linked because economic development aimed at reducing poverty can at the same time threaten the environment. A rising level of economic development generates increased pollution, at least until a country reaches a GDP of about $5,000 per person. Consequently, twentieth-century environmental improvements in the more developed countries of North America and Western Europe are likely to be offset by increased pollution in LDCs during the twenty-first century.

(469)
Critical to world pollution in the twenty-first century is China. The rapid economic transformation of China has resulted in rapidly raising levels of pollution. The country has 16 of the 20 most polluted cities. Sulfur dioxide emissions from China are even crossing the Pacific Ocean and being deposited in the western U.S. The World Bank estimates that 10 percent of China's GDP is being lost to direct damage from pollution, including destruction of crops, medical bills, and sick leave payments. The Brundtland Report was optimistic that environmental protection could be promoted at the same time as economic growth and social equity. In recent years the World Bank and other international development agencies have embraced the concept of sustainable development. Planning for development involves consideration of many more environmental and social issues today than was the case in the past.

Sustainability's Critics
Some environmentally oriented critics have argued that it is too late to discuss sustainability.

The World Wildlife Federation (WWF) claims that the world surpassed its sustainable level around 1980. Others criticize sustainability from the opposite perspective: Human activities have not exceeded Earth's capacity because resource availability has no maximum, and Earth's resources have no absolute limit because the definition of resources changes drastically and unpredictably over time.

Environmental improvements can be achieved through careful assessment of the outer limits of Earth's capacity. Critics and defenders of sustainable development agree that one important recommendation of the UN report has not been implemented — increased international cooperation to reduce the gap between more developed and less developed countries.

Biodiversity

Biological diversity, or **biodiversity** for short, refers to the variety of species across Earth as a whole or in a specific place. (470) Sustainable development is promoted when biodiversity of a particular place or Earth as a whole is protected.

Biological and Geographic Biodiversity

Species variety can be understood from several perspectives. Geographers are especially concerned with biogeographic diversity, whereas biologists are especially concerned with genetic diversity. Estimates of Earth's total number of species range from 3 to 100 million, with 10 million as a median "guess," meaning that humans have not yet "discovered," classified, and named most of Earth's species. For geographers, biodiversity is a measurement of the number of species within a specific region or habitat. A community containing a large number of species is said to be species-rich, whereas an area with few species is species-poor. Two communities may have the same number of species and the same total population of individuals, yet one may be more diverse than the other, depending on the distribution of the total population among the various species. Strategies to protect genetic diversity have been established on a global scale. Strategies to protect biogeographic diversity vary among countries. Frustrated by the inability to precisely measure environmental impacts, Millennium Ecosystem Assessment has undertaken a multiyear effort to establish systematic data sets.

Biodiversity in the Tropics

The characteristics of the tropical forest biome contribute to the presence of more species than in temperate or polar biomes. Thus, reduction of biodiversity through species extinction is especially important in tropical forests, where six species per hour are extinguished in the tropics, and more than 5,000 species are considered in danger of extinction. Although tropical forests occupy only 6 percent of Earth's land area, they contain more than one-half of the world's species, including two-thirds of vascular plant species and one-third of avian species. The principal cause of the high rate of extinction is cutting down forests, which is the result of changing economic activities in the tropics, especially a decline in shifting cultivation (see Chapter 10). Governments in LDCs support the destruction of rain forests, because they view activities such as selling timber to builders or raising cattle for fast-food restaurants as more effective strategies for promoting economic development than shifting cultivation. Until recently, the World Bank has provided loans to finance development proposals that require clearing forests.

Key Terms:
Acid deposition (p. 452)

Acid precipitation (p. 452)
Active solar energy systems (p. 463)

Air pollution (p. 451)
Animate power (p. 441)
Biochemical oxygen demand (BOD) (p. 456)
Biodiversity (p. 469)
Biomass fuel (p. 441)
Breeder reactor (p. 460)
Chlorofluorocarbon (CFC) (p. 452)
Conservation (p. 467)
Ferrous (p. 449)
Fission (p. 459)
Fossil fuel (p. 441)
Fusion (p. 461)
Geothermal energy (p. 462)
Greenhouse effect (p. 451)
Hydroelectric power (p. 461)

Inanimate power (p. 441)
Nonferrous (p. 450)
Nonrenewable energy (p. 441)
Ozone (p. 452)
Passive solar energy systems (p. 463)
Photochemical smog (p. 454)
Photovoltaic cell (p. 463)
Pollution (p. 451)
Potential reserve (p. 442)
Preservation (p. 468)
Proven reserve (p. 441)
Radioactive waste (p. 459)
Recycling (p. 465)
Renewable energy (p. 441)
Resource (p. 440)
Sanitary landfill (p. 458)
Sustainable development (p. 467)

Test Prep Questions

1) What country has the world's largest proven reserves of coal by a large margin?
A) China
B) The United States
C) Russia
D) Canada

2) Which of the following is a nonferrous metal?
A) copper
B) titanium
C) molybdenum
D) tungsten

3) Which of the following is an example of air pollution at the local level?
A) the greenhouse effect
B) ozone depletion
C) acid precipitation
D) photochemical smog

4) Which of the following is NOT an industry that generates large amounts of waste water?
A) food processing
B) paper products
C) automotive assembly
D) steel

5) Which of the following is NOT a renewable energy source?

A) biomass
B) nuclear fission
C) geothermal
D) nuclear fusion

6) What is the world's second most widespread energy source for generating electricity, after coal?
A) natural gas
B) biomass
C) wind
D) hydroelectric

7) Which of the following is NOT presently an alternative source of fuel for automobiles that is becoming commercially available?
A) solar power
B) batteries
C) hydrogen fuel cells
D) biofuel

8) Which of the following is least commonly recycled in the U.S.?
A) glass
B) ferrous metals
C) paper
D) aluminum

9) Which of the following is NOT a primary recycling collection method?
A) buyback centers
B) dropoff centers
C) incineration
D) curbside

10) While tropical forests occupy only 6 percent of Earth's land area, they contain _____ of the world's species.
A) two-thirds
B) over half
C) 30 percent
D) one-fourth

Short Essay

1) Identify the two main groups of mineral resources important to human activities, and describe their relative importance, and, in particular, how they are used.

_____

_____

_____

_____

_____

_____

_____

_____

_____

2) Explain how air pollution occurs at three different scales.

_____

_____

_____

_____

_____

_____

_____

_____

3) Describe the problems associated with nuclear power that impede its adoption as an alternative to fossil fuels.

_____

_____

_____

_____

_____

_____

_____

_____

Answers to Test Prep Multiple Choice Questions

Chapter 1:
1. Answer: B
2. Answer: A
3. Answer: D
4. Answer: C
5. Answer: A
6. Answer: C
7. Answer: A
8. Answer: B
9. Answer: D
10. Answer: A

Chapter 2:
1. Answer: A
2. Answer: B
3. Answer: D
4. Answer: B
5. Answer: C
6. Answer: D
7. Answer: B
8. Answer: D
9. Answer: C
10. Answer: B

Chapter 3:
1. Answer: B
2. Answer: B
3. Answer: C
4. Answer: A
5. Answer: D
6. Answer: C
7. Answer: A
8. Answer: D
9. Answer: B
10. Answer: C

Chapter 4:
1. Answer: B
2. Answer: A
3. Answer: D
4. Answer: B
5. Answer: C
6. Answer: A
7. Answer: D
8. Answer: A
9. Answer: B
10. Answer: C

Chapter 5:
1. Answer: B
2. Answer: A
3. Answer: B
4. Answer: C
5. Answer: C
6. Answer: B
7. Answer: D
8. Answer: B
9. Answer: D
10. Answer: A

Chapter 6:
1. Answer: C
2. Answer: A
3. Answer: D
4. Answer: C
5. Answer: A
6. Answer: B
7. Answer: D
8. Answer: A
9. Answer: C
10. Answer: B

Chapter 7:
1. Answer: B
2. Answer: A
3. Answer: B
4. Answer: D
5. Answer: C
6. Answer: A
7. Answer: C
8. Answer: D
9. Answer: A
10. Answer: C

Chapter 8:
1. Answer: B
2. Answer: A
3. Answer: C
4. Answer: B
5. Answer: D
6. Answer: A
7. Answer: C
8. Answer: A
9. Answer: B
10. Answer: C

Chapter 9:
1. Answer: B
2. Answer: A
3. Answer: D
4. Answer: A
5. Answer: C
6. Answer: B
7. Answer: A
8. Answer: B
9. Answer: D
10. Answer: A

Chapter 10:
1. Answer: C
2. Answer: B
3. Answer: A
4. Answer: C
5. Answer: D
6. Answer: D
7. Answer: A
8. Answer: C
9. Answer: B
10. Answer: A

Chapter 11:
1. Answer: D
2. Answer: A
3. Answer: C
4. Answer: B
5. Answer: C
6. Answer: A
7. Answer: A
8. Answer: D
9. Answer: C
10. Answer: A

Chapter 12:
1. Answer: B
2. Answer: A
3. Answer: B
4. Answer: D
5. Answer: A
6. Answer: B
7. Answer: B
8. Answer: B
9. Answer: C
10. Answer: A

Chapter 13:
1. Answer: B
2. Answer: C
3. Answer: B
4. Answer: D
5. Answer: A
6. Answer: D
7. Answer: B
8. Answer: B
9. Answer: D
10. Answer: A

Chapter 14:
1. Answer: B
2. Answer: A
3. Answer: D
4. Answer: C
5. Answer: B
6. Answer: D
7. Answer: A
8. Answer: B
9. Answer: C
10. Answer: B